The Transformation of Plantation Politics

SUNY series in African American Studies

John R. Howard and Robert C. Smith, editors

The Transformation
of Plantation Politics

Black Politics,
Concentrated Poverty, and
Social Capital in the Mississippi Delta

Sharon D. Wright Austin

State University of New York Press

Published by
State University of New York Press, Albany

Printed in the United States of America

Marcella Plantation, Mileston, Mississipi cover photo courtesy of the Library of Congress.

For information, address State University of New York Press,
194 Washington Avenue, Suite 305, Albany, NY 12210-2384

Production by Diane Ganeles
Marketing by Michael Campochiaro

Library of Congress Cataloging-in-Publication Data

Wright Austin, Sharon D., 1965–
    The transformation of plantation politics : Black politics, concentrated poverty, and social capital in the Mississippi Delta : Sharon D. Wright Austin.
    p. cm. — (Suny series in African American studies)
Includes bibliographical references (p.   ) and index.
ISBN-13: 978-0-7914-6801-2 (hardcover : alk. paper)
ISBN-10: 0-7914-6801-1 (hardcover : alk. paper)
ISBN-13: 978-0-7914-6802-9 (pbk : alk. paper)
ISBN-10: 0-7914-6802-X (pbk : alk. paper)
    1. Plantation life—Mississippi—Delta (Region) 2. African Americans—Mississippi—Delta (Region)—Politics and government. 3. Poverty—Political aspects—Mississippi—Delta (Region) 4. African Americans—Mississippi—Delta (Region)—Social conditions. 5. Elite (Social sciences)—Mississippi—Delta (Region) 6. Whites—Mississippi—Delta (Region)—Social conditions. 7. Social capital (Sociology)—Mississippi—Delta (Region) 8. Delta (Miss. : Region)—Race relations. 9. Delta (Miss. : Region)—Politics and government. 10. Delta (Miss. : Region)—Social conditions. I. Title. II. Series.

F347.M6A94 2006
307.72089'9607307624—dc22

                                              2005024114

10 9 8 7 6 5 4 3 2 1

*To Mama, Mother Austin, Al Jr., Al Sr., my family,
and to my dear friend and mentor, the late Jim Button*

CONTENTS

ILLUSTRATIONS

FOREWORD

Sharon D. Wright Austin has produced a comprehensive study of rural Mississippi, focusing on its traditional Delta "Black Belt." That long sliver of fertile crescent located along the Mississippi River seems, in this graphic and copious descriptive analysis, to roll along almost out of sync with real time. The plantations remain the driving force in the region, with even family names appearing immutable. And there also are the dependent African Americans bound to the former plantations like so many post feudal clients. So thick is this fog of racialized tradition that even the contrary new myth of gaming is but a vehicle to sustain the old arrangements. In short, the Mississippi Delta remains the Delta, barely interrupted by the displacement of cotton as "king." The new kings all fit into a well-wrought scheme where whites dominate in virtually all spheres of life, while African Americans remain powerless and often subservient in virtually all spheres of life.

How is this possible Austin asks, in light of the prevalence of an opposing and quite widely dispersed vision of a "new Mississippi? In fact this new story line emphasizes racial integration, buttressed by the evidence that African Americans in this state lead other states in political empowerment. In this previously "unredeemed" state, an outlier on all things racial, African Americans now are regularly elected to a wide range of political offices, and with such success that the scope of this electoral achievement outpaces all other states. So could Austin be incorrect about the Mississippi Delta? After all this region of the state had been one of the great centers of leadership and activism during the civil rights movement that swept the state in the 1960s. Aaron Henry founded a branch of the National Association for the Advancement of Colored People (NAACP) branch in the town of Clarksdale in the heart of the region and went on to lead a confederation of movement affiliates that broke the cycle of segregated partisan organization in the state. Moreover, all the major towns in the region had strong NAACP, Student Nonviolent Coordinating Committee (SNCC), and/or Congress of Racial Equality (CORE) centers of activism that effectively registered most voting age African American citizens by the end of the 1960s. Clarksdale, Greenwood, Greenville, Cleveland, Ruleville, and so forth. Despite all this contrary data, which Austin surveys, she still finds something amiss in the empowerment of African Americans in the region.

But how can both of these portrayals be true? What is the meaning of such a contradictory situation for social, economic, and political change in Mississippi? In some senses what it means is that this state, like some others, have found an uneasy and often deficient accommodation of African American claims for inclusion. They have struck the ultimate bargain-the more things change, the more they remain the same. While it is true that Mississippi outdistances other states in the number of African American political officeholders, that in itself hardly signifies political empowerment or even that any fundamental alteration of the racial caste system has occurred. Political officeholding is not the same thing as delivering political benefits to one's constituency. It simply means that as access to those formal offices has been conceded, real power has moved to other places; or, that real power was never vested in such positions in the first place. Austin shows that power remains illusive for African Americans because it is, and always has been, significantly determined by economic power or wealth; and that while political offices may have been vacated, hardly any of the wealth has been reallocated. So it is not so complicated after all—whites remain the power base in the Mississippi Delta. And for African Americans, even when there is some favorable change other factors and circumstances conspire in such a way that their real conditions only get worse. And here is the real anomaly of the situation-that in places where apparently there is greater access to formal political offices, overall empowerment (defined in the terms Austin has adopted) is significantly worsened. So in thinking about the question of African American betterment, still something else is required and she provides some useful ways of thinking this through.

The analysis is significant in a number of important ways. It brings to bear a number of theories (some old and some new) to amplify the power arrangements in the Delta and applies them in novel ways. Her deft combination of political and economic factors shows how these twains are rarely separated in the local power equation. The historical sweep of this project is vast and is absolutely vital in revealing how the past and present resonate with each other. And there is a mix of methods that get the benefit of both worlds of political inquiry, although clearly the weight of the project is on the development of the region/industry as a case or cases. All told this provides us with an illuminating contemporary study of the Mississippi Delta, with definite implications for an analysis of African Americans located in rural areas. The latter remains a very important, but vastly understudied area, because of the still sizable number of African Americans and their officeholders.

In the early theoretical part of the analysis, Austin offers a comprehensive and targeted analysis of some of the most prominent theories in the discipline and shows that they do not work satisfactorily to illuminate her data or the study of racial politics in general. Among those she considers are pluralism, regime, and incorporation theories. She then borrows from aspects of two conceptualizations that seem promising for explaining the Mississippi Delta. She reaches back to the well-wrought concept of elitism and the relatively recent iteration of social capital as her tools. She uses elitism to reveal the continuing racial hegemony of Southern planters and the new partnership they developed to accommodate geopolitical conditions; and, uses social capital to interrogate the terrain of relative African American electoral success and internal social and economic community organization. She then applies these theories to the circumstances she uncovers in the northern Mississippi Delta. Clearly a Delta elite remains the prime mover in public affairs, economic control, and public benefits distribution. Austin uses personal interviews to uncover who these figures are, and time and time again they remain the same families, even to the point of bearing many of the same surnames. And while African Americans command considerable social capital, which they deploy to organize their racialized communities, this capital does not seem to be transferable across racial lines. There is therefore little alteration of the historical status arrangements between the two racial groups.

The methodologies employed in this analysis seem to be especially appropriate. Austin adopts a mix of personal interviews, historical, and quantitative techniques for the study. This mix makes it possible for her to delve deeply into several cases in the northern tier of the state; and, to make modest use of aggregate cross-region data that strengthens the broader claims for her findings and for the conceptualizations she employs. As such we get to know the case of Tunica County and its new industry (gaming) thoroughly. She used Floyd Hunter's reputational technique to produce a list of local elites, and then used structured interviews to collect information from, or on, these leaders. The historical material was developed from secondary sources, archives, and interviews. Meanwhile, she collected and coded a considerable amount of aggregate data on socioeconomic/political factors for the state and for the Delta region. The combination of methods produced a richly detailed analysis of the subject that will open it up for greater attention by scholars-a much-deserved examination.

This book falls into an important category of studies that focus on racial politics in the United States, and specifically the manner in which Mississippi fits into this scheme. The state has always had a large African American population and has had a reputation for being particularly recalcitrant in finding cross-racial accommodation. Moreover it has a particular place in the study and analysis of Southern regional politics. This provides a body of work on which Austin relies and offers her the opportunity for updating and reassessment. She does this comprehensively, demonstrating a remarkable command of the extant literature and builds on it usefully. In chapter 2, she brings together a huge amount of material on the plantation system, reorganizing it in a way that makes it understandable. Chapter 3 explores the transition period when racial change finally came to Mississippi-revealing its principals, accomplishments, and the distinct limits on the redistribution of power and wealth. The new "industry" of gaming is considered in chapter 4, with special reference to Tunica County and Tunica City. Chapters 5 and 6 are substantive discussions of what has happened to plantation relations; and, how African Americans develop and deploy social capital for public ends. This prodigious effort is thought provoking and challenging, inviting us to think anew about the place of Mississippi in racial, national and regional politics. It reveals in great detail what has changed and what has remained the same, and to what end for the political empowerment of local African Americans.

Minion K. C. Morrison

ACKNOWLEDGMENTS

As a proud Memphis native and the daughter of two Tunica County, Mississippi-born parents, I became acquainted with the Mississippi Delta history and political development at an early age. I first of all need to thank my Lord and Savior for blessing me in so many ways. Also, I would like to thank my mother Annie Ruth Wright and my late father Willie James Wright for making countless sacrifices on my behalf.

I would also like to thank all of the educators in elementary, middle, and high school who touched my life over the years with special thanks to Jim Fisher, Patricia Terry, Martha Chandler, Cynthia Gentry, Carol Maynard, and Elma Hill at Westwood High School in Memphis, Tennessee. I have taught hundreds of students at the Universities of Florida, Louisville, Michigan, Missouri, and Yale who have challenged me to think in ways I never before imagined, including Candice Myesha Richie and Damon Terrell Rucker White at the University of Missouri who lost their lives because of senseless violence only months before their college graduations.

At the University of Missouri, Carol Anderson, Diann Jordan, Charles Menifield, Minion KC Morrison, Helen Neville, Robin Remington, Anna Riley, Julius Thompson, Paul Wallace, Clenora Hudson-Weems, and Robert Weems helped me cope with many difficult situations. I'm grateful to Hanes Walton Jr. of the University of Michigan, a true friend who provided me with excellent advice during the academic year I served as a visiting scholar in the Department of Political Science. I also received a lot of helpful advice from Stephanie Taylor and from some of the brightest graduate students in the country - Encarnacion Anderson, DeAundria Bryant, Ruth Nicole Brown, Alana Hacksaw, Zenzele Isoke, Harwood McClerking, Brian McKenzie, Michael Moore, and Ishmail White to name a few. In addition, Reynolds Farley, Al Anderson, Lisa Neidert, and Michael Bader of the University of Michigan's National Poverty Center provided assistance in the analyses of census data in chapter 4 and the graphics in this book during a summer 2004 workshop, "Analyzing Poverty and Welfare Trends Using Census Bureau Data."

William E. Nelson, James Jennings, and Wilbur C. Rich have been my mentors since the beginning of my academic career. Denise Dugas and Richard Hart of the Joint Center for Political and Economic Studies provided data for the analysis in chapter 5. Also, I would like to thank all of the Delta residents, elected officials, economic development officers, and community activists who consented to interviews.

At the University of Florida, Les Thiele and Michael Martinez gave me the opportunity to serve as a visiting scholar in the Department of Political Science. It was such a delight to work in a department that was filled with collegiality and professionalism from its faculty, staff, and students. The students in my African American politics, American government, multiracial politics, and urban politics courses provided significant insight into my research during class discussions, especially Basil Binns II, Gloria Reina Bowens, Lisa Brown, Christopher Busey, Hannah Carter, Hughes Desir, Natalie Domond, Jordan Hale, Karen Harmel, James Holloway III, Jorge Irala, Natassia Kelly, Sisteria Mixon, Kelli Moore, Desiree Noisette, Funmi Olorunnipa, Vincent Onuoha, DeAngelo Parker, Roseberte Pierre, Janelle Rahyns, Ana Rangel, Tashiba Robinson, David Ruiz, Mark Villegas, Lydia Washington, and Antonio Whatley, to name a few. Also, the members of our department's ethnic working group, the McNair Scholars Program, and the Black Political Science Association were a wonderful group of people to have as friends, students, and colleagues. The environment and the people by who surrounded me made it much easier for me to complete my book. I would especially like to thank Michael Chege, Larry Dodd, David Hedge, Samuel Stafford, Richard Scher, and Philip Williams for their help over the years and other political science faculty members at the University of Florida who always made me feel welcome. My closest friends Fatima and Tony Conard; Russell Benjamin; Angela Lewis; and Richard T. Middleton IV; my church family at Cherry Street Church of Christ; my colleagues and friends in the National Conference of Black Political Scientists; my mother Ruth; brother Chris; sister-in-law Megan; sister Janice; brother-in-law Donald; nieces Victoria and Maya; nephews Andrew and Austin and in-laws (Ludetha, Nathaniel, Fannie, Trina, Ricky, and Rita) continue to enrich my life each day. My colleague, the late Professor James W. (Jim) Button, was more than a friend, but was like a big brother to me before his untimely death. Lastly, my wonderful husband Alfred and our son Alfred Jr. have taught me the true meaning of happiness.

ABBREVIATIONS

AAA	Agricultural Adjustment Act
CCA	Corrections Corporation of America
CIO	Congress of Industrial Organizations
CMT	Community Management Team
CPMT	Community Policing Management Team
COFO	Council of Federated Organizations
COPS	Communities Organized for Public Service
CQE	Citizens for Quality Education
CORE	Congress of Racial Equality
DCVL	Drew Community Voter's League
EZ/ECs	Empowerment Zone/Enterprise Communities
FARM	Farmers Advocating Resource Management
IAF	Industrial Areas Foundation
LMDDC	Lower Mississippi Delta Development Commission
MACE	Mississippi Action for Community Education
MDEZA	Mid-Delta Mississippi Empowerment Zone
MEWG	Mississippi Education Working Group
MFDP	Mississippi Freedom Democratic Party
MRC	Mississippi Redistricting Coalition
NAACP	National Association for the Advancement of Colored People
PLI	Persistently Low-income
SDE	State Department of Education
SNCC	Student Nonviolent Coordinating Committee
STFU	Southern Tenant Farmers' Union
TANF	Temporary Aid for Needy Families
TCRC	Tallahatchie County Redistricting Committee
TERC	Tallahatchie Education and Redistricting Committee
THI	Tallahatchie Housing Incorporated
TIL	Tunica Institute for Learning
VAP	Voting-Age

PART ONE

THE THEORETICAL FRAMEWORK

CHAPTER 1

THE INFLUENCE OF LOCAL ELITES
IN THE MISSISSIPPI DELTA

Introduction

Most of the research examining relationships between white elites and black nonelites in the Mississippi Delta has been of a historical nature. In recent years, three superior books have examined these relationships. The historian James C. Cobb's comprehensive history of the Delta from the 1820s to the early 1990s allowed for an understanding of the region's reputation as the "most Southern place on earth"[1]. *The Most Southern Place on Earth* (1992) explained the manner in which black Deltans endured poverty and racism, but failed to significantly improve their economic situation despite the aid of federal laws, U.S. Supreme Court decisions, and federal programs.

Clyde Woods's book, *Development Arrested* (1998), also analyzed the historical conflicts among impoverished African American residents and wealthy white elites. Woods's research indicated that African Americans in the Delta continued to pursue social and economic justice during an era of vehement and massive resistance from the plantation bloc. In addition, *Development Arrested* is one of the few books that discussed the establishment of the Lower Mississippi Delta Development Commission (LMDDC) in October 1988 and its mixed results in alleviating poverty in 214 of the poorest counties in Arkansas, Illinois, Louisiana, Kentucky, Mississippi, Missouri, and Tennessee. Like *The Most Southern Place on Earth*, *Development Arrested* explained the way in which African Americans coped with unbearable conditions during slavery, the end of federal Reconstruction, Jim Crow, and the peonage system by developing the blues musical tradition.

Frederick M. Wirt examined the Delta's sordid history of racism, political exclusion, and labor exploitation, but also the emergence of a New South. *We Ain't What We Was* examined the changes that occurred after the publication of Wirt's 1970 study

3

of Panola County, Mississippi, *The Politics of Southern Equality*.[2] Although evidence of a closed society remained apparent in the Delta by the 1990s, significant changes had taken place beginning in the 1960s because of the civil rights revolution and black political empowerment in several Delta counties. Nevertheless, the problems associated with poverty and segregated schools have always been insurmountable in the Mississippi Delta.

A few books have analyzed political relationships in the Mississippi Delta and in other rural areas especially in African American communities. Minion KC Morrison's *Black Political Mobilization* (1986) and Lawrence Hanks's *The Struggle for Black Political Empowerment in Three Georgia Counties* (1987) are two notable books on African American politics in rural areas.[3] Despite these studies of politics in rural, predominantly black, Southern communities, more research is needed. One scholar discussed the absence of political science scholarship on rural predominantly African American counties as well as the need for more such studies:

> By the late 1960s, social scientists had abandoned the critical investigation of rural relations in the predominantly African American plantation counties of the South. When they are examined, there is a tendency to superimpose categories created for the study of Northern manufacturing-based cities onto the social and institutional histories of these rural regions. What is lost in the process is not only an appreciation of the continuity of plantation-based economic systems and power relations, but also the critique of these relations.[4]

The Transformation of Plantation Politics will provide more than simply a description of race relations in the Mississippi Delta. It will also comprehensively examine the impact of black political exclusion, institutional racism, and white elite resistance on the Delta's economic, political, and social relations. A significant portion of the book will examine political and socioeconomic conditions in Tunica County where the most dramatic economic changes have occurred since the early 1990s and where white elite-black nonelite divisions remain apparent.

The elitist theory of community power depicts decision making in most Delta counties because the local political scene has always been dominated by a small group of white elites. One of the seminal studies of this theory is C. Wright Mills's *The Power Elite* (1956), which found that local elites rather than local elected officials controlled the major economic institutions and manipulated political officials to give them what they wanted. Mills's study characterized local affairs in the Mississippi Delta. Most of the white Delta residents were "plantation bloc millionaires" who inherited their wealth and privilege from their families, benefited from the cheap labor provided by black sharecroppers, selected local politicians, and determined the manner in which local revenues would be spent.[5] The terms plantation elites, landowning elites, and the plantation bloc will be used interchangeably throughout this book in reference to these families.

As plantation owners, these individuals guaranteed the exclusion of African Americans from any influence in local affairs. For several decades, generations of black sharecroppers were trapped in a cycle of poverty where they earned low wages and lacked alternative employment opportunities. The sharecropping system also resulted in illiteracy, substantial school dropout rates, and other indicators of low educational achievement because most black children had to leave school and work in the fields for most of the year. Thus, black Delta families never had a reason to place a high value on education. Also under this oppressive system, African Americans found it almost impossible to own land, businesses, or even their homes. The sharecropping system mostly meant that they lived in substandard housing or "nigger town slums," did fieldwork from morning until night, were kept indebted, and had no opportunities to improve their standard of living.[6] Thus, chapter 1 analyzes pluralist, elitist, regime, and political incorporation theories and explains why the elitist and political incorporation theories paradigms best characterize the relationships among whites and African Americans in the Mississippi Delta. The pluralist and regime frameworks have weaknesses that render them inappropriate for examining relationships among white elites and black nonelites in rural Mississippi.

Theories on the Role of Race in Local Decision making

Pluralist Theory

Over the years, political scientists have developed many theories in order to study the relationships among dominant and subordinate groups in local communities. The complex question of who governs cities and counties, has been debated repeatedly in the political science literature because the individuals who govern cities determine who will hold the major elective offices and which group(s) receive the most economic resources. In his study of power relations in New Haven, Connecticut, *Who Governs?* (1961), Robert A. Dahl examined whether the city of New Haven was governed by a small number of elites. He analyzed twenty-four important decisions in the areas of urban renewal, education, and the selection of party nominees for mayor during the 1940s and 1950s in order to determine whether the same individuals made the most important local decisions most of the time. He found that power and decision making in New Haven was noncumulative in the sense that no one individual made all of the decisions, but that a plurality of groups-such as the members of labor unions, political parties, banks, manufacturing plants, churches, school systems, and government agencies-competed for power.

During the Nineteenth century, New Haven had been dominated by an "oligarchy" or a system of "cumulative" inequalities in which a few privileged individuals possessed most of the wealth and power; yet, this system was later replaced by one of "noncumulative" power and "dispersed" inequalities during the twentieth century.[7] A system of dispersed inequalities existed in New Haven because, despite the existence of some inequalities, every group in the city possessed some resources and thus had some measure of influence. On this point, Dahl found that:

> No minority group is permanently excluded from politics or suffers cumulative inequalities. Our system is not only democratic, but is perhaps the most perfect expression of democracy that exists anywhere. . . No minority group is permanently excluded from the political arena or suffers cumulative inequalities. . . . Different citizens have many different kinds of resources for influencing officials.[8]

Who Governs? also discussed the ability of Irish "ex-plebes"-working class Irish politicians-to mobilize the Irish vote and to control city patronage jobs during the heyday of machine rule. Irish mobilization allowed them to take control of the local political machine. Dahl pointed out that Irish machine bosses used the political mobilization of the Irish and the patronage system in the city of New Haven to advance the social and economic position of the Irish. Using machine patronage, the Irish gained middle-class status rapidly considering their meager job skills and the discrimination they encountered. The implication was that other ethnic and racial groups could also mobilize themselves politically in order to improve their disadvantaged plight in local communities.[9]

Pluralist theory was found to be an invalid theoretical model for understanding the impact of race on local decision making in the years following the publication of *Who Governs?*[10] First, the finding that local decision making is noncumulative because several groups rather than a few elites make most of the major decisions is not the case in rural Southern communities. Power in these areas is more likely to be concentrated in the hands of a few elite individuals who make most of the major decisions with little or no input from most local residents. This is especially the case in areas with histories of polarized racial relationships and with substantial populations of poor African American residents. For most of the Mississippi Delta's history, wealthy white elites excluded black nonelites from even the slightest role in local policy making.

Second, Dahl's finding of dispersed inequalities-that all groups have some measure of influence in local politics because of the resources they possess-is an even more inadequate characterization of power relationships in the Mississippi Delta. Until recently, the members of elite families were the only individuals who possessed any power in the region. The most influential members of these families effectively prevented African Americans from gaining political and economic power by using legal, physical, and economic forms of intimidation.

Third, the belief that African Americans can emulate Irish Americans in translating their political power into economic power is problematic. The political and economic discrimination endured by the Irish was much less severe than that endured by African Americans in the rural South who experienced insurmountable de facto and de jure obstacles when attempting to mobilize politically. Even after African American citizens overcame these impediments and held most of the major elective offices in cities and counties, the communities they governed were plagued by extreme poverty, crime, unemployment, and other socioeconomic ills. For example, African Americans held the major political offices in most of the Mississippi Delta's counties beginning in the 1970s, but failed to gain economic power because of factors such as a lack of financial capital, industrial redlining, and a permanently low-income workforce.

Elitist Theories

Dahl's findings contrasted with those of Mills, Floyd Hunter, and others who found that individuals known as elites controlled the major economic institutions and manipulated political officials to give them what they wanted. Elitist theories explained the way in which individuals became elites, the amount of influence they possessed, and the method by which they exercised their power. Most of this research defined elites as "unitary" actors who worked together and who conspired to promote their interests to the detriment of the masses.[11] Whether they were social elites,[12] specialized elites,[13] or governing elites,[14] they were at the top of any "socially significant hierarchy and always determined the amount of resources that groups received in local areas.[15] The following discussion outlines the elite theories that originated in sociological research and that were later used in political science research. This overview will provide a theoretical framework for the analysis of relationships among white elites and black nonelites.

Classical elite theory originated in the works of the sociologists V. Pareto, Gaetano Mosca, and Roberto Michels. Their research was among (the earliest to find that a small group of individuals determined the way in which their society would be governed.[16] The classical elite studies identified who the elites were and questioned whether they established and maintained their power base through consent of the masses, right of birth, or force. Subsequent research examined the manner in which elites reacted when nonelites threatened their power base and the reasons why some individuals lost their elite status.

G. William Domhoff, in *Who Rules America?* (1983), discussed the activities of the ruling elite and the governing class. The ruling elite were the "minority of individuals whose preferences regularly prevail in cases of differences in preference on key political issues."[17] Domhoff found that the same persons from upper class families determined the outcome of a wide variety of issues. Together these "ruling elites" made up a governing class, "a social upper class which receives a disproportionate amount of a country's income, owns a disproportionate amount of a country's income, owns a disproportionate amount of a country's wealth, and contributes a disproportionate number of its members to the controlling institutions and key decision making groups in that country."[18]

In *The Power Elite*, Mills discussed critical elite theory. He found that most American communities whether small or large were dominated by a small group of individuals and families whom he defined as, ". . . Men whose positions enable them to transcend the ordinary environments of ordinary men and women. They are in positions to make decisions having major consequences. . . . They are in command of the major hierarchies and organizations of modern society."[19] Mills found that the earliest elites were white men who controlled the local and/or national economic and political scene by using a variety of leadership and governing styles. Some of the elites were born into privileged families. Others were born into families that were outside the strata of elites, but that gained influence by accumulating wealth in the business establishment, acquiring an education at a prestigious institute, marrying someone from an elite family, or ascending to the highest military rankings.[20]

Hunter's book, *Community Power Structure* (1953), was the first major empirical study to utilize elitist theory and the first attempt to analyze elite and nonelite relationships in a major city. In order to determine which leaders ran "Regional City"—a fictional city with several similarities to Atlanta, Georgia,—Hunter used the "reputational approach." He identified all of the city's business, civic, and political leaders and asked six other leaders who were familiar with them, to select the most influential persons from the list.[21] Because Hunter described the city's power structure as a "stratified pyramid," his theory is also referred to as the stratificationist theory.

According to Hunter, business elites had more power than local governmental officials. Therefore, political leaders were in the second tier of the pyramid. The business elites manipulated government officials to give them what they wanted. Political leaders then carried out the instructions of those in the first tier of the pyramid. Thus, the key to gaining influence in Regional City and in others was to first gain influence in the business establishment and later in the political sphere.[22] This elite power structure initiated most of the development that occurred in Regional City and that successfully kept most projects it disapproved of from coming to fruition.

Both normative elite theorists and the technocratic approach to elite theory pointed out some of the positive aspects of elite rule. Rule by a small minority reduced conflict among the masses, and elites were necessary for the management of society.[23] Since around the mid-1970s, a number of scholarly articles and books have examined the neo-elite perspective that found that elites have been constrained by such factors as the economy and public opinion.[24]

In sum, classical, critical, normative, and technocratic elite theories examined the relationships between influential and powerless individuals in large cities. The manner in which elites acquired, maintained, and utilized their power differed in rural cities and counties; however, because elites in these areas are not always business or political figures, they find different avenues to attain power. In the rural South and especially in the Mississippi Delta, they are usually born into wealthy landowning families.

Regime Theory

Regime theory analyzed the relationships among local elected officials and business-people. Regimes have been defined as "the informal arrangements by which public bodies and private interests [functioned] together in order to be able to make and carry out governing decisions."[25] Clarence N. Stone in "Atlanta and the Limited

Reach of Electoral Control" (1997) discussed the need for cooperation among the public and private sectors:

> Achieving electoral influence is significant, but popular control of
> elected office is only one element in the actual governance of a city.
> The need for private investment in business activity makes control of
> economic institutions a second element of great consequence. Gover-
> nance comes out of the interplay between electoral and economic
> power. Neither stands alone. Governance . . . requires cooperation and
> accommodation among a network of institutions, especially political
> and economic ones.[26]

These partnerships between politicians and business-people were
difficult to establish and maintain especially in cities governed by
African American politicians and predominantly white business communities. Major conflicts arose when black politicians attempted to
deliver economic benefits to lower- and middle-income black communities. They usually encountered massive resistance from the white
middle-class citizens and majority white business communities.[27]
    The regime theoretical framework has been more appropriate
for analyses of public-private partnerships in urban cities rather than
in rural counties. As previously mentioned, few business elites remained in the Mississippi Delta after the 1960s because of factory closures and overall declines in the farming industry. Whereas in cities,
business-people and elected officials cooperated in order to pursue
economic growth, political figures catered to the whim of wealthy
landowners rather than to business-people in rural counties. Because
of the polarized race relations in the Delta, landowning elites per-
suaded political elites to reject industries that would result in economic parity among African Americans and whites for most of the
region's history. Therefore, the regime analysis of the partnerships
among political and business elites in cities has had little relevance
for examining relationships among political elites and landowning
elites in rural Mississippi.

Political Incorporation Theory

    According to Rufus Browning, Dale Rogers Marshall, and David
Tabb in *Protest Is Not Enough* (1984), African Americans possessed political power in local areas when they achieved strong levels of political incorporation. Such incorporation occurred when African
American citizens had "an ability to participate in a coalition that
dominated city policymaking and . . . an ability to have issues of great-

est concern to [them] furthered by this coalition."[28] Levels of political incorporation ranged from no minority group representation to "a dominant role in a governing coalition strongly committed to minority interests."[29]

Incorporation required more than simply electing black representatives; it also required these political figures to pursue initiatives to raise the socioeconomic status of black citizens. After African American voters elected black representatives on local city councils, aldermanic boards, city commissions, and as city mayors, they expected tangible benefits from them, such as the establishment of civilian police review boards, minority citizen appointments to city boards and commissions, and increased opportunities to win city contracts.[30]

As previously mentioned, pluralist and regime theories fail to adequately characterize political relationships in the Mississippi Delta. Studies that have utilized political incorporation theory to determine African American political behavior and empowerment have mostly assessed black political power in cities rather than in rural counties. Although political, social, and economic relationships differ in rural counties and cities, political incorporation theory is an adequate framework for examining the political and economic relationships among white elites and black nonelites in the Mississippi Delta.

According to the theory, African Americans and Latinos first mobilize their communities so that they can elect minority representatives, then gain varying degrees of political power and substantive benefits from their elected representatives.[31] The discussion in chapter 5 will demonstrate the manner in which African American residents in Delta counties have mobilized themselves and elected representatives just like the African American residents of cities; however, rural citizens have had more obstacles to overcome when attempting to gain political power. First, rural counties have been more likely to have governmental systems in which most candidates are elected in at-large rather than in district elections. Second, it has been difficult to find viable black candidates to run for office because of their belief that they cannot win due to a lack of funding, racial bloc voting, and disappointing black voter turnout rates. Many predominantly black rural counties in the South still have majority white political establishments because of these obstacles.[32] Third, the political incorporation framework discussed the importance of coalitions in cities as a way to gain political power. When African Americans joined coalitions with whites, Latinos, and Asians in cities, they were more likely to have their needs met and their interests served. In the rural counties of Mississippi, biracial coalition politics was never a feasible option in the search for black political and economic empowerment because of the unwillingness of white voters to join coalitions with African Americans. In most Delta counties, blacks and whites have remained residentially segregated because wealthy whites have always lived in separately annexed towns. Also, poor whites and African Americans joined coalitions on the basis of race rather than class. Poor whites seldom supported black candidates even when these candidates promised to uplift the plight of the poor. Thus, it is impossible for African Americans in the Delta to follow the example of African Americans in Los Angeles, New York, New Haven, and in other cities where black candidates have developed multiracial coalitions. Moreover, it is more difficult for African American rural county residents to gain political incorporation because of the unique challenges their preferred candidates encounter when seeking offices and when attempting to govern.

The Limitations of Black Political Power and the Emphasis on Social Capital

Scholarly research has almost universally found that low-income minority citizens must gain political power and use it to address their social and economic dilemmas in American communities.[33] Political and economic transformations may not occur, however, even in cities and counties with a powerful African American political base. For example, African Americans became members of the political elite in many cities and counties during the 1970s, 1980s, and 1990s, but inherited a "hollow prize."[34] Their cities benefited in some ways from black political officeholding, but were also plagued by middle-class flight, population declines, and escalating unemployment, poverty, and crime rates. Added to these problems, majority white business establishments have oftentimes opposed political agendas designed to aid impoverished African Americans. Despite these limitations on black political mobilization, it is clear that minority communities that lack such empowerment will not experience any significant economic improvements.

Because of the difficulties that many black Deltans have faced when attempting to mobilize politically and the disappointments they have had with the inability of black elected officials to improve their quality of life, a larger number of African American Delta residents are addressing their community's ills by working in community development organizations more so than in political organizations. In *Blacks and Social Change* (1989), a finding by James W. Button provided the rationale behind the current social capital efforts in the

Mississippi Delta, "Since powerless groups are generally precluded from achieving significant change through conventional political approaches, such groups tend to develop unconventional strategies in the attempt to influence change."[35]

Because of a "paradox of political power," black Delta residents are now focusing on black social capital and intergroup social capital efforts. In this book, the paradox of political power is defined as follows: For African Americans in Tunica County, a lack of a political base has meant that few of gaming's substantive benefits have trickled down to the poor. Massive resistance from elites and from a governmental system in which most officials were elected at-large prevented them from gaining political power. Partly because they have held few municipal or countywide political offices until recently and have essentially been ignored by white politicians, the black residents of Tunica County failed to receive equitable benefits from the lucrative legalized gaming industry beginning in the 1990s. On the other hand, African American candidates in most of Tunica's neighboring Delta towns won most of the local political offices and were committed to the interests of the black citizenry, but failed to raise the socioeconomic status of their constituents because of a lack of financial capital. Currently, some Delta counties with predominantly black governing coalitions are listed among the poorest counties in the nation because of the lack of a middle-class tax base, jobs and other fiscal resources, as well as a large sector of "permanently low-income" (PLI) residents.

Even if the black residents of Tunica County had political power, it may not have made much of a difference for the poorest residents of the county because black elected officials usually pursue the same type of agendas as white elected officials in cities and counties. The emphasis of these officeholders is usually on economic development strategies that benefit the middle class and the business community, often at the expense of the poor.[36] For these reasons, the impoverished black residents of neglected communities engage in nontraditional political activities. Robert D. Putnam defines the concept of social capital as "features of social organization, such as trust, norms, and networks, that can improve the efficiency of society by facilitating coordinated actions."[37] By strengthening their social capital ties, African Americans can develop strong networks within their communities and accomplish more by working together in community empowerment groups while continuing to elect black officeholders.

In one of the few studies that analyzed social capital efforts in a predominantly African American community, Marion E. Orr distinguished between black social capital-the trusts, norms, and networks within black communities-and intergroup social capital-the trusts, norms, and networks of cooperation among black citizens and white elites.[38] In *Black Social Capital* (1999), Orr pointed out that black communities usually have strong levels of social capital, but have had difficulty working with white elites.[39] *The Transformation of Plantation Politics* will demonstrate that it is even more difficult for African Americans to establish successful collaborative relationships with white elites in rural counties with histories of polarized race relations and massive elite resistance to black political and economic gains.

Overview

Each of the chapters in this book reveals the transformation of the Delta's plantation political culture from one of complete African American political exclusion to one of majority black representation in many small towns. The plantation political structure of the Delta has undergone five phases. During the first phase from the 1800s to the early 1960s, African Americans were denied the right to participate in any kind of local or state political activity. The second phase took place during the height of the modern civil rights movement when activists sought to improve the economic, educational, and political conditions for black Mississippians.

During the third phase, the years immediately following the Voting Rights Act of 1965, an initial transition from majority white to majority black political governance took place in many Delta towns after the black voter registration rates increased and black candidates sought elective offices. After the ratification of the Voting Rights Act of 1965, African American citizens had high expectations that black political figures would more sufficiently address their needs, but were soon disappointed because of the lack of economic resources in towns governed by African American politicians and the insurmountable problems experienced by most Delta residents.

During the fourth phase from the 1970s to the present, African Americans held most of the political offices in many Delta towns, but few countywide positions. Members of the plantation elite class continued to control these positions which were the most powerful in the region. During the fifth and final phase from the 1980s to the present, Delta community residents have focused on "politicizing [their] black social capital and transforming it into a force of policy change."[40] In other words, they have attempted to strengthen their levels of black social capital while still engaging in political activities as a way to improve their economic status in the Delta.

Chapter 2 discusses the establishment of a "cotton-obsessed, Negro-obsessed" society that was maintained through an exploitative sharecropping system and blatant institutional racism. The plantation bloc of white landowning elites profited from the cheap labor of black sharecroppers. During this time, the Delta had a prosperous economy that was sustained by the profitable cotton industry as well as by the oats, soybean, and wheat-farming industries. Conditions for black sharecroppers, however, were never ideal in the Mississippi Delta. Studies have found that African Americans in rural counties in Mississippi and in other Southern states have remained impoverished primarily because of the legacy of slavery, the sharecropping system, and institutional racism.[41] In the current Delta society, the legacy of the sharecropping system remains apparent because of the continuing economic disparities among the white wealthy and the black poor.

Chapter 3 discusses the disfranchisement of African Americans by white elites during the first and second phases of the plantation political structure. Many black Deltans chose the option of "exit" over "voice" during this time period.[42] For several decades, thousands of local residents moved out of the area because of the lack of employment, educational, and political opportunities rather than remaining to transform a seemingly unchangeable system.

At this time, civil rights activists attempted to challenge black political exclusion in the entire state of Mississippi, but found it more difficult to persuade the African American residents of many rural towns of the Mississippi Delta to participate in civil rights and political empowerment protests than the black residents of cities. The elites had instilled such a great amount of fear in black Delta residents that most refused to participate in the earliest empowerment efforts. Civil rights activism did occur in many Delta towns and counties despite threats of reprisal from local elites because of the involvement of historically black colleges and universities in the state, independently-owned churches, and charismatic leaders. However in Tunica County, no visible efforts occurred because churches were owned by local elites and were located on their property. No student activism occurred and no leaders emerged to the forefront. The discussions of black political and civil rights efforts in chapter 3 indicate the existence of strong levels of social capital within the Delta's black communities during the 1960s. Through their work in groups such as the Council of Federated Organizations (COFO), Delta residents of color developed networks to survive the harshness of plantation life in Mississippi and took the initial steps toward gaining political and civil rights.

Chapter 4 discusses the abject poverty in the Delta during the 1980s, the decline of the agricultural industry, industrial redlining, and the unsuccessful governmental efforts to revitalize the region's economy. Because of these problems, local and state officials were desperate for a new industry to revitalize the Delta. At the time, the Delta had an abundance of cheap land and a need to enhance cultural tourist sites, but no means to attract new industries.

Beginning in the 1990s, several major changes occurred because of legalized gaming. The proponents of casino gaming promoted it as an "industry" that would revitalize the economies of counties throughout the Delta, the Gulf Coast, and the entire state of Mississippi. Gaming became a godsend, but also a double-edged sword for the Delta. After the legalization of gaming, an abundance of jobs and financial capital existed in Tunica County, but the poverty rate in the entire Delta region continued to double and even triple the national average. While gaming revenues alleviated unemployment and welfare dependency, it exacerbated the problems of crime, alcohol addiction, drug addiction, gaming addiction, and traffic fatalities. The main research questions in this chapter are as follows: Has one of the poorest areas in the nation been transformed into an entrepreneurial state? Is there any evidence that the elites were threatened by "outsiders"-casino executives and owners-whose industry resulted in a myriad of changes in a society that had traditionally resisted change? To what extent has gaming resulted in an economic transformation in the Delta? Third and most importantly, has gaming brought about a transformation of economic power relationships among white elites and African American nonelites-that is, a greater amount of economic power for African Americans as a group?

Chapter 5 analyzes the question of whether a lack of black political power contributes to the remaining high poverty levels in some Delta communities. Despite the alleged benefits of gaming, the region's poverty rates remain among the highest in the nation. The improvement in the economic and political standing of black Deltans by the end of the 1990s should have resulted in significantly lower black poverty rates, especially in counties with strong amounts of political power and with casinos. This chapter essentially questions why this has not happened as expected in the Mississippi Delta.

Chapter 6 discusses the efforts of black Deltans to enhance their social capital after the legalization of gaming during the fifth and current phase of the plantation political system. Unlike the social capital efforts of the 1960s, the most recent activities are concerned with economic empowerment more so than political and civil rights gains. In Tunica County, black residents solicited the assistance of regional and national organizations and formed new local community empowerment groups in order to reap more of gaming's benefits. In neighboring Delta counties, black political power and gaming revenues failed to improve the overall quality of life. The social capital activities of these community residents mostly involved winning the local and statewide support to build new prisons-the only industry that would provide reliable jobs, higher wages, decent working conditions, and revenues to sustain the local economy. This chapter examines the significance of this study. What can we learn from this analysis of plantation politics in the Mississippi Delta and how does it contribute to our understanding of elite-nonelite relationships, rural African American political development, and the concept of social capital?

Conceptualizations of Black Political Power and Black Social Capital

The Joint Center for Political and Economic Studies publication, *Black Elected Officials*, listed the names and offices of all African American political figures in the United States. As mentioned earlier, political incorporation theory equates African American political power with an ability to elect black mayors, City Council members, aldermen, and other political representatives over a period of several years and the power to demand that these representatives implement the preferred policies of African Americans.[43] However, African American citizens with the strongest measures of political incorporation still may not have had the kind of unchallengeable political power possessed by wealthy white elites in some cities and counties. This latter form of political power involved more than electing officeholders and promoting group interests, but also a capacity to "determine whether certain questions ever reach the competition stage" and to guarantee "the quiescence of the powerless."[44] Thus, these individuals possessed what EE Schattschneider and later John Gaventa referred to as "power's second face"-the ability of the elite class to exclude certain issues from the decision making process and to suppress opposition from nonelites.[45]

In a study of elite-nonelite relationships in Appalachia, Gaventa found that most powerful elites not only implemented a political, economic, and institutional structure beneficial to them at the expense of others, but also kept the issues, grievances, and interests of nonelites off of the decision making agenda.[46] Appalachia's elites maintained a "quiescence" of its nonelite class through its "mobilization of bias"—that is, its ability to promote issues and decisions favored by elites and to suppress nonelite challenges to the elite-dominated power structure.[47] These power relationships could only be altered when either the elites lost power or the nonelites gained power.[48]

In the analysis of the possible impact of black political power on black poverty in the Mississippi Delta in chapter 5, African American political power is defined as the ability to elect sympathetic black political representatives over a period of several years, but also by the number of African American landowners because of the importance of land ownership in the Delta. To assess the amount of black political power according to this definition, the author first analyzed the Joint Center's roster of the number of black elected officials in each Delta county and the years in which they were elected. Second, chancery court clerk records that included the names, but not the racial backgrounds, of elected officials were examined to determine the names and titles of politicians elected after publication of the Joint Center study. Local residents who were knowledgeable about local politics looked at these lists and were able to identify the officeholders's races.

To determine the third component of political power in the Mississippi Delta, land ownership, 1998-2003 annual reports of the Delta Council and of the most recent Delta Farmers Advocating Resource Management (FARM) organization report were reviewed in order to determine the names of the owners of the most acreages of land. The membership of the Delta Council, established in 1935 to promote agricultural interests, has traditionally consisted of the most prominent landowners, business people, and professionals in the area.[49] Delta FARM originated in 1997 to protect the region's natural resources; its members are owners of the Delta's largest farms. Throughout most of their histories as organizations, both the Delta Council and Delta FARM have had all-white memberships.

In the analyses of the social capital efforts of African American Delta activists during the modern civil rights movement and the post gaming eras in chapters 3 and 6, an attempt will be made to estimate the levels of social capital relationships. Scholars have encountered several obstacles when "measuring" social capital ties among community residents. One body of research found that "a single 'true' measure [of social capital] is probably not possible or even desirable" mostly because of the difficulties of defining and measuring concepts such as "community," "trust," "relationships," and "networks."[50] Some research has estimated the extent of social capital relationships from surveys assessing the levels of trust individuals have in their neighbors; their voter registration and turnout rates; and the numbers of individuals belonging to civic, political, religious, and social institutions in local communities.

In this book, social capital will be defined as the concern of individuals for the welfare of their communities and by their willingness to work cooperatively to solve their problems. This definition, like others of social capital, includes the numbers of active participants in churches, social, and in political, community empowerment, and civic organizations.[51] Interviews conducted by the author found clear indications of strong social capital ties because of the participation of most African American Delta residents in churches and a sizable number in other groups. Before African Americans were allowed to form community development groups or to participate in political organizations, their strong social capital ties were shown in their concern for their neighbors and in their active participation in churches.[52]

Robert D. Putnam's research pointed out the impossibility of strong social relationships among community residents, but the possibility of weak political participation rates. In his view, weak social capital ties resulted in "civic disengagement" or in a declining interest in political participation.[53] The experience of Mexican American activists in San Antonio, Texas's poorest neighborhoods, however, demonstrated that a minority group with strong social capital ties could also possess low political participation rates. Vibrant social capital relationships exist among the thousands of mostly poor, Latino, and Catholic members of COPS (Communities Organized for Public Service). This organization has become one of the most powerful community groups in the nation because of its ability to win federal block grants and to persuade local elites to empower their neighborhoods. The participants in COPS have enhanced their social capital by holding neighborhood meetings, writing proposals for community development projects, securing federal block grants, using these grants to enhance their neighborhoods, and pressuring the city's political leaders to fulfill their needs.[54] However, the members of COPS have had some of the lowest voter registration and turnout rates in San Antonio's local elections. This low involvement in the political process has been attributed to the unique socioeconomic profile of its members-that is, their low incomes and status as recent immigrants.[55]

Chapters 5 and 6 will echo the finding that communities with strong social capital relationships can also have low political participation rates. After the Voting Rights Act of 1965, the Mississippi Delta had record high black voter registration rates. Although these levels declined in subsequent years, the social capital efforts of local citizens continued.

Data and Methods

The rich data source of this qualitative book consists of interviews, U.S. census data, dissertations, scholarly articles and books, theses, and unpublished papers. Numerous scholarly analyses of concentrated poverty, elite, and social capital theories are referred to in the analysis of the research questions in this book. These sources provide historical, political, and theoretical information that are relevant for this examination of politics, poverty, and social capital in the Mississippi Delta.

Over the past four years, approximately one hundred face-to-face and telephone interviews were conducted by the author with community activists, current and former residents, journalists familiar with Delta politics, and political officeholders. Appendixes A, B, C, and D provide a list of questions that were asked during the interviews. Each ranged from approximately 30 to 60 minutes and some individuals were interviewed more than once.

The "reputational approach" developed by Hunter in one of the earliest studies of nonelite-elite relationships in the South was useful for identifying the Mississippi Delta's elite class and for determining prospective interviewees. Hunter's approach stipulated that the names of local elites can be ascertained by first compiling a list of prominent individuals in civic, business, and political affairs; then allowing knowledgeable community residents to rank in hierarchical order the most influential persons or the "top power structure" and the "understructure personnel" of less powerful individuals in local communities.[56]

After reading several newspaper articles and conducting the first round of interviews in December 1999 with current and former Delta residents, the author compiled a list of political and landowning elites in the top power structure, community activists and others in the understructure personnel, and the least influential residents of Delta communities or nonelites. During the second round of interviews in the summer of 2000, many of these persons were interviewed. The author conducted subsequent sessions with these local elites and with nonelites between 2000 and 2004. During each round of interviews, many of the those interviewed provided additional names of influential landowning politicians, community residents, activists, and journalists.

The information gathered in these meetings is referred to in this book, but especially in chapters 2 and 3 that discuss the plantation economic and political history of the region. In addition, taped interviews that were part of oral history projects at Delta State University, the University of Mississippi at Oxford, and the Mississippi Valley Collection of the University of Memphis Ned R. McWherter Library provided insight about the attitudes of the Delta's elites and nonelites. In these interviews, local activists, citizens, and politicians explained the manner in which the plantation bloc continues to dominate the economic and political arenas of Delta counties. Although they have not exhibited the overt resistance to black political and economic gains as in previous years, this book argues that the legacy of their past resistance to these gains continues to negatively impact the socioeconomic status of African American residents.

Like any study of this nature, this research has limitations. Many of those contacted agreed to participate only after receiving assurances of anonymity. Their desire to have their names withheld and/or to not be quoted directly was understandable considering the peculiar race relations in the Mississippi Delta's small counties and the fear on the part of nonelites of retribution from elites. In addition, few plantation elites consented to interviews. Therefore, the author questioned others about the governance and wishes of the plantation bloc. In addition, many of the journalists cited ethical reasons for their refusal to be interviewed; they instead referred the author to their published newspaper and magazine articles.

Chapters 4 and 5 include an analysis of data from the U.S. census and from the Mississippi State Tax Commission to determine the changes in the Delta's median household incomes, per-capita incomes, poverty, and unemployment rates of Delta residents. The census data provides a socioeconomic profile of the Mississippi Delta's residents-that is, its white upper and middle classes and its black impoverished population. Second, this data indicate the declines in the region's unemployment and poverty rates after the legalization of casino gaming, but the persistence of double-digit black poverty in all of the Delta's counties. Third, the census data, and the Joint Center for Political Economic Studies information, provide evidence in chapter 5 that poverty rates were higher in some areas with greater percentages of black elected officials.

PART TWO

THE PLANTATION
POLITICAL AND ECONOMIC CULTURE

CHAPTER 2

THE "COTTON-OBSESSED, NEGRO-OBSESSED" DELTA PLANTATION ECONOMY

Introduction

The Mississippi Delta has been called a "police state," "cotton-obsessed, Negro-obsessed", and "the most southern place on earth" because of white resistance to black political participation and economic advancement.[1] For most of the state's history, black Delta families were sharecroppers who lived in shacks, picked cotton from morning until night, and had no political voice. The current prevalence of concentrated poverty, low educational achievement, and industrial redlining in the Mississippi Delta results in part from the legacy of the sharecropping system.

This chapter discusses the relationships among elites and non-elites during the two phases of the sharecropping system. During the first phase of the sharecropping system, the Delta's elite class heavily relied upon black labor, opposed federal governmental aid, and prevented the formation of labor unions out of fear that federal aid and unions would require higher wages and improved working conditions for black laborers. During the second phase, federal governmental programs were supposed to end the dependencies of black sharecroppers on Delta plantation elites, but instead resulted in even greater dependencies because the elites administered these programs for their own personal gain. The plantation bloc no longer had much of a need for sharecroppers due to acreage-reduction and agricultural mechanization. Also, after federal laws stipulated that field-workers receive a minimum wage, civil rights, and political rights, the once valued black labor force became a liability.

In order to understand the current status of the Mississippi Delta's politics and economy, one must understand the sharecropping system. The main goal of this system was to keep the landowning elites rich and powerful and the black nonelites poor and powerless. As a result of the actions of elites during the first two phases of the sharecropping system, abject poverty continued to be widespread in later years. By the 1980s, the Mississippi Delta's counties ranked among the most impoverished in the nation providing evidence of the sharecropping system's legacy in the region.

A Portrait of the Mississippi Delta

The Mississippi Delta's 18 counties, (figure 2.1), are bounded by the Mississippi River to the west and the Bluff Hills to the east. Tunica County is the first of the "core" counties in the Mississippi Delta from the North. The Delta consists of 11 "core" counties and 7 "peripheral" or "fringe" counties, is 200 miles long and 70 miles wide.[2] Only parts of Carroll, Holmes, Grenada, Panola, Tallahatchie, Tate, and Yazoo counties lie within the Delta region.

For most of the Mississippi Delta's history, the agricultural industry sustained the local economy. The abundance of fertile land adjacent to the Mississippi River and the warm climate was ideal for farming. The Delta has always provided an ideal life for the few, but difficult life for the majority. Currently, some neighborhoods have a picturesque scene of beautiful plantation homes on large parcels of land surrounded by cotton fields while nearby neighborhoods grapple with blight, decay, and hopelessness. For most of the region's history, the wealthy white families in the elite class heavily relied on black laborers to cook their food, wash their clothes, chop their cotton, tend to their children, and maintain their property. Willie Morris in "My Delta. And Yours?" observed that the Delta could not have functioned without black laborers:

> Almost every house had its black maid, who, for fifteen cents an hour, left her own dwelling early in the mornings and did not return until late afternoons-cooking, laundering, mopping, sweeping. . . . Their labors never ceased. Then almost every second house had its yardman, Jap and Redey and Shorty and Potluck and Shenandoah, who wore sweaty bandanas and had their own private jelly glasses to drink tap water from. From the womb to the tomb, blacks tended to the whites of the town: their women raising the white infants, their men digging white graves, mowing the cemetery grass, clipping the hedges surrounding the very plots of the dead. In the proper seasons, the town blacks went out in trucks to the plantations to work from dawn to dusk. . . . If, through some precipitous act of nature, the blacks of our town suddenly vanished from the earth, [wealthy whites in the Delta] would have been strangely empty and bereft.[3]

Figure 2.1   Map of the Mississippi Delta

The Delta began relying on an agriculturally based or "plantation" economy during the mid-1800s. By 1860, most Delta counties
had been created, but were sparsely populated. The earliest Delta
farmers created the first flood control measures and instituted the
plantation economy.[4] The sharecropping system was instituted sup-
posedly to provide job opportunities, wages, and housing for ex-slaves
as a way to keep their labor in the area. During the Reconstruction
years and after the turn of the century, many whites abused black

workers, but the landowning elites did not want to alienate black workers to such an extent they would leave because of the need for a cheap labor force.

Before the 1960s, a traditionalistic plantation political culture and the sharecropping system dominated the region's political and economic affairs. Even before the implementation of the Delta's agriculturally based economy, the plantation bloc established a monopoly that still controls the agricultural, manufacturing, and banking industries as well as the allocation of local, state, and county revenues. Generations of plantation elites amassed their wealth and power first and foremost by purchasing acres of land for farming purposes. Second, these landowners maintained control of local affairs by working with the few white middle-class professionals in the region to promote their self-interests.[5] However, these professionals or "town industrialists" were not fully accepted into the plantation bloc, but simply assisted the elites, many of whom were local officeholders, in maintaining the status quo. The relationship among plantation elites and industrialists can be described in the following manner; "[The plantation] complex was defended by politically and economically active planters and their family members who also served as sheriffs, judges, lawyers, and merchants. Alliances within the plantation bloc were cemented through culture, schooling, and marriage. These families expanded into other businesses such as cotton gins, cottonseed oil mills, real estate, insurance, publishing, banking, and cotton footage."[6] Third, the plantation bloc had a cohesive, monolithic leadership style that vehemently resisted any kind of change, especially that involving the region's black majority. The next two sections explain the manner in which generations of black sharecroppers in the Delta were subjugated by the plantation elites during the height of the sharecropping system.

The First Phase of the Sharecropping System

The sharecropping system in the Mississippi Delta has had two distinct phases. The first was the heyday of the system when the landowning elites had an unchallenged, invincible domination of local affairs from the 1800s until the early 1960s. The second phase took place from the late 1960s and the 1970s when major reforms and changes impacted the sharecropping system, the agricultural industry, and the Delta's labor force.

During the first phase of the system, the landowners employed black laborers to do back breaking labor in temperatures that surpassed 100 degrees on many summer days plowing land with mule-drawn planters (and tractors in later years) and chopping cotton. At daybreak, truck drivers transported workers to the fields. In the middle of the day, women were taken back to their homes and were allotted two hours to cook and eat lunch while men had one hour.[7] Most workers could not afford watches and therefore determined the time by looking at their shadows that grew smaller as the hours passed. At sunset, sharecroppers weighed cotton in the fields, dumped it in baskets, and transported it to a "cotton house."[8] They then received $1 per 100 pounds. Most adult field-workers picked between 300 and 350 pounds of cotton a day.[9]

Black sharecroppers remained impoverished during this time mainly because of their dependency on the plantation elites for their farming supplies, food, housing, and other needs. Usually, the landowner furnished sharecroppers with the necessary supplies, deducted the costs from their pay at the end of the season, and gave them a portion of the harvest at settlement.[10] In Tunica County, five families have owned most of the land-the Harveys, the Keelers, the Leathermans, the Moores, and the Owens. Usually sharecroppers owed money to the landowner for food and for other commodities received before settlement. The living conditions of sharecroppers were "no different from those in Africa" because of the poverty, lack of running water, heat, lights, air-conditioning, electricity, and indoor toilets.[11] Sharecroppers were compelled to also obey other local customs, "Avoid white areas. Don't associate with them. Call white kids Mr. and Ms. after age 13 and don't go in the front door of a white person's house."[12] The strictest unwritten rules, however, were for black men:

> Black men couldn't interact with white women. One black man had to leave Sledge [Mississippi in Quitman County] because a white woman wrote a letter to her father and said that he had tried to rape her. He was framed and was beaten with ax handles by some of the white men in town. The white people did this because they were jealous of him for working in a nice store. He had to put pepper in his shoes so that dogs couldn't track his scent and had to swim away in a swamp.[13]

For a brief time during the Reconstruction years, black workers believed that the sharecropping system would enable them to eventually become independent landowners. Sharecropping, they believed, was a chance to escape the close supervision and physical abuses reminiscent of slavery, acquire livestock, own farm equipment, receive portions of crops, work at their own pace, and bargain with plantation owners for higher wages.[14] James C. Cobb in *The Most Southern Place on Earth* described the contrasting hopes of African Americans and whites during the post-Civil War years:

> Recognizing the Delta's potential as a perpetually fertile plantation paradise, ambitious antebellum planters had envisioned vast fields of cotton tended by legions of servile blacks while projecting themselves as members of an omnipotent white gentry whose affluence allowed them to live as graciously and extravagantly as they chose. The destruction of slavery interrupted this dream for whites but created a new one for blacks, that of a rich cotton region where demand for their unfettered labor might provide them with opportunities for significant progress toward independent land ownership and facilitate their social and political advancement as well.[15]

White elites in the antebellum South, however, had no intention of allowing African Americans to gain this or any other kind of independence. In their view, good race relations and a prosperous agricultural economy would only be maintained if black workers remained completely subservient to whites rather than attempting to own land and exercise their political rights. In a society in which landowners possessed the most wealth, political influence, and economic power, several factors prevented black workers from owning land. First, most black workers earned such low wages that they could not afford to purchase land. Even in the unlikelihood that they possessed the funds to buy land in the Delta, white landowners would have refused to sell it to them because "controlling land [was] crucial for maintaining segregation"[16] In addition, African Americans were charged higher prices for land than whites.[17] The average price of land in the Mississippi Delta in 1940 was $19 per acre for whites and $25 per acre for African Americans.[18] Also, unlike whites who desired to buy land, black Mississippians were not able to obtain loans from white-owned banks.[19]

All of the Delta's field-workers were not sharecroppers, however. Share-tenants owned the mules, seeds, tools, and other farming materials they used when working in the fields. The landowners allowed them to cultivate their land in exchange for one-fourth to one-third of the crop.[20] Cash-renters, on the other hand, were field-workers who rented their farming materials and received higher cash payments than sharecroppers for their field labor.[21]

The landowning elites preferred the labor of sharecroppers over share-tenants and cash-renters because of the cheaper costs of securing their labor. At the end of the year, the landowners "settled crops" with their sharecroppers by giving them money and/or a share of the crops. Sometimes, the owners had to lend money to the sharecroppers on the next year's crops if a family of sharecroppers failed to make any money on the crop.[22] In other words, the family often worked for an entire year, received nothing at settlement, and had to borrow money from the landowner.

Thus, black sharecroppers were locked in a status of inescapable debt. For many years, the elites could claim that their sharecroppers still owed them money for loans they had acquired in the past. The sharecropper faced harsh punishment including imprisonment if they left the landowner's plantation without paying their debts. Their only option was to continue working for the landowner during subsequent farming seasons to pay off their debts. Black Deltans had to use the "exit" over "voice" option because sharecroppers literally had to escape from their plantations in order to remove their families from the system and to find a better life elsewhere. Usually, fathers moved to Northern cities and sent for their families later, "Many black males and families moved North for jobs. Others went to the army. Younger black males left their families because it was too hard for the whole family to leave. Finding a way to leave was the only way to protest."[23] One study pointed out that:

> By mid-winter, not only were many sharecroppers in debt after nine months of work, but cash advances were typically reduced or suspended. Many sharecroppers secretly moved during this post-harvest period to escape these manufactured debts, the likelihood of imprisonment for refusal to pay or attempted escape, and the specter of starvation if they acquiesced. . . . Those who challenged this year-in and year-out system of exploitation often found themselves or their family members imprisoned, beaten, or murdered.[24]

In most of the Delta's counties, all or most of the sharecroppers were African American. Most of the white farmers left the Delta in the years following the turn of the century because the wealthy white landowning class earned the most money, monopolized political offices, and allocated local revenues. Some white farmers unsuccessfully attempted to challenge the dominance of wealthier Delta landowners over their control of local and state political and economic affairs during the "revolt of the Rednecks"; however, these farmers soon realized that Delta affairs would always be controlled by wealthy landowning elites who were unwilling to share power with poor white farmers.[25] Thus, most of the remaining poor white farmers worked as "overseers" who watched the sharecroppers as they worked in the fields.

The sharecropping system also resulted in the disruption of black families after fathers migrated to other towns looking for work during the winter off-season, illiteracy, and low educational achievement.[26]

Joyce E. Allen-Smith in "Blacks in Rural America" found that the legacy of slavery, the sharecropping system, and institutional racism were the main factors contributing to the persisting poverty of African Americans in the rural Southern counties: "The heavy concentration of rural blacks in specified areas, notably the Mississippi Delta and the Black Belt, has its roots in plantation agriculture and the systems of slavery and sharecropping that provided a cheap input, labor. For decades, many counties in these areas have been among the poorest in the country."[27]

By the turn of the century, the Delta's landowners experienced prosperity because of the cotton industry and the supply of inexpensive labor provided by sharecroppers, but African Americans failed to benefit from the lucrative agricultural industry. Because the plantation elites also owned all of the local stores and housing, they could charge the sharecroppers exorbitant prices for goods and high rents for substandard housing. As a result, the sharecropping system became a type of legal slavery after the formal institution of slavery ended. Most white Delta families lived a comfortable if not prosperous lifestyle, however, due to the booming agricultural industry.

The plantation elites also objected to "Communist" racially mixed labor unions like the Southern Tenant Farmers' Union (STFU) formed in 1934 in the Arkansas Delta and the Congress of Industrial Organizations (CIO) of Memphis, Tennessee, during the first phase of the sharecropping system.[28] The STFU organized fieldworkers in both the Arkansas and Mississippi Delta areas, mobilized strikes, and demanded that the federal government grant to agricultural workers those rights given to their counterparts in the industrial sector: Social Security, collective bargaining, minimum wage, maximum work hours, and child labor regulations.[29]

Because they feared the "infiltration" of labor unions in the Mississippi Delta, the plantation elites, led by the Delta Council, decided to provide improved job training and working conditions to black workers. In 1935, the plantation bloc had founded the Delta Council to coordinate agricultural production, handle flood control issues, improve race relations, and pursue economic growth in the region.[30] By the 1950s and 1960s, the elite class feared that the burgeoning labor union, civil rights, and political activism in other Southern counties would eventually surface in the Delta. Therefore, the Delta Council wanted to capitalize on the Delta's "fine black soil, good black labor, and outstanding white leadership" and to implement resolutions that were made as early as 1944.[31] A 1944 Delta Council report summarized the main dilemmas faced by the region's black workers and the suggested solutions for transforming them from semi skilled to skilled laborers:

Within the Delta the labor is predominantly black, agricultural, and semi-skilled. . . . As mechanization on the farm increases and diversification in production continues, more and more of the agricultural labor of the Delta will acquire specialized activity. With very little industry in the area, no great percent of the labor has had the opportunity to learn machine trades. . . . Contrary to popular belief, Negro labor is industrious and, when properly trained, reliable and skillful. The attitude of the Negro laborer is no different than that of any worker of the nation who desires a good job at a reasonable rate of pay and takes pride in work well done. Their amenability to supervision and management is among the highest of any type of workers.[32]

One of the first objectives of the plantation elites was to teach leadership skills to black ministers. In this way, the ministers would convince the masses of sharecroppers to obey the wishes of the elites. For example, the Delta Council made the eradication of the STFU a primary goal and used the Reverend H. H. Humes, its executive staff associate, to spy on post offices to learn which sharecroppers received union literature.[33]

Plantation elites then began a campaign to improve the living conditions of field-workers by building new homes and by encouraging residents to improve the appearance of their homes. Also, the Delta Council financially supported an African American newspaper, the Delta Leader. Many planters subscribed to it for their tenants.[34] The Reverend H.H. Humes, the newspaper's editor, wrote articles encouraging sharecroppers to remain on the plantation and to accept their political status.[35] Nan Elizabeth Woodruff pointed out that the reforms instituted by the plantation elites were actually paternalistic measures designed to thwart federal intervention:

Through the Delta Council, planters opposed the S.T.F.U. and sought to regain complete control over their employees' wages and hours. They also sought to . . . reclaim some of the control they feared had been lost as a result of agricultural policies and migration. Combining pragmatism with paternalism, the Delta Council developed a program to reform the plantation by improving the housing, health, education, and "moral" condition of their workers. The pragmatic side sought to destroy any grass-roots political movement and aimed for a more efficient work force, while the paternalistic side sought to extend employers' authority into all realms of their workers' lives—their churches, lodges, schools, and homes.[36]

During the first phase of Delta politics and in the years thereafter, the plantation elites handpicked political figures who would ignore poverty, oppose new industries, resist federal governmental intervention, and oppose the development of labor unions. They feared that as a result black workers would have economic and political power and thus completely restructure their Southern society. The main goal of elite landowners and of the local politicians during this time was to have African Americans work in the fields so that the landowners would reap profits while the laborers remained impoverished. Black workers lacked the power to change the conditions in which they lived because of the dominance of plantation politics and because of their dependency on the plantation elites for their farming supplies, food, and housing.

The Second Phase of the Sharecropping System

The Mississippi Delta experienced massive floods in 1916, 1920, and 1927 as well as an outbreak of boll weevil attacks on its crops in 1920. The 1927 flood and the Great Depression devastated the Delta's once thriving agricultural economy by the end of the 1920s. Cotton production stalled and many counties experienced a labor shortage after field-workers left the region in search of Northern industrial jobs. After Northern industries began recruiting Delta workers during the World War I years, these former farmworkers migrated en masse to Northern cities.[37]

In order to restore the Delta's economy, the elites had no alternative but to rely on federal aid during the late 1920s and the 1930s. During the depression, New Deal, and World War II years, the federal government attempted to revitalize the Delta's struggling farm-based economy and to decrease the wide economic disparities among landowning elites and sharecroppers. Between 1933 and 1939, the federal government spent $450 million in the state and cleared or insured loans for an additional $260 million.[38] Bank deposits doubled during the 1930s, as did the value of farm real estate and farm incomes rose by 134 percent. By 1934, federal aid had become the state's major source of revenue, and it was the major reason why the state's treasury had a surplus by the end of 1935.[39] As a result of governmental spending during the 1930s, the state of Mississippi's economy was restored by the mid- and late 1940s.

During the Reconstruction years, the Delta plantation bloc had rejected federal aid for fear the government would have the power to intervene in its local affairs. The main fear was that the government would enforce federal civil rights and suffrage laws and uplift the region's black underclass. In later years, however, plantation elites discovered that federal programs and funds could be used to reinforce rather than undermine the status quo. For example, after the 1927 flood resulted in deaths, property and land damage, and a mass exodus of Delta workers, Congress appropriated $325 million in relief dollars and allowed local officials to administer these funds to the poor and to create a flood control system for the region.[40] Local elites were allowed to distribute Red Cross assistance and supplies, but were supposed to abide by a moral obligation to administer federal aid programs fairly. However, white elite control of these assistance programs made the region's African American residents more vulnerable to reprisal and intimidation than at any time in their history. Many of the region's wealthiest residents charged the homeless black population for Red Cross supplies that they had received at no cost. This was yet another way for white elites to keep poor African Americans indebted and to use this indebtedness to hold onto their labor.[41] Thus, the federal government, by allowing the elites to distribute these supplies exacerbated the problems of white power and black dependency.

The acreage reduction requirements, agricultural mechanization, and in later years a federal minimum wage law exacerbated the dependency of black laborers on white elites even more so than the flood relief efforts. The elites became the prime beneficiaries of these new government initiatives that not only increased their incomes through acreage-control payments but also reduced their labor needs. The goals of the Agricultural Adjustment Act of 1938 (AAA) were to enhance the Delta's agricultural economy by paying landowners to reduce their acreage, to reduce their workforce, and to pay these field-workers higher wages. Both planters and field-workers were expected to benefit from acreage reduction. Planters would receive higher profits because of the reduced production and increased demand for cotton. The increased efficiency and higher prices would more than offset the reduced production while the field-workers would receive higher wages and work shorter hours.[42] The government also expected former sharecroppers to find work in the new factories they hoped would relocate to the area.

While the AAA's acreage-reduction requirements benefited planters, they disadvantaged sharecroppers. The AAA awarded federal funds to the plantation owners with the expectation that they would administer them fairly to their sharecroppers.[43] Despite the AAA's good intentions, the administration of funds was wrought with corruption. Many landlords kept their sharecropper's portion of the AAA payment. Also, any field-worker who filed a complaint alleging that he had been cheated by his landlord was a prime target for eviction because such complaints ultimately were investigated by local AAA county investigation committees.[44] The members of these committees were chosen by the landowning elites who easily evicted those who complained from their plantations. As a result, these workers and their families no longer had a place of residence or a means of making a living.[45]

Agricultural mechanization had an even more detrimental impact on black sharecroppers than acreage-reduction. Its goal was to provide an efficient, affordable, mechanical "cotton picker."[46] Rather than employing numerous sharecroppers, plantation owners now only needed a few individuals to operate the large cotton pickers. One of two machines picked and harvested much larger amounts of cotton than several sharecroppers could in one day. Agricultural mechanization mostly resulted in population declines and widened the gap between the very rich and the very poor Delta families. When mechanization, especially the mechanical cotton picker, became more widespread and when subsidies for weed control became common, landowners had to hire agricultural workers and to pay them higher wages than sharecroppers. The subsequent decline in sharecropping jobs motivated large numbers of black workers to leave the Delta. And because of the inadequate living conditions and lack of job opportunities in the Delta, a pattern developed in which young people, especially the more skilled and educated, left the region.[47]

On February 1, 1967, a minimum wage law took effect that worsened the economic plight of black Delta workers. Its intention was to end the indebtedness of black sharecroppers to white plantation owners and to give them a fair wage. Instead of receiving $3.50 for a 12-hour day, workers would be paid $1.00 an hour and overtime pay. Before passage of the new law, sharecroppers worked for approximately 30 days at $3.50 a day in June or July.[48] After the minimum wage law took effect, planters hired less workers for shorter hours and days a month because they either could not afford to or had no desire to pay them $12.00 a day for 12 hours of work. For example, a family of ten sharecroppers who worked for 8 hours a day earned $80.00 a day or $400.00 for a 5 day work week. Share-tenants would have received the $1.00 wage plus a percentage of the crop at the end of the season. Plantation elites believed that this was too much money for any black family in the Delta and would almost assuredly result in the type of economic independence they had always sought to prevent.

Ironically by the 1960s, white landowners in the Delta viewed their large black population as a liability and wanted them to leave the region. Acreage-reduction and mechanization had reduced the Delta's labor needs dramatically and the black civil rights movement continued to challenge the political supremacy of the Delta's white elite. The white establishment in Mississippi wanted to depopulate the Delta area to the point where African Americans were no longer a threat to the political structure.[49] Thousands of plantation owners were evicting black farm workers and replacing them with mechanized cotton pickers and choppers. In a 1959 study, the Mississippi Employment Security Commission reported that more than 60,000 black sharecroppers worked in Mississippi (primarily in the Delta region). By October 1966, only 2,000 black sharecroppers were employed in the state's cotton fields and because of acreage reduction, mechanization, and the unwillingness of landowners to pay their employees a minimum wage.[50] In 1967, the number of cotton choppers employed was less than one-fourth the number hired in 1964 and the number of days worked was also reduced considerably.[51]

Delta residents had begun their outward exodus during the post-World War I years, but the most dramatic population declines occurred in subsequent decades. After World War II, labor shortages resulted in an abundance of jobs in eastern, midwestern, and Southern cities. A mass exodus from the Delta took place during this time as many individuals fled from a rural to an urban environment. The population of the United States grew steadily from 1940 and 1990, but the population of the counties of the Mississippi Delta declined by large percentages during this same time period (see table 2.1).[52] These population declines were higher in the Delta's core counties that had larger black populations and a heavier reliance on the agricultural industry than in its peripheral counties.

The Plantation Model and Industrial Redlining

The population declines, poor race relations, and unskilled workforce alienated potential industries from relocating to the Delta throughout the region's history:

> With regards to economic development, the entire Southern region suffered from racial conflicts and violence. . . . Several states lost out on prospective industries because of their strong resistance to social change. As a result, the South, particularly the rural areas, continued to lag behind the rest of the nation, both socially and economically. The Mississippi Delta is perhaps the best example of resistance to social and economic changes.[53]

The racial conflicts in the Delta have been such a turnoff to industries that many refused to relocate to the region's predominantly black counties. New industries, especially those with more lucrative jobs, adhered to the 30 percent rule and avoided areas where minorities comprise more than 30 percent of the population.[54]

Table 2.1 Population Changes in the United States, Mississippi, and Mississippi Delta Counties, 1940–2000

Area	Population					Percent Change		
	1940	1960	1980	1990	2000	1940–1960	1960–1980	1980–2000
U.S.	131,164,569	179,323,175	226,542,199	248,709,873	287,421,906	+36.2	+26.3	+26.8
MS	2,183,796	2,178,141	2,520,770	2,573,216	2,844,658	−0.2	+15.7	+12.8
Delta	623,737	524,568	455,478	441,212	452,243	−15.8	−13.1	−0.7
				Core Delta Counties				
Bolivar	67,574	54,464	45,965	43,302	40,633	−19.4	−15.6	−11.6
Coahoma	48,323	46,212	34,270	34,270	30,622	−4.3	−25.8	−10.6
Humphrey	26,257	19,093	13,363	13,363	11,206	−27.2	−30.0	−16.1
Issaquena	6,433	3,576	2,513	2,129	2,274	−44.4	−29.7	−9.5
Leflore	53,400	47,142	41,525	41,004	37,947	−11.7	−11.9	−8.6
Quitman	27,191	21,019	12,636	10,237	10,117	−2.7	−39.8	−19.9
Sharkey	15,433	10,738	7,964	7,331	6,580	−30.4	−25.8	−17.3
Sunflower	61,007	45,730	34,844	36,517	34,369	−25.9	−23.8	−1.3
Tallahatchie	34,166	24,081	17,157	15,604	14,903	−29.5	−28.7	−13.1
Tunica	22,610	16,826	9,652	8,648	9,227	−27.9	−42.6	−4.4
Washington	67,576	76,638	72,344	68,798	62,977	+13.4	−5.6	−12.9
				Peripheral Delta Counties				
Carroll	20,651	11,177	9,776	9,733	10,789	−45.8	−12.5	+18.5
Grenada	19,052	18,409	19,854	21,043	21,555	−3.3	+7.8	+8.5
Holmes	39,710	27,090	2,970	21,962	21,609	−31.7	−15.2	−5.9
Panola	34,421	28,164	27,244	29,748	34,274	−18.1	−3.2	+25.8
Tate	19,209	18,138	20,119	21,766	25,370	−5.5	+10.9	+26.0
Warren	39,585	42,200	51,627	51,110	49,644	+6.6	+22.3	−3.8
Yazoo	40,091	31,653	27,349	25,690	28,149	−16.0	−13.5	+2.9

Source: U.S. Bureau of the Census. Resident Population and Apportionment of the U.S. House of Representatives. www.census.gov; U.S. History. Com. U.S. Population, 1790–2000. *www.u-s-history.com/pages/h980.html.*

As a result, Mississippi Delta counties and towns with majority black populations (which includes most of them) had an extremely difficult time attracting new industries both before and after the legalization of gaming. These counties were viewed as high-risk areas for industries that feared they would not be able to find qualified employers for many of their positions.

Second, plantation elites hampered efforts to attract industry. Traditionally, economic development in the rural South, particularly in the Delta, has been controlled by certain elite groups who would determine whether industry will be allowed to locate in a particular area. Fearing an upset of the existing status quo, factories that may have improved conditions for black workers in the Delta were always opposed. Before the late 1960s, the plantation bloc only allowed approval of the relocation of new factories after receiving assurances that only white workers would be hired in all but the most menial of positions.[55] In this way, the plantation bloc would only attract industries that they could control and that posed no threats to the elite power structure.[56]

Conclusion

Elites in the Delta generally benefited economically from discriminating against black workers and exploiting their labor during the two phases of the sharecropping system. In the Delta, black workers held the low-paying, dead-end jobs that were undesirable to whites.[57] Most of the region's plantation elites preferred the field labor of black sharecroppers rather than that of share-tenants and cash-renters because the cheaper labor of sharecroppers increased the landowner's profits and decreased his labor costs. It was also easier to manipulate black workers because they had no rights that white elites had to respect. Because the elites believed that the social and economic arrangements that maintained their positions were the correct ones, they resisted any kind of societal change. In subsequent years, this resistance led to a myriad of additional problems and made conditions in the Delta worse than those in many underdeveloped countries.

CHAPTER 3

BLACK MOBILIZATION AND
ELITE RESISTANCE DURING THE HEIGHT
OF TRADITIONALISTIC PLANTATION
POLITICAL RULE

Introduction

Both historically and currently, two factors have primarily led to
the pervasive racial socioeconomic disparities in the Delta-economic
subordination and institutionalized racism. Chapter 2 discussed the
brutal exploitation of black labor under the sharecropping system
that resulted in the existing low educational levels and poverty among
black Deltans. This chapter examines the civil rights and political discrimination experienced by black Deltans during the first and second
phases of the plantation political structure as well as their successful
and unsuccessful efforts for civil rights and political mobilization and
the response of white elites during the second phase.

At this time, the plantation bloc's dominance of local and state
politics seemed invincible. The wealthy white elite class collaboratively promoted their racial and class interests to the detriment of
the black majority by opposing black enfranchisement, officeholding, and economic advancement. They prioritized the growth of the
agricultural industry for their financial gain and for the maintenance of the sharecropping system for its cheap black labor pool.
Although black Deltans remained completely dependent on plantation elites for their livelihood, they and their Northern white allies
engaged in the region's first successful efforts to develop black and
intergroup social capital relationships in the struggle for black civil
rights and political mobilization.

The Traditionalistic, Transitional, and Modern Phases
of Mississippi Politics

Mississippi's political system has undergone a complete evolution from the traditionalistic or plantation politics to transitional and modern politics. During the traditionalistic period, the elites disfranchised African Americans; advocated segregationist principles; subjugated poor farmers and sharecroppers; maintained the dominance of the Democratic Party; and staunchly opposed significant political changes in the state.[1] As chapter 5 will explain, the transitional and modern periods were characterized by the ratification of the Voting Rights Act, the first African American voting and political officeholding since Reconstruction, ideological divisions in the Democratic party, a decline in Democratic Party membership, and a concomitant rise in Republican Party influence.

Individuals excluded from the elite class continued to experience a "politics of frustration" because of the remaining vestiges of the traditionalistic political era.[2] From 1965 to 1970, the percentage of black registered voters statewide increased from 5 percent in 1965 to 68 percent in 1970.[3] These increases in registration were the largest in the Deep South. An increase in the voter registration rates of poor and working-class whites coincided with the increase in black registered voters largely because less affluent, "redneck" whites were prodded to register by conservative whites as a means of maintaining a white majority in many jurisdictions."[4] The Democratic Party consisted of two factions: the "regulars" who were opposed to integration and "loyalist" Democrats-African Americans, and liberal and moderate whites.[5] Conservative Democrats and "Republicrats"-"economically conservative country-club whites, socially conservative religious fundamentalists, and the pickup truck whites," voted for Republican candidates in national elections (president, Senate, and House) and for conservative Democrats in countywide, state, and local contests.[6]

It is important to understand some of the key events of each period of Mississippi's political development. Subsequent sections of this chapter discuss the specific measures that laid the framework for maintaining plantation elite political dominance in the Mississippi Delta. During the transitional period, the Civil Rights Act of 1964 prohibited legalized segregation that was maintained through the use of physical and economic intimidation of black Mississippians. The Voting Rights Act of 1965 forever changed Mississippi's closed political society of black disfranchisement and battles among the residents of the Delta and the Hills. During the modern period, however, institutional racism and a continuation of black poverty remained after the end of blatant discrimination. Moreover, Mississippi eventually gained the distinction of having the highest number of black elected officials in the nation.

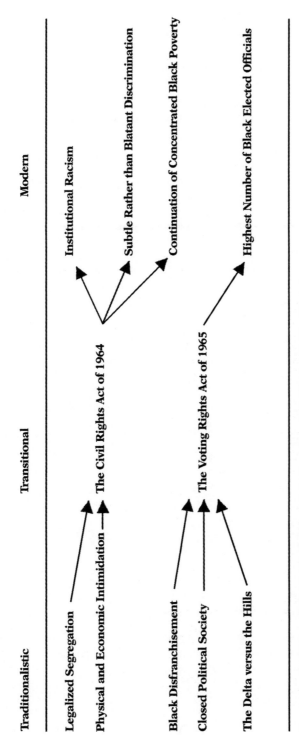

Figure 3.1   The Status of Mississippi's Traditionalistic, Transitional, and Modern Political Periods

The Disfranchisement of Black Mississippians during the Traditionalistic Era

During the traditionalistic period and for much of the state's history, Mississippi politics was characterized by the divisions among residents of the Delta and the Hills or "the planters versus the rednecks."[7] Although a high percentage of African Americans have always lived in the Delta area, the Hills have a substantial population of poor and working-class whites. William C. Havard described this regional conflict between the white residents of the Delta and the Hills in *The Changing Politics of the South* (1972):

> The division is more ideological and economic than geographic, however, and has taken the form of conservative versus radicalism, the wealthy versus the poor, large planters versus small farmers, in a number of campaigns. Some of the most celebrated political battles of the state, notably those between James K. Vardaman and LeRoy Percy and between Theodore Bilbo and Earl Brewer, have involved individuals and issues representing these divisions.[8]

Despite the ideological cleavages between the Delta and the Hills, white Mississippians in all areas of the state had a strong contempt for black political and civil rights. The state of Mississippi has been described as a "closed society" because of the harsh conditions for its black residents in all aspects of life.[9] Historically, they have tolerated more oppressive treatment in Mississippi than in any other state. Whites subjugated African Americans through economic and physical intimidation, state-sanctioned segregation, political disfranchisement, and other means.[10]

White Mississippians knew that the most successful way to maintain the status quo during the traditionalistic era was to prevent its black citizens from voting. Therefore, strategies to disfranchise African Americans became an obsessive goal of local and state political elites who approved of many unique and corrupt measures to preserve the status quo throughout the state's history:

> Many political observers have viewed local government as being backward and unresponsive to socially disadvantaged citizens, reflecting its rural nature. Such unresponsiveness is rooted in a traditionalistic political culture entailing a government with few responsibilities and limited to preserving the status quo, which benefits the political and social elite. Government is also based on interpersonal relations and oriented toward a patron-client structure. In such a culture there has historically been great public tolerance of corruption that served the ruling political elite.[11]

In 1890, the members of a constitutional convention in Mississippi adopted a state constitution that disfranchised the overwhelming majority of black Mississippians from the post-Reconstruction
years until the mid-1960s. This chapter will discuss the 1890 Mississippi Constitution and other disfranchisement methods in the state
of Mississippi that resulted in weak minority political incorporation as
evidenced by the total exclusion of black registered voters and black
elected officials before the 1960s. This discussion points out the fact
that African Americans in Tunica County continue to lack political
power in part because of the legacy of the 1890 constitution and a
1902 law that required all-white primary elections.

In 1890, black citizens constituted the majority population in thirty
counties in the state of Mississippi. Whites feared that they would use
their approximately 58 percent majority population to challenge the
mores of their conservative Southern society.[12] The black electorate
had shown their political savvy by electing two black U.S. senators, one
U.S. representative, one lieutenant governor, and two African Americans in the Offices of Secretary of State and State Superintendent of
Education during the Reconstruction era.[13] However, Vernon Lane
Wharton in *The Negro in Mississippi* (1947) found that black voters were
never able to elect a large number of black representatives even when
they lived in predominantly black counties.[14] After the adoption of the
1890 constitution, African Americans in Mississippi were deprived of
their suffrage rights and would not again elect black political figures
until the late 1960s.

In 1890, the primary purpose of the new constitution was to disfranchise black voters without violating the Fifteenth Amendment or
disfranchising white voters.[15] White residents of the Hills and the
Delta's landowning elites worked together to disfranchise African
Americans; however, to the landowner's political advantage, many
poor whites were also disfranchised by the poll tax, literacy test, and
other suffrage requirements. The chair of the 1890 Constitutional
Convention, SS Calhoon, expressed the explicit view of most of the
delegates, "We [came] here to exclude the Negro. Nothing short of
this will answer."[16] The constitution accomplished this goal for many
decades by disfranchising "idiots," the insane, Native Americans,
and women.[17] Although never ratified by the people of Mississippi,
the 1890 Constitution was adopted anyway. The convention's
Judiciary Committee felt that such ratification was not necessary for
lawful adoption.[18]

In addition, voters had to contend with residency requirements,
character tests, grandfather clauses, poll taxes, and white primaries.[19]
Five provisions of the constitution in particular disfranchised the

majority of the state's black citizens and some white voters. In order
to be eligible to vote, the constitution required that its citizens

> 1) live in the state for at least two years and in the district for at least one
> year before being eligible to register to vote; 2) have no previous con-
> victions for crimes that African Americans were thought to be more
> likely to commit such as arson, bigamy, bribery, burglary, embezzle-
> ment, forgery, obtaining money under false pretenses, perjury, murder,
> and theft; 3) register to vote at least four months before election day; 4)
> pay a poll tax-usually a two-dollar fee; 5) prove their literacy by reading
> a section of the state Constitution chosen by the registrar and by pro-
> viding a "reasonable interpretation" of it.[20]

Although these requirements appeared to be fair, the few black Mississippians who met them were prohibited from voting because of the
discriminatory ways in which local registrars enforced these requirements. Poor and illiterate whites were able to avoid the constitution's requirements because of these tactics.[21] If the registrar desired to
disfranchise potential black voters, numerous tactics could be employed
to this end such as finding spelling and other errors on the long and
complicated registration form or by refusing to accept their poll tax payments.[22] In addition, the constitution contained complex language that
"damn few white men and no niggers at all can explain," according to
former Mississippi governor and senator Theodore G. Bilbo.[23] William
Alexander Mabry, in "Disfranchisement of the Negro in Mississippi," observed that "The 1890 Constitution discriminated not against the
Negro, but "against his characteristics and limitations."[24] The poll tax,
literacy, and interpretation provisions were probably the most burden-
some for black voters. Before the 1960s, the highest wage sharecroppers
earned was $2.00 a day. In 1890, $2.00 was a tremendous amount of
money that neither black nor poor white workers could afford.

The suffrage requirements of the constitution resulted in a sharp
decrease in the number of black registered voters in Mississippi's
counties and partly in the institution of the "one-party system" of
Democratic political dominance in Mississippi (see table 3.1).
Stephen D. Shaffer and Dale Krane in "The Origins and Evolution of
a Traditionalistic Society" (1992) found that

> Only 8,600 of 147,000 eligible blacks were registered in 1892. . . .
> Whereas the poll tax helped disfranchise people of both races for fi-
> nancial reasons, especially during the difficult economic times of the
> 1890s, the literacy test was administered in an unequal manner to dis-
> franchise primarily blacks. The white elite in Mississippi had succeeded
> in limiting mass participation in politics. Indeed, as late as 1964, only[7]
> percent of blacks of voting age were registered to vote.[25]

Table 3.1   Mississippi Voting-Age Population (VAP) and Voter Registration, by Race, 1868–1964

	Black		White	
	Registered Voters[1]	Percentage VAP Registered[2]	Registered Voters	Percentage VAP Registered
1868	86,973	96.7	68,587	80.9
1892	8,922	5.9	69,641	57.7
1896	16,234	8.2	108,998	72.4
1899	18,170	9.1	122,724	81.5
1940	2,000	0.4	—	—
1947	5,000	1.0	—	—
1955	21,502	4.3	423,456	59.6
1964	28,500	6.7	525,000	70.2

[1]Figures for 1868, 1892, 1896, and 1955 are official; others are estimates.
[2]These figures are the voting-age populations of African American men, ages 21 years and older from 1868 to 1899 and of African American men and women, ages 21 years and older from 1940 to 1964. [Source: Reprinted in Neil R. McMillen, *Dark Journey: Black Mississippians in the Age of Jim Crow.* (Urbana: University of Illinois Press, 1989), 36.]

Twelve years after the ratification of the state constitution, the state legislature drafted a "mandatory, statewide, direct primary law." The purpose of the primary law was to ensure that political figures be elected by the majority of voters in a particular area.[26] It mandated that primary elections be held no later than August 10th of an election year. If none of the candidates received a majority in the primary election, a second election would be held three weeks later.[27]

Eventually in 1907, African Americans were completely excluded from Democratic primary elections. For many years, the winners of Democratic primary elections in the South were almost assured of victory in countywide, local, and statewide races in the "solid South." For this reason, white Mississippians believed that it was of vital importance to prevent black registered voters from participating in these elections.

In the 1944 *Smith v. Allwright* decision, the U.S. Supreme Court invalidated white primaries; yet, during the next two years, the Mississippi legislature enacted additional measures to avoid obeying the *Allwright* decision.[28] Laws were enacted that allowed the executive committee of the Democratic Party to only allow persons to vote if they had been eligible to vote in primaries within the two preceding years. A person's qualifications could also be challenged at the polls.[29] In 1948, the Democratic Party adopted principles endorsing racial segregation arguing that the exclusion of black members was necessary in order to preserve "peace and tranquility" in the state.[30] Thus, the *Allwright* decision essentially failed to end the white primaries in Mississippi.

After the passage of the Civil Rights Acts of 1957 that authorized the U.S. attorney general to file lawsuits to prevent disfranchisement on the basis of race, color, or national origin and the Civil Rights Act of 1960 that required states to keep a record of their registered voters and authorized the appointment of voting referees in areas with evidence of discrimination, the U.S. Department of Justice began to challenge the disfranchisement of black voters in Mississippi. The state legislature responded by passing more restrictive suffrage laws in 1962 which:

> 1) implemented the good moral character requirement that had already been included in the state Constitution; 2) reinforced the rule that applicants complete a "letter-perfect form wholly without assistance"; 3) required that the names of applicants be published in the local newspaper; and 4) directed the registrar not to provide rejected applicants with explanations for their rejection with the exception of individuals who were rejected because of bad moral character.[31]

The 1890 constitution, the 1902 white primary law, and other state laws laid the framework to disfranchise Mississippi's black voters before the mid-1960s. Also, an environment of terrorism existed in Mississippi that frightened African Americans to such an extent that they dared not attempt to register to vote. For example, between the years 1882 and 1952, 534 black men, women, and children were lynched in Mississippi-more than in any other state in the nation.[32] Various forms of corruption were apparent in Mississippi politics because of the Delta plantation bloc's manipulation of the political process for their personal and financial gain. Even U.S. Supreme Court decisions and the passage of federal laws failed to secure suffrage rights for most black Mississippians. The elites and their hand-picked officeholders found methods to ensure that poor whites lacked a significant voice in government and that black citizens had absolutely no voice.[33]

The Modern Civil Rights Movement Reaches the Mississippi Delta

During the 1960s, civil rights activists began an aggressive campaign to improve conditions for black Deltans. It was common knowledge that the economic, political, and social conditions for African

Americans in the Delta were among the worst in the country. Not only was there black poverty in the midst of white wealth, but the atmosphere of fear, terrorism, and strained race relations meant that a change in the status quo was unlikely. The activists believed that if they could ensure civil and political rights for African Americans in the Mississippi Delta, they could also ensure the same rights in all areas of the South. For the first time in Mississippi's history, white elite rule was being aggressively challenged by biracial yet mostly black groups of "agitators who did not understand the South."[34]

This section discusses the civil rights movement in the Mississippi Delta in the early and mid-1960s. During and before the early 1970s, local organizers who led these mobilization efforts became the first black officeholders in many of Mississippi's cities, towns, and counties. The civil rights activities in the Delta were crucial in black political development because their participants learned leadership and mobilization skills. Also, the black community was later able to establish a strong political base in these rural, predominantly black towns.[35] In later years, this political base resulted in black politicians holding most of the local elective offices. Because Tunica County's African American residents were not involved in these kinds of activities, they failed to develop a leadership class, to stress the importance of voting, and to mobilize a black political base. As a result, the black residents of Tunica County's small towns failed to elect black political figures in later years.

Probably the most important activities that challenged elite rule in the area of political rights occurred during the early and mid-1960s. During the modern civil rights movement in Mississippi, groups of volunteers informed local residents about the importance of voting, used independently owned churches to mobilize the community, involved students in leadership roles, attracted media attention to white violence, and attempted to change the feelings of hopelessness among the lifelong residents of the Delta. By 1961, Mississippi became the main target of the Student Nonviolent Coordinating Committee (SNCC's) staff and resources. In August of that year, its workers went into the state under the leadership of Project Director Robert Moses and later expanded their activities into all five of Mississippi's congressional districts.[36]

These civil rights workers encountered more challenging obstacles when attempting to mobilize the black residents of rural counties than those of cities. During this time, the dilemmas for activists in Southern cities were not less severe than those for Southern rural activists because of the prevalence of police brutality, arrests, firings, and other reprisals, but in rural areas, organizing was more problematic.

First of all, most Delta sharecroppers had a "plantation mentality"-a belief that they were helpless in their attempts to change their plight because of their complete powerlessness and dependency on the plantation elites.[37] The landowners also had convinced many sharecroppers that they had no need for educational or political opportunities and should be grateful to the elites for "taking care of them."[38]

Their paralyzing fear of activism was understandable considering the context of the times. Delta residents risked losing their livelihood and their lives if their involvement in voter registration or in other political activities was discovered by the landowning elites. According to Unita Blackwell, former SNCC member and mayor of Mayersville, Mississippi, in Issaquena County, many sharecroppers who lost their jobs and homes on one plantation because of their activism, were ostracized all over Mississippi and sometimes blamed the movement for their predicament:

> . . . you found people had fear. . . . There was the fear of not having a
> place to stay. . . . Cause some people was put off the plantation. People
> were throwed out of jobs; all these things happened because of this
> order. Some folks never did get settled again; it sort of threw them off
> psychologically, you know; they went out and tried to vote and stuff like
> this, try to register, and they'll vote and things like that, but they still re-
> member just being told to get out, get off, you know. And so they are
> still bitter, you know, about some of this stuff, but I think we did
> it true.[39]

Despite these fears, a few Delta residents engaged in protests with the assistance of activists living outside the Delta region. As the protests continued during the 1960s and in subsequent years, a greater number of African American residents participated as a way to enhance their quality of life through the development of social capital.

Second, organizers found it almost impossible to inform sharecroppers about planned meetings and activities. On most Delta plantations, an unwritten rule denied the police of the right to arrest sharecroppers from plantations without the landowner's consent.[40] Many sharecroppers thought that the landowners were protecting their welfare by prohibiting others, even the police, from entering their property without authorization; but in actuality, the landowners were able to keep the people they deemed as trespassers off their property.

Yet, the most significant problem for rural organizers was that wealthy white elites owned the shacks in which most sharecroppers lived and the commissaries in which they shopped. Because the residents did not own their homes, they could be asked to leave at any time and for any reason. Charles M. Payne in an award-winning on the Mississippi organizing tradition pointed out the peculiar dilemmas for individuals seeking to mobilize Delta sharecroppers:

> [In Delta cities], canvassing might only be a matter of taking a group to a section of town and assigning a different street to see who was willing to canvass that day. "Out in the rural" was a different matter. The plantations were white-owned, and civil rights workers were trespassing. They had to either sneak past the landlord or lie their way past ("I'm just going to visit my cousin.") There was always the possibility that someone would tell the owner what was really going on, and if plantation workers were even suspected of talking to civil rights workers, they would be fired and evicted.[41]

In addition, sharecroppers would have had little success in boycotting plantation stores both because they lacked economic power and because their limited spending made such a strategy futile. Also, they risked offending store owners who had the ability to deny them government surplus commodities such as flour, meal, and rice if they participated in boycotts and voter registration activities.[42] In cities and towns in Mississippi like Clarksdale, Greenwood, Jackson, and Natchez, local activists such as Medgar and Charles Evers, under the direction of the National Association for the Advancement of Colored People (NAACP) boycotted stores that discriminated against black customers and employees. As a result of these boycotts, national chain stores were pressured into hiring black employees in positions other than janitorial, implementing policies requiring that black customers be addressed with respect, and allowing them to try on clothes.[43] In the rural towns of the Delta, however, these policies were not realized because no boycotts of commissaries were attempted.

Fully aware of these challenges in the rural towns and counties of the Mississippi Delta, representatives from the Congress of Racial Equality (CORE), the NAACP, the Southern Christian Leadership Conference (SCLC), and SNCC united to translate local black social capital relationships into societal and political change in the Council of Federated Organizations (COFO) by the fall of 1963.[44] A distinction has been made between two kinds of social capital relationships that are relevant for this book-black (bonding) and intergroup (bridging). Black social capital ties exist among African Americans in their communities while intergroup relationships exist among individuals of different races.[45] Numerous scholarly studies have found that predominantly African American communities possess relatively strong social capital ties, but encounter opposition from white elites when attempting to develop intergroup ties. As chapter 6 will explain in further detail, both forms of social capital are necessary in order for significant improvements to occur because African Americans lack the financial resources possessed by white elites and therefore must find a way to gain elite support for their efforts. This has proven to be quite a challenge in the Mississippi Delta because of the historically uncooperative relations among white elite "haves" and black nonelite "have-nots."

Strong black social capital ties had been evident throughout the Delta's history because of the interactions of African American sharecroppers at Delta churches and their close-knit living arrangements on plantations. In small Delta towns, neighbors knew each other and had no need to lock their doors because of the trusting relationships in their neighborhoods. After working in the fields all week, local sharecroppers spent their Friday and Saturday nights in "town" at small, black-owned cafes and their entire Sundays at church services. Destitute families appealed mostly to the elites for food and clothes when such were lacking, but churches also contributed collections to the needy.[46]

An evolution of social capital has occurred in the Mississippi Delta since the early 1960s. Beginning then, the members of COFO encouraged African American citizens to mobilize their social capital bonds for political participation or for "civic engagement." Throughout the late 1960s and early 1970s, black social capital activities were mostly geared toward increased educational opportunities, voting, and electing black representatives to change Mississippi's plantation political and economic system.[47] African American communities continued to develop their social capital to increase the numbers of black officeholders, but mostly participated in community development organizations to address their community's problems by the 1990s.

Before the Delta civil rights campaign began, the representatives of COFO discussed the state of race relations, provided information on the dismal plight of African Americans in Mississippi, and appealed for suffrage and civil rights from then governor Ross Barnett. Few changes occurred in the aftermath of this meeting, however, because of Barnett's unwillingness to address their concerns.[48] This meeting confirmed what COFO's representatives already knew about the local and state elite political establishments' indifference about issues of concern to black Mississippians and about their cohesive opposition of any and all political and civil rights gains for black Mississippians.

After realizing that Governor Barnett and other politicians would do nothing to help them accomplish their goals, COFO began its ambitious campaign to open community centers and freedom schools, and to organize literacy projects and voter registration drives in various Delta counties and in other counties throughout the state. The main goal of the Delta campaign was "the development of leadership for politically emerging communities."[49] The members of COFO used what would later be referred to as the relational organizing strategy that "[worked] from the bottom up"-that is, found leaders within targeted communities, equipped them with the resources to achieve their goals, and brought residents together to develop solutions to their problems.[50] The members of COFO practiced a common tactic for mobilizing poor communities by building upon the existing social capital relationships in African American neighborhoods in newly formed community empowerment organizations.[51]

In Biloxi, Canton, Carthage, Clarksdale, Greenville, Greenwood, Hattiesburg, Holly Springs, Holmes, Laurel, McComb, Meridien, Moss Point, Ruleville, Madison, Shaw, and Vicksburg, literate local residents and COFO volunteers established 41 "freedom schools" to provide Mississippi with a "nucleus of leadership committed to critical thought and social action."[52] Students in the 10th, 11th, and 12th grades attended "daytime freedom schools" that provided remedial education in reading, math, grammar, political science, the humanities, journalism, and creative writing. More advanced high school students attended "resident schools" that had the same curriculum as the day schools, but that stressed political involvement.[53] In addition to the freedom schools, community centers operated in Batesville, Canton, Clarksdale, Greenville, Greenwood, Harmony, Hattiesburg, Holly Springs, Meridian, Mileston, Ruleville, Shaw, and Vicksburg and provided services normally denied to black Mississippians such as civic, educational, literacy, health care, cultural, and vocational training programs.[54]

COFO, a biracial group, primarily addressed the educational, political, and economic plight of the black poor, but also addressed the small percentages of white poor families and the repeal of racially discriminatory laws. About thirty Southern white college students who had recently joined the civil rights movement, attempted to organize the few poor white areas of the Delta in the battle against bigotry, poverty, and ignorance in the White Community Project.[55] The Law Student Project consisted of law students from around the country who challenged every Mississippi law that deprived black Mississippians of their rights and sued state and local officials who discriminated against potential voters and candidates.[56] Lastly, the Federal Programs Research Program, which operated in the Delta towns of Canton, Carthage, Greenwood, Itta Bena, and Jackson, monitored the success rates of existing programs and determined if new programs were needed.

Most of COFO's activities targeted the mobilization of black social capital for political gains. As Robert D. Putnam, a leading scholar in the concept of social capital, found, the work of individuals in these projects resulted in more of a desire to participate in the political process.[57] These efforts included the support of a black congressional candidate, the Reverend RLT Smith who only received 2,000 votes while his white opponent received 15,000 votes.[58] Although he had no realistic chance of winning the election, the main purpose of his candidacy was to prove that African Americans possessed the ability to both run for office and use the local media to promote their campaigns in Mississippi.

COFO also conducted voter registration campaigns throughout the Delta and eventually held a Freedom Vote mock election in 1963. In 1962, COFO's first black voter registration campaign took place in Leflore County, Mississippi. They conducted the campaign in this county because only 1.98 percent (268 of its 13,567 black adult residents) were registered to vote compared to 70 percent of white voting-age adults.[59] This campaign ended without a significant increase in the number of black registered voters because of the refusal of the county election officials to register black voters and because of the amount of retaliation black participants received from whites.

Its second black voter registration campaign, also in 1962, occurred in the counties of Bolivar, Coahoma, Holmes, Leflore, Marshall, Sunflower, and Washington, in Mississippi. African American SNCC and COFO organizer Robert Moses selected these counties because of their large black populations, large number of independently owned churches, and evidence of unsuccessful African American attempts for voter registration.[60] This campaign also resulted in only a slight increase in the number of black registered voters. Approximately 70,000 African Americans attempted to register, but only 7,000 met the eligibility requirements.[61]

In 1963, COFO supervised two freedom elections in which Aaron Henry, an African American Clarksdale pharmacist and NAACP member, ran for governor and the Reverend Edwin King, a white Methodist minister at historically black Tougaloo College, for lieutenant governor.[62] Approximately 100 black and white college students traveled throughout the state distributing and collecting ballots. Mail ballots were sent to places that were extremely dangerous for the workers. Most of the balloting took place in local black churches over a period of several days about the same time as the regular election.[63] Because approximately 93,000 voters participated in the elections, the

plantation bloc could no longer perpetuate the stereotype that
African Americans in Mississippi had no desire to vote.

During the summer of 1964, civil rights activists in Mississippi carried out their most ambitious political effort since the Reconstruction
years. Approximately 1,000 white students traveled to Mississippi to
assist with voter registration efforts. This undertaking was called Freedom Summer. Its goals were to expand black voter registration efforts, build a statewide political organization (the Mississippi
Freedom Democratic Party or MFDP) that would be open to all citizens, and serve as an alternative to the Mississippi Democratic Party
that excluded black members and that would send representatives to
the 1964 Democratic National Convention in Atlantic City, New Jersey, in August 1964.[64]

During the summer of 1964, approximately 80,000 African Americans participated in the Freedom Summer campaign; 17,000 black
citizens attempted to register, but only 1,600 succeeded.[65] Over 1,000
persons were arrested, at least 80 persons were assaulted, 35 churches
were burned, 30 homes and other buildings were bombed, 35 shoot-
ing incidents occurred, and three civil rights workers-Andrew Goodman, Michael Schwerner, and James Chaney-were murdered in
Mississippi.[66] On a positive end, by the end of 1964 the one-party system was coming to an end in Mississippi with three major factions
competing for political power: state Democrats, state Republicans,
and the MFDP.[67] Moreover, the work of COFO demonstrated that interracial groups could work together to politicize black social capital
in its sponsored community empowerment projects-the White Community Project, the Law Student Project, the Federal Programs Research Program, mock elections, and Freedom Summer activities in
1964. Despite the diligent involvement of white volunteers, evidence
of improved intergroup social capital relationships remained unchanged in the Mississippi Delta because of the monolithic opposition from local plantation elites. In addition, the racial cleavages
among the region's black and white poor populations inhibited them
from collaborating in a class-based rebellion against elite rule.

The Absence of Civil Rights Activism in Tunica County

While these activities took place in other Delta counties, the
members of COFO failed to carry out any organizational work in Tunica County. In Delta towns such as Clarksdale, Cleveland, Ruleville,
Itta Bena, Greenwood, and Belzoni, the mobilization efforts of the
1960s were aided by the presence of historically black colleges and

their students' activism, a working-class sector of residents who worked in occupations other than as field-workers, and church congregations that were more supportive of civil rights activities than their rural counterparts.[68] Also, strong, independent, charismatic individuals such as Fannie Lou Hamer, Annie Devine, Winson Hudson, Dovie Hudson, Dr. Aaron Henry, and Amzie Moore were able to gain the support of the locals because they were well-known gifted orators, and lifelong residents of their communities.

The mobilization efforts of African Americans in Holmes County, Mississippi were typical of those in other Delta counties. The U.S. census reported that African Americans constituted 72 percent of the population, but that no black officeholders served in the county. For this reason, small groups of residents met in a few communities with the ultimate goal of registering people to vote. The emphasis was on building social capital by "finding one person other than yourself" who could work as organizers in the movement.[69] After several informal meetings in seven or eight communities, the members of the Holmes County Freedom Democratic Party held countywide meetings once a month to strategize about getting everyone registered to vote.[70]

They then decided to draft candidates to run for office and cast a cohesive bloc vote in their favor. Before the late 1960s, these candidates had no chance of winning the elections in which they ran, but the HCFDP learned important mobilization skills. Their objective was to register as many voters as possible even if they failed to elect their preferred candidates with the hopes that their candidates would win elections in the future.[71]

The civil rights activities that occurred in other Delta counties did not occur in Tunica County, however. In other Delta towns and counties, civil rights groups such as SNCC, CORE, and the NAACP worked with the clergy, students, and other local activists to mobilize communities in the fight for civil rights. Most of the organizational meetings occurred in independently owned churches. In other Delta counties, black congregations owned their churches.[72] In Tunica County, however, the plantation elites owned the churches on their property and were fully aware of all activities within them.[73] Every plantation had an overseer who kept a record of each worker's cotton production. Most of these overseers were white, but sometimes African American overseers informed the landowners about their employees' daily activities both in and out of the fields.[74] With the exception of Tunica County, civil rights volunteers convinced sharecroppers in other predominantly black counties to participate in the movement by using religious images:

We'd stand up and go to singing and get everybody loosened up, and we'd sing and pat our hands, and then we'd talk about the Lord want[ing] us to register and this kind of thing, you know, and folks would say I'll be ready in the morning, and so they'd be ready in the morning, some would back out and some would keep on, you know, that kind of things. The church was the only place we could get in; a lot of them we couldn't get in, because the ministers were told by the plantation owners, and some of the white community to tell us to stay out, and we would sit down and talk to us and tell [us to] leave this stuff alone, let the Lord fix it. As so we all [had] these ups and downs, you know. . . We had the black community movement, and you look around, some of the blacks would go tell it, you know, what we were planning to do to the whites, and then the whites would be there to cut us off, things like that.[75]

One factor that kept political and civil rights activism out of Tunica County, besides fear and intimidation, during the height of the civil rights movement was the lack of civic education. Tunica County had few high school and college student activists. Because few families owned televisions before the 1970s, people lacked an awareness of the protests challenging unjust conditions in other communities. One former Tunica County resident attributed the lack of protests to the lack of education, "Schools didn't teach it [the importance of civil rights and political protests]. Parents weren't educated. People had to make a living and were scared of politics. Plus, as long as you obeyed them, they took care of you."[76] Another former Quitman County resident agreed that the lack of protests stemmed from the lack of education about the importance of protests, "There were no protests because most people were illiterate and thought they weren't entitled to vote."[77]

Even today, the county has a small contingent of African American political figures. Moreover, no community empowerment organizations existed in Tunica County before the 1980s and the amount of racial polarization that has always existed among African Americans and whites in Tunica County has made it impossible for the black community to form electoral and governing coalitions with whites. With the exception of the local chapter of the National Association for the Advancement of Colored People (NAACP) which had few members and was not active, the only groups that black sharecroppers could join were nonthreatening religious groups such as the Masons and the Eastern Stars and traditionally the black clergy has avoided active political participation.[78] Thus, both the local political scene and the economic scene have always been dominated by white elites.

Conclusion

After the height of the modern civil rights movement, Delta elites used the following strategy to resist change: reject federal enforcement of federal civil rights laws, manipulate federal aid programs to their advantage, send their children to elite private academies rather than to public schools, maintain their wealth while ignoring the plight of the poor, develop tactics to dilute the black vote, and maintain their separate society in counties where black residents are the numerical and political majorities. The greatest challenge for most of the Mississippi Delta's black residents in later years would not be a lack of political power, but a struggle to survive widespread impoverishment in a region plagued by industrial redlining.

PART THREE

THE TRANSFORMATION AND LEGACIES
OF THE PLANTATION CULTURE

CHAPTER 4

THE TRANSFORMATION
OF THE DELTA'S ECONOMY?
LEGALIZED GAMING, ECONOMIC CHANGE,
AND THE PERSISTENCE OF BLACK
CONCENTRATED POVERTY

Chapters 2 and 3 pointed out that white wealth and black poverty was always the norm in the Mississippi Delta partly because of the opposition of elites to nonelite political and economic gains. Neither federal laws, social programs, nor U.S. Supreme Court decisions brought about significant improvements in the quality of life for black Deltans. The Delta was perceived as an essentially hopeless region with insurmountable social, political, and economic problems. In the past, the elites found ways to avoid any outside forces that challenged the society of white wealth and black poverty and the dominance of Delta planters over local and state political affairs. Over the years, it was believed that a significant reduction in the poverty rate would occur if the Delta attracted a new industry capable of providing jobs and higher wages. An ideal situation would occur in Delta communities that had a majority of African American political establishments because black elected officials with a commitment to their mostly black and poor constituents would use gaming revenues to improve their economic standing.

This chapter discusses the fact that legalized gaming was a mixed blessing for the Mississippi Delta in many ways. On a positive end, the elites accepted legalized gaming because they benefited from selling their land to casino owners and lived in their own separate world outside the county. On a negative end, however, poverty levels in most Delta counties remained among the nations highest by the end of the 1990s. Many of the region's poor residents were transformed from the unemployed poor to the working poor after the legalization of gaming. Thus, the Delta continues to be a society of white wealth and black poverty.

A discussion of the way in which gaming became legalized in the state of Mississippi follows the examination of the chronic poverty that persisted in the region by the 1980s. Members of the state legislature practiced the entrepreneurial style of leadership in order to capitalize on the Deltas greatest resources-an abundance of cheap land and a location along the Mississippi River. These individuals convinced casino owners to build facilities in the Delta and Gulf Coast areas, found support for legalized gaming in the legislature, and found ways to suppress the opponents of gaming.

This chapter examines the economic transformation that occurred in many Mississippi Delta counties after gaming's evolution as a lucrative, nonagricultural industry. It is common knowledge that both white elites and African Americans, the latter traditionally the poorest group in the region, experienced an improved quality of life because of the gaming jobs and revenues. But exactly which benefits did the people of the Delta receive from gaming? In this chapter, three issues will be addressed. First, has one of the poorest areas in the nation been transformed into an entrepreneurial state? In other words, to what extent has gaming resulted in an economic transformation in the Delta? Second, is there any evidence that the elites were threatened by "outsiders"—casino executives and owners— whose industry resulted in a myriad of changes in a society that had traditionally resisted change? Third and most importantly, has the gaming industry markedly changed the economic power relationships among white elites and African American nonelites-that is, led to a greater amount of economic power for African Americans as a group?

America's Ethiopia: Chronic Poverty in the Mississippi Delta

In "Race and Economic Development," William Fletcher and Eugene Newport pointed out that "The crisis threatening Afro-America is not simply that there is black poverty rather it centers around the chronic nature of that poverty. . . ."[1] Areas with chronic poverty not only have large populations of poor residents, but also must grapple with other problems that disproportionately affect the poor such as low educational achievement, substandard housing, inadequate schools, and high crime levels. Widespread poverty that existed in the Delta in previous years, continued to exist after 1970 (see table 4.1). From 1970 to 1990, substantial percentages of mostly African American residents lived in the regions poorest neighborhoods. Although the poverty rate decreased, record high poverty rates remained by 1990.

Table 4.1   Poverty Rates in the Counties of the Mississippi Delta, 1970–1990

Core Counties			
Delta County	*1970 Poverty	1980 Poverty	1990 Poverty
Bolivar	44.3	31.8	53.4
Coahoma	42.8	30.6	47.6
Humphreys	53.8	35.1	46.2
Issaquena	42.0	27.8	45.4
Leflore	36.3	27.0	38.6
Quitman	49.8	30.9	46.8
Sharkey	47.2	37.0	50.4
Sunflower	46.2	30.0	49.9
Tallahatchie	49.9	34.4	44.3
Tunica	55.6	44.8	56.0
Washington	34.1	26.3	35.7
Peripheral Counties			
Carroll	42.6	25.0	50.5
Grenada	27.9	25.1	21.2
Holmes	53.0	39.1	57.1
Panola	38.3	35.0	29.2
Tate	33.0	20.8	21.6
Warren	22.2	13.9	21.0
Yazoo	42.4	27.6	39.8
State of MS	28.9	10.1	25.2
U.S.	12.6	13.0	13.1

*The U.S. Census did not keep records of black and white poverty in America before 1970.

Source: U.S. Census Bureau. Poverty Status in 1969 of Families and Persons by Race and Spanish Origin for Counties: 1970. *Characteristics of the Population. General Social and Economic Characteristics. 1970 Census of the Population* (Washington, DC: U.S. Department of Commerce, 1973); ibid. Poverty Status in 1979 of Families and Persons by Race and Spanish Origin for Counties: 1980. *Characteristics of the Population. General Social and Economic Characteristics. 1980 Census of the Population* (Washington, DC: U.S. Department of Commerce, 1983); ibid. Poverty Status in 1989 of Families and Persons by Race and Spanish Origin for Counties: 1990. *Characteristics of the Population. General Social and Economic Characteristics. 1990 Census of the Population* (Washington, DC: U.S. Department of Commerce, 1993); ibid. Persons Below the Poverty Level and Below 125% of Poverty Level. *Statistical Abstract of the U.S.: The National Data Book, 19th ed.* (Washington, DC: U.S. Department of Commerce, 1999); www.census.gov.

Although poverty levels throughout the Delta have ranged from over 20% to less than 60% since 1970, the residents of Tunica County, Mississippi were worse off than many other Delta residents because of the chronic nature of its poverty. By 1990 approximately 56% of its population lived below the poverty level; 45.9% of the adult population lacked a high school diploma; and the median annual family income was only $10,965 (see table 4.2).[2] Also during the 1980s, Tunica County's infant mortality rate was the eighth highest in the nation and its number of births to unwed teenaged mothers was the fourth highest in the nation.[3] A 1984 report of the Lower Mississippi River Delta Commission found that infant mortality in Tunica and in three other Delta counties exceeded 25 deaths per 1,000 live births; this outnumbered the infant mortality rate in Cuba, Malaysia, and Panama, respectively.[4] By 1999, the average socioeconomic status of most county residents had improved as witnessed by the decreased poverty rate and increased median household and per-capita incomes, but poverty, low educational achievement, and low incomes remained the norm for many residents.

During the mid-1980s, the striking disparities among the approximately 30 wealthy white families and the larger masses of poor black residents in the county received national attention. In 1985, the Reverend Jesse Jackson referred to Tunica County as "America's Ethiopia" and requested that Tunica County be declared a disaster area to make it eligible for immediate federal assistance.[5] Jackson was referring mostly to conditions in Kestevan Alley or in the "Sugar Ditch Alley" where conditions were particularly deplorable. The Sugar Ditch was a drainage ditch where neighborhood residents of the seventeen houses along the alley dumped their trash and waste. Their homes, that were eventually condemned and destroyed, lacked indoor plumbing, electricity, and heat and the county refused to provide garbage collection services to the area.[6] When Jackson and former U.S. representative William Gray (D-PA) toured the area in 1985, they found houses with holes in the floors and roofs, rodents, and roaches. A Memphis Commercial Appeal newspaper article described the home of one Sugar Ditch Alley resident, ". . . The floor full of holes was warped and rotting. . . . Books went under furniture legs to keep it all upright. It was always cold and it smelled. . . . There were dead dogs, old furniture and raw sewage in the open ditch next to the house. When the ditch flooded, it all came into her yard."[7]

The conditions near the Sugar Ditch were typical of those for Tunica and for most of the other black Delta residents as well. These individuals had lived in these conditions for most of the Delta's history, but only received redress after the visits of Jackson and Gray. After many national newspapers and after the popular newsmagazine show 60 Minutes exposed the nation to the plight of Sugar Ditch

Table 4.2   Socioeconomic Index for Residents of Tunica County, Mississippi, 1960–2000

	Poverty Rates			
	1970	1980	1990	2000
Persons below poverty level	55.6	44.8	56.0	33.1
Persons above poverty level	44.4	55.2	44.0	66.9

	Educational Attainment			
	1970	1980	1990	2000
High school graduate or higher	19.8	30.8	45.9	60.5
Bachelor's or higher	4.8	6.5	8.5	9.1

	Income Levels			
	*1970	**1980	1990	2000
Median Household Income	$2,896	$7,685	$10,965	$23,270
Per-capita income	$1,156	$5,757	$15,040	$11,978
Less than $10,000	88.7	66.5	61.6	35.1
$15,000–$24,999	16.9	18.7	14.3	17.5
$25,000–$34,999	11.0	8.6	9.5	13.3
$35,000–$49,999	6.7	2.3	6.9	11.9
$50,000–$74,999	2.9	0.7	3.9	25.6
$75,000 or more	1.7	3.2	3.7	8.5

*The income levels are less than $3,000; $3,000–$4,999; $5,000–$6,999; $10,000–$14,999; $15,000-$24,999; $25,000 or more.

**The income levels are less than $10,000; $10,000–$19,999; $20,000–$29,999; $30,000–$39,999; $40,000-$49,999; $50,000 or more.

Source: U.S. Census Bureau. "Household Income in 1999 (Black Alone)". *American Factfinder, 2000.* www.factfinder.census.gov; ibid. "Household Income in 1999 (White Alone)". American Factfinder, 2000. www.factfinder.census.gov; ibid. "Sex by Educational Attainment for the Population 25 Years and Over (Black Alone)." *American Factfinder, 2000.* www.factfinder.census.gov; ibid. "Sex by Educational Attainment for the Population 25 Years and Over (White Alone)". *American Factfinder, 2000.* www.factfinder.census.gov; U.S. Department of Commerce. "Counties-Civilian Labor Force and Personal Income". *City/County Data Book* (Washington, DC: Government Printing Office, 1972, 1982, 1994); ibid. "Counties-Education and Income". *City/County Data Book* Washington, DC: Government Printing Office, 1972, 1982, 1994; ibid. "Counties - Money Income and Local Government Employment". *City/County Data Book* (Washington, DC: Government Printing Office, 1972, 1982, 1994); ibid. "Labor Force Characteristics by Race and Hispanic Origin". *City/County Data Book* (Washington, DC: Government Printing Office, 1972, 1982, 1994).

residents local and state political figures were embarrassed about the negative publicity for the county and for the state of Mississippi as a whole. After years of ignoring the plight of most Tunica residents, local and state leaders pretended to sympathize with them after the national media exposure. According to Clyde Woods, this feigned sense of compassion was ironic to the extent that these leaders almost exploited Tunica's Americas Ethiopia reputation:

> Although the New South leaders had never lifted a finger to assist the people of Tunica or the people living in the dozens of Tunicas in all seven states, they shamelessly exploited it as a symbol of depression. Tunica was repeatedly used as an example of the dreaded past, as the epicenter of poverty, as Americas Ethiopia, and even worst, as a disease.[8]

Poverty and evidence of low educational achievement were the norm in Tunica's neighboring counties as well. Despite the increases in the Deltas high school and college graduation rates, less than half of Tunica County s residents earned high school diplomas in 1990 (see table 4.3). The lack of educational achievement was equally or more evident in Tunica's neighboring counties. By 2000, the Delta's high school graduate rates had improved, but still lagged behind statewide and national rates, especially in predominantly African American core counties.

By the late 1980s and early 1990s, the elites had created a society of irreversible poverty for its black residents by exploiting their labor as sharecroppers, by denying them educational opportunities, and by resisting new industries in the Delta. Conditions in the Mississippi Delta mirrored those in many other rural Southern counties. Although the economies of many metropolitan areas of the Sunbelt thrived, extremely high rates of poverty plagued most rural Southern communities. The already existing problems of population declines, low wages, industrial redlining, and factory closures were exacerbated by reduced federal funding, manufacturing and service job losses, and the decline of the agricultural industry during the 1980s.[9]

A desperate need existed for an alternative industry to revitalize the economy, but to also be supported by the wealthiest elite families in the area.

The Campaign to Legalize Gaming in Mississippi

One of the major issues in the Mississippi Delta since the legalization of gaming concerns whether one of the poorest areas in the nation has been transformed into an entrepreneurial state. During

Table 4.3 Educational Levels of Delta Residents, 1970–2000

Delta County	1970 H.S.	1970 College	*1980 H.S.	1980 College	1990 H.S.	1990 College	2000 H.S.	2000 College
				Core Counties				
Bolivar	31.1	8.0	45.8	14.1	54.9	15.2	65.3	18.8
Coahoma	31.2	8.9	43.8	12.1	54.0	14.7	62.2	16.2
Humphreys	23.7	4.8	38.7	9.1	46.4	10.4	53.7	11.6
Issaquena	24.9	2.4	37.9	5.7	43.7	5.6	58.8	7.1
Leflore	36.5	8.6	44.7	13.2	55.3	15.7	61.9	15.9
Quitman	23.6	5.8	36.5	8.2	45.5	9.0	55.1	10.6
Sharkey	31.6	7.4	42.2	13.3	51.3	12.4	60.6	12.6
Sunflower	28.1	6.5	41.1	11.3	49.2	12.4	59.3	12.0
Tallahatchie	23.5	5.1	36.9	8.6	48.2	7.9	54.4	10.9
Tunica	19.8	4.8	30.8	6.5	45.9	8.5	60.5	9.1
Washington	36.7	8.4	50.0	12.5	58.8	14.3	66.5	16.4
				Peripheral Counties				
Carroll	26.6	4.4	40.3	7.3	54.0	10.3	66.6	10.9
Grenada	36.8	6.5	49.2	10.0	56.5	10.8	63.8	13.5
Holmes	28.0	6.1	39.6	10.3	48.0	9.7	59.7	11.2
Panola	30.7	4.7	40.9	7.7	54.3	8.7	63.5	10.8
Tate	32.6	5.9	49.7	9.2	61.0	11.7	71.7	12.3
Warren	47.1	9.9	59.5	15.7	67.7	19.1	77.0	28.8
Yazoo	33.7	6.8	46.5	11.5	53.4	12.0	65.0	11.8

(*continued*)

Table 4.3 (*continued*)

Delta County	1970 H.S.	1970 College	*1980 H.S.	1980 College	1990 H.S.	1990 College	2000 H.S.	2000 College
				Peripheral Counties				
State of MS	41.0	8.1	54.8	12.3	64.3	14.7	72.9	16.9
U.S.	52.3	10.7	66.5	16.2	75.2	20.3	80.4	24.4

*Percentage of persons ages 25 and over with a high school education.

Source: Courtenay M. Slater and George E. Hall, eds., "Counties-Education and Money Income," *1993 County and City Extra. Annual Metro, City and County Data Book* (Lanham, MD: Bernan Press, 1993); ibid. "Counties-Labor Force and Personal Income"; U.S. Census Bureau. "Educational Characteristics by Race for Urban and Rural Residence: 1970". *Characteristics of the Population. General Social and Economic Characteristics. 1970 Census of the Population* (Washington, DC: U.S. Department of Commerce, 1973); ibid. "School Enrollment and Educational Attainment: 1990". *Characteristics of the Population. General Social and Economic Characteristics. 1990 Census of the Population* (Washington, DC: U.S. Department of Commerce, 1993); ibid. "State and County Quick Facts: Counties in Mississippi." http://www.quickfacts.census.gov; ibid. "State and County Quick Facts: U.S.A". http://www.quickfacts.census.gov; U.S. Department of Commerce. "Counties-Civilian Labor Force and Personal Income." *City/County Data Book* (Washington, D.C.: Government Printing Office, 1983); ibid. "Counties-Education and Labor Force." *City/County Data Book* (Washington, D.C.: Government Printing Office, 1983); ibid. "Counties-Education." *City/County Data Book* (Washington, DC: Government Printing Office, 1972).

the early 1990s, the residents of a number of poor rural areas used the casino industry to revitalize their economies and tourist industries. Local politicians in these counties practiced the entrepreneurial style of leadership by creating a demand for new products, capitalizing on opportunities that would benefit the economy, creating new investment opportunities, and mobilizing the resources that were necessary to pursue growth. An entrepreneur is one who

> Not only identifies new opportunities-new products to invent and sell, new markets to penetrate-but also mobilizes, organizes, and may even supply the resources necessary to exploit these possibilities. . . . What guides the entrepreneurial state is attention to the demand side of the economic growth equation. [There is an] assumption that growth comes from exploiting new or expanding markets. The states role is to identify, evaluate, anticipate, and even help to develop and create these markets for private producers to exploit, aided if necessary by government as subsidizer or coinvestor.[10]

Areas with slumping economies became entrepreneurial states after new industries were identified. Spin-off businesses, jobs, and revenues then resulted. In Mississippi, casino gaming emerged as the industry capable of transforming its Delta and Gulf Coast counties into an entrepreneurial state. It was hoped and expected that the economies of the poorest counties would be the first to rebound as a result of gaming's revenues. Eventually, counties throughout the state would receive portions of these revenues and ultimately become entrepreneurial states after local political and business leaders identified, developed, and attracted opportunities for economic growth.

The Delta's greatest resources were its land, cultural traditions, and location along the Mississippi River. Although several of Mississippi's counties would have casinos, most would be located in Tunica County because of its abundance of cheap, vacant land along the riverfront and its proximity to the Memphis metropolitan area. In order to create new investment opportunities and to become entrepreneurial states, rural counties in other states had publicized their locations; their environmental amenities (lakes, rivers, and other scenic features); their ability to become tourist centers and historic sites (museums and homes of distinguished persons); or their unusual population characteristics (university towns and technical schools).[11] Casino gaming would be crucial for the states economic development because of its positive effects on the economy and because the state would gain a new image as a place of historic beauty, economic prosperity, and Delta folklore rather than as a state of racial terrorism, political factionalism, poverty, and labor exploitation.

By providing higher wages to poor workers in the Delta, many hoped that gaming would prohibit white elites from trapping black nonelites in poverty. Because the Delta plantation elite class had always opposed initiatives that would bring about significant changes, the state legislators who advocated legalized gaming in the Delta and Gulf Coast counties had to carefully construct a plan in order to gain support from elected officials, the public, and most importantly from Delta elites. Influenced by the experiences of counties lying along the Mississippi River in Iowa and Illinois, legislators from three Mississippi Gulf Coast counties and from eleven of the poorest counties in the Mississippi Delta formed an alliance with the ultimate goal of legalizing casino gaming during the late 1980s.[12] Before 1980, only two states had legalized on-land casino gaming-Nevada which became the first state to legalize casinos statewide in 1931 and New Jersey, which legalized gaming in Atlantic City in 1977.[13]

Casino gaming oftentimes produced mixed results in Iowas' and Illinois' economically depressed areas, but provided much needed revenues. In March 1989, the state of Iowa legalized riverboat casino gaming mostly because of the states massive unemployment rate after the closure of several farm equipment manufacturing plants during the 1980s especially in the Delta cities of Davenport and Bettendorf.[14] Soon thereafter, the Illinois legislature legalized gaming in Joliet and in its neighboring river cities in order to stem the patronage of Illinois residents of Iowa casino industry.

Realizing the potential of riverboat casinos to generate revenues, individual members of the Mississippi legislature began a campaign to legalize gaming by using the entrepreneurial leadership style. According to one analysis, an entrepreneur politician must

> (1) Persuade businessmen to locate enterprises in his city to facilitate job training and persuade labor unions to open places in apprenticeship programs to minority groups, (2) Exercise control and direction over the City Council and relevant departments (police, schools, etc.), (3) Attempt to stretch his legal jurisdiction as far as possible, (4) Achieve nongovernmental support for his efforts by promising rewards and sanctions, (5) Control his political party to further his policy preferences, and (6) Use publicity in order to appeal to the public to support him against his opponents.[15]

Politicians in major urban areas are more likely than rural politicians to practice the entrepreneurial leadership style because it is easier for them to lure businesses and corporations to urban rather than rural cities. The representatives of Mississippi's rural counties engaged in this form of leadership by persuading other legislators to ratify a gaming bill, convincing the public and casino owners of the potential profitability of Mississippi casinos, and convincing landowning elites to sell and lease their land to the casino industry. The most complex part of this process involved the passage of a gaming bill because business-people could only erect casinos if gaming were legalized. One of the main actors in the effort to legalize gaming was former representative Sonny Meredith of Washington County, Mississippi, who was responsible for "conceiving it and rocking it to birth."[16] Meredith advocated the legalization of gaming in Mississippi River's and Gulf Coast counties in order to discourage the states residents from traveling to other states to gamble. Because of the inevitability of casino gaming in the South, he reasoned, Mississippi would lose millions of tourists and revenue dollars if Louisiana became the first Southern state to legalize casino gaming.[17] Meredith and Representative Tommy Walman of McComb, Mississippi, sponsored the first proposal to legalize dockside gaming in the House of Representatives and Senator Denny Jacobs of Moline, Mississippi sponsored a proposal in the Senate; however, their bill lacked specific provisions for a gaming commission.[18] Another proposal by Senator Tommy Gollott of Biloxi contained a provision for a five-member gaming commission after the legalization of gaming.[19]

The other chief proponents for casino gaming in the state legislature were House Ways and Means Committee Chair Charlie Williams and Speaker of the House Tim Ford. The proponents of gaming realized that they faced an uphill battle in the effort to legalize gaming in Mississippi. Their more conservative colleagues in the legislature would find gaming objectionable because of its mixed economic results in Iowa, Illinois, and New Jersey, and because of gaming's tendency to exacerbate existing addiction, crime, and traffic problems. Other legislators objected to gaming on moral grounds. In their view, by legalizing gaming the state of Mississippi would give the appearance that it not only sanctioned gaming, but also encouraged it.

Although a political entrepreneur usually solicits publicity for his legislative initiatives, the state legislators who spearheaded Mississippi's legalized gaming campaign did not want extensive media attention because this might have triggered mobilization among anti gaming factions. Fortunately, state legislators were preoccupied with discussions about a possible statewide lottery in Mississippi. As a result, they were able to mobilize gaming supporters in the legislature and across the state with little media attention during the early stages

of their campaign to legalize gaming.[20] In their arguments before
the state legislature, those who advocated legalized gaming empha-
sized the merits of casino gaming rather than a statewide lottery.
These legislators referred to gaming as an industry that would attract
investments from the private sector, employ many people, and attract tourists to the state. The casinos would be located in counties
with the greatest need for revenues, provide public school funds and
finance other public services and roads, and support other public
services through taxes.[21] Lotteries, on the other hand, employed few
people, attracted few investments from the private sector, and
brought in few tourists.[22]

The gist of the arguments in favor of gaming lay in its ability to
stimulate economic growth and tourism. By this time, most Americans were aware of the plight of Tunica County's poor population,
but several Gulf Coast counties that included the cities of Biloxi and
Gulfport, also had experienced severe fiscal stress for several years.
Mississippi's Gulf Coast had been devastated by natural disasters such
as Hurricane Camille in 1969 that resulted in 256 deaths and that destroyed the hotels and shrimp factories that were vital to the areas
tourist and seafood industries.[23]

Twenty years later, the stagnant and declining economies of Gulf
Coast counties still had not recovered from the devastation left by the
hurricane. Biloxi was on the verge of bankruptcy and three of its
largest hotels filed for bankruptcy during the 1980s.[24] Instead of visiting Biloxi and Gulfport, tourists frequented the newer hotels, resorts,
and sites in the Alabama Gulf Coast, the Florida Panhandle, and
Louisiana.[25] Also, federal defense budget cuts had severely affected
the coast's naval bases and ship-building industries.

In 1990, the Mississippi legislature enacted the Mississippi Gaming
Control Act which allowed legalized gaming, but mandated "1) that
the majority of voters in counties approve of gaming, 2) that legalized
gaming take place only in areas along the Mississippi River and Gulf
Coast, and 3) that casinos either float on the water of the Mississippi
River or Gulf of Mexico or remained docked near them."[26]

The Mississippi Gaming and Control Act did not stipulate that
residents of counties along the Mississippi River and Gulf Coast to
vote on legalized gaming, but only that they indicated their approval
in some way. Also, the legislature refused to allow gaming on Mississippi soil, but many owners bypassed this requirement by building
their casinos on large barges over land that contained holes filled
with the waters of the Mississippi River. Mississippi's casinos would
also have lower tax rates, lower licensing fees, and less restrictions
than casinos in Iowa and Illinois.[27] The casinos would be open twenty-

four hours a day. No limits would be placed on the number of casinos that were located in Mississippi's Delta and Gulf Coast counties nor on the amount of bets patrons could make. These lax restrictions were designed to lure a greater number of casinos into these counties. Also, the Mississippi legislature placed few restrictions on the states casinos because of the uncertainty that gaming would be a successful venture. According to Senator Bob Montgomery, "Nobody thought gambling would catch on in Mississippi. Not knowing any better, we wanted the thing open."[28]

After the 1990 Gaming Act was ratified, the state's politicians had to convince casino owners to build casinos in Delta and Gulf Coast counties to garner public support. In a few Delta counties, religious groups and the clergy led anti gaming efforts, but no visible opposition was evident in Tunica County from the clergy or from anyone else. Tunica mayor Bobby Williams stated that the lack of resistance stemmed from the fact that "We needed it. The county didn't have anything and we had a 30 percent unemployment rate."[29] Like other institutions in Tunica County, churches struggled for funds because of the impoverished financial status of their members. Most of the local, predominantly black churches had many vacant pulpits. Small churches were having a hard time and couldn't pay their pastors."[30] For three weeks, the board of supervisors issued a legal notice giving county residents the option of gathering signatures to oppose the proposed casinos.[31] Local residents could have prohibited the opening of a casino if either 1,500 or 20 percent of a county's registered voters petitioned for a referendum to bar casinos from the county.[32] Because of the lack of opposition to casinos in Tunica County, no need existed for a referendum vote. Hence, the County Board of Supervisors began negotiations with private casino owners to open the first casino in 1992. The overwhelming majority of Tunica County's residents viewed the casino industry as a way to transform their stagnant economy, create jobs, provide higher wages, and produce revenues for public schools and for the local infrastructure. All of these benefits would in turn result in a reduction in illiteracy, welfare dependency, and poverty. Thus, it was not difficult to win the support from the public especially in the Delta region.

In addition, the elite families did not have to be coaxed into selling their land. In each subsequent decade after the 1960s, the region's wealthiest families had been receiving less profits from the agricultural industry and were looking for a way to diversify their incomes-to rely on something other than cotton, corn, and soybean farming.[33] The farming industry provided less profits because the cotton, soybean, and rice industries had suffered from falling prices in an increasingly competitive world market. Many of the Delta's elite families had already begun efforts to build hotels, condos, and housing subdivisions on their land.[34] Casino gaming would provide a new method to use their land for something other than farming.

By the 1990s, the Delta was experiencing a decline in the number of full-time farms as a family's only source of income. For example, a report by the U.S. Department of Agriculture found that full-time farms declined by 16% (12% statewide) from 1992 to 1997.[35] Smaller farmers had to rely on farm assistance because of their need for government subsidies to boost sliding commodity prices, for help in paying for crop insurance, and to help pay for costly projects to lessen flooding. Moreover, many of the youngest members of the Delta's elite families had chosen to work outside of the agricultural industry.[36]

Little apparent evidence exists that the elites were threatened by "outsiders"-casino executives and owners-because they made millions selling and leasing their land to casino owners. For example, in 1992, two business-people, Fernando Cuquet and Evert Macaulay, proposed an idea for casinos to two wealthy landowning farmers, RB "Dick" Flowers and his partner DB "Dutch" Parker. Flowers owned approximately 300 acres of land that included Mhoon Landing-inexpensive farmland that was seldom used because of its proximity to the Mississippi River and to its high risk of flooding.[37] Cuquet and Macaulay negotiated a deal with Flowers and Parker to lease 46 acres of their land for the development of the Mhoon Landing casino complex in exchange for 4 percent of the complex's annual revenues.[38] In 1990, Mhoon Landing was one of the cheapest land acreages in Tunica County with a value of less than $35,960; however, 24 of its acres were worth $600,000 by the end of 1992.[39] During the first year of the Mhoon Landing casino complex's operation, Flowers and Parker received a $5.6 million profit.[40] James Dunn, an African American member of the Tunica County Board of Supervisors, explained the rationale behind the landowning class acceptance of the casino industry:

> The average wealthy landowner makes money off their land so he s willing to deviate from his old ways [resisting industries to maintain the status quo]. The landowners make the most profits. They changed [their attitudes about race] as times and society changed. They realized that we don't need as many people on farms. Plus, the price of cotton and soybeans has declined and they needed new ways to get funds. New demands made it possible for people to have to change their ways.[41]

By the end of 1992, and the beginning of 1993, the owners of once useless Delta farmland now owned a gold mine because "Splash was raking in millions every week and the land rush was on."[42] For example, the Delta farmland purchased by Thomas W. Swindoll of Robinsonville, Mississippi, for $20,000 in 1957 was worth less than $40,000 in 1990.[43] By July 1993, however, Swindoll sold one and three-fourths acres of his land for $250,000 to Boyd Tunica Inc., developers of Sam's Town Hotel and Gambling Hall. Also, Shea Leatherman, one of Tunica County s wealthiest landowners sold 150 acres of Delta farmland that was worth less than $1 million in 1990, to Boyd Gaming Corporation, owner of Sam's Town Casino and Gambling Hall for $25 million in 1993.[44]

In addition, the elites accepted gaming with open arms because they were not as threatened by outsiders during the late 1980s as they had been in previous years. As long as they could live in a separate affluent, all-white society, they no longer were as threatened by black economic and political gains. The casinos in North Tunica County were in close proximity to impoverished, all-black neighborhoods, but a world away from the affluent, all-white neighborhoods where the wealthiest families resided. Therefore, the casinos, traffic, and increased crime would not affect the quality of life of the regions wealthy landowning families. Casino owners, local elites, elected officials, and the public all felt that they would profit from gaming.[45]

State legislators and the public believed that gaming would revitalize the economy of Tunica County, other Delta counties, and the entire state of Mississippi by providing jobs and higher wages. This new industry was also expected to end the legacy of poverty and joblessness that resulted from the sharecropping system and from elite resistance to African American political and economic gains. The main issue concerns whether the gaming industry has revitalized the economy of Tunica County and other Mississippi Delta counties by providing jobs and higher incomes.

An Economic Transformation in the Delta?

Figure 4.1 reveals the locations of Mississippi's twenty-nine casinos. Nine are located in Tunica County and seven in the Delta counties of Coahoma, Warren, and Washington. Although many of the county's residents praised gaming's revenues and jobs, this section examines whether workers in the Delta have earned higher incomes, and experienced lower poverty and unemployment rates by the end of the 1990s. One Tunica County resident referred to the changes resulting from legalized gaming as an "economic miracle."[46] Another stated, "In an impoverished area which was desperate for some type

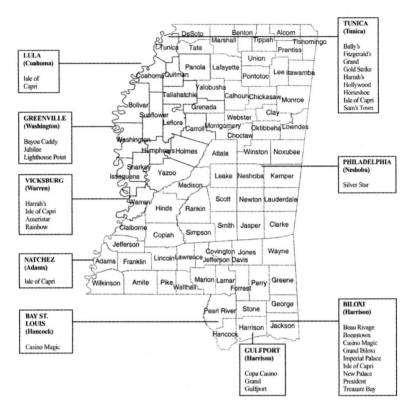

Figure 4.1   Casinos in Mississippi's Towns and Counties

Source: Mississippi Gaming Commission. Directory of Current Operators. http://
www.mgc.state.ms.us.

of industry and opportunity, it has created it. Gaming is good for
Tunica County. It's not for everyone, but it really helped Tunica."[47]

As expected, gaming has been an extremely lucrative industry
in Mississippi. During fiscal year 2003, the state collected $329,433,
967.65 in total gaming revenues and local governments received
$109,508,420.52.[48] Because gaming has been such a profitable indus-
try for the state, it has produced higher tax revenues each year since
they were first collected in fiscal year 1993.[49] Additional revenues are
collected by the county in the form of license fees on slot machines
and on other gaming devices.[50] Half of these funds are placed into the
states general fund. Counties with casinos receive a third of the revenues for their roads, infrastructure, public schools, and law enforcement agencies.[51] Figure 4.2 shows the manner in which gaming
revenues are allocated in Tunica County. Eighty-five percent of these

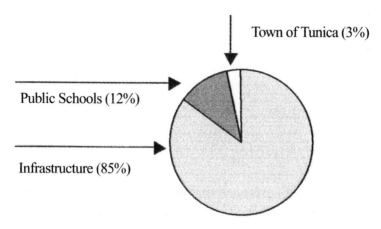

Town of Tunica (3%)

Public Schools (12%)

Infrastructure (85%)

Figure 4.2   Allocations of Gaming Revenues in Tunica County, Mississippi.

funds are devoted for road and infrastructure maintenance, 12% for public schools, and 3% for the town of Tunica.[52]

Because counties with no casinos get no direct revenues, an African American elected official from Bolivar County, Mississippi, believed that its local residents are worse off after the legalization of gaming "It [gaming] has not benefited us. It's been detrimental because our folks gamble there, but we don't benefit from the resources. We don t get any [revenues]. However, quite a few people are employed there. They commute the 64 miles to Tunica because they want to live here, but some people don't want to work in Tunica because it requires a 12-hour day of commuting to and from work and working for 8 hours or longer."[53] Robert Ingram of the Greenwood-Leflore County Industrial Board pointed out that Leflore County also has received no substantive financial benefits from gaming "Only counties with casinos receive revenues. We don't get any. Casinos pay a 12% tax—8% goes to the state of Mississippi, 2% to the local county, and 2% to the local city. . . . If you don't have a casino in your county, you get limited benefits from gaming."[54]

Gaming has provided the most significant economic turnaround in Tunica County, which receives the largest amount of funds because, unlike those in the Gulf Coast area, its casinos have consistently earned substantial revenues each year since 1992.[55] In fiscal year 2000 alone, Tunica County casinos paid more than $100 million into city, county, and state coffers.[56] Because the County received the highest revenues from the multibillion-dollar gaming industry in comparison to other Mississippi counties, increases in per-capita and median household incomes and decreases in unemployment, poverty, and welfare dependency should have been more evident there.

At first glance, legalized gaming ended the lifelong, seemingly irreversible dependency of Tunica County residents on welfare. In the years before the 1980s, at least half of the county's population received some kind of assistance. Table 4.4 shows that the percentage of households receiving food stamps decreased from 51.2% in 1992 to 17.81% in 1999, the percentage of households receiving Temporary Aid for Needy Families (TANF) decreased from 19.8% in 1992 to 2.1% in 1999, and the collected amount of child support payments doubled from 1992 to 1999. Tunica County also has several new upscale apartments and housing subdivisions, a new school, arena, fitness center, library, fire station, police station, post office, community center, jail, hotels, gas stations, fast-food restaurants, and an outlet mall. Plans are also underway to expand the local airport and to build a $22 million riverfront park.[57]

The changes in the per-capita incomes of Delta residents have not been as positive as the public assistance rates, however. According to the data in table 4.5, the average per-capita incomes of most Delta residents consistently ranked among the lowest in the state of Mississippi and in the entire nation from 1970 to 1990. For example, in 1980, the per-capita incomes in the counties of Carroll, Holmes, Humphreys, Issaquena, Tallahatchie, and Tunica in Mississippi, were approximately half the national average of $10,495. By 1990, the incomes in these and in other counties had risen, but most Delta counties still lagged far behind Mississippi's average per-capita income of $12,830 and even farther behind the national average of $18,696.

Table 4.6 reveals the increase in per-capita incomes by 1999. By this time, the incomes of many individuals in Delta counties were closer to the state's average ($15,853); however, most Delta workers earned half the incomes of workers in the United States ($21,587). Another troubling fact is that glaring disparities existed among the 1999 incomes of whites and African Americans in Delta counties. While most white workers earned per-capita incomes that were higher than the state average in 1999, most of the Delta s black workers earned incomes that were approximately half of the state average and a third of the national average. For example, African Americans workers in Tunica County earned an average of $7,929 annually in 1999. This figure was only a third of the 1999 average per-capita income of white workers ($22,715) in Tunica County and approximately a third of the 1999 average per-capita income of all U.S. workers ($21,587). Black workers in the County's neighboring counties-Coahoma, Quitman, and Panola-earned higher incomes than Tunica County's workers, but even in these counties the annual per-capita incomes were only half of the state average and a third of the U.S. average. Thus in 1999, black workers in the Delta

Table 4.4   Households Receiving Public Assistance in Tunica County, Mississippi, 1992-1999

Food Stamp Participation			
Year	Number of Households	Percentage	Amount
1992	1348	51.2	$259,551
1993	1231	44.5	$214,981
1994	1017	37.1	$168,054
1995	1005	35.3	$162,758
1996	903	30.8	$149,833
1997	729	24.2	$107,979
1998	633	19.5	$88,359
1999	609	17.81	$72,200

T.A.N.F. Participation			
Year	Number of Households	Percentage	Amount
1992	541	19.8	$71,294
1993	445	14.7	$57,178
1994	369	12.7	$49,061
1995	308	10.3	$41,355
1996	295	9.2	$37,504
1997	225	6.6	$31,418
1998	118	3.3	$11,233
1999	64	2.1	$7,700

Child Support		
Year	Cases	Amount Collected
1995	1412	$46,558
1996	1412	$80,157
1997	1741	$85,405.07
1998	1786	$92,870.61
1999	1882	$108,306.26

Source: Mississippi Department of Human Services.

earned higher per-capita incomes than in previous decades, but still had much lower incomes than whites in the Delta, other workers in the state of Mississippi, and other workers in the United States.

Moreover, the poverty rates of Delta counties continued to double the state and national averages by the end of the 1990s. Table 4.7 shows that the poverty rate decreased in all of the Delta's counties from 1990 to 1999 with the most significant occurring in Carroll

County (34.5%), Tunica County (22.9%), and Bolivar County (20.1%). Coahoma, Quitman, and Panola - had 11.7%, 3.9%, and 13.7% decreases, respectively, from 1990 to1999. Despite some of the most impressive declines in poverty in the Deltas history, disproportionately high poverty rates remained. By 1999, all of the core counties and three peripheral counties had poverty rates that doubled the national average of 12.4% and the rates in three Delta counties also doubled the statewide average (19.9%).

Table 4.5   Per-Capita Incomes of Mississippi Delta Residents by Race, 1970–1990

	Core Counties					
Delta County	1980 Black	1980 White	1980 All	1990 Black	1990 White	1990 All
Bolivar	2,231	6,947	6,009	4,060	11,764	11,265
Coahoma	2,209	7,569	6,839	3,761	13,610	12,644
Humphreys	2,055	—	5,752	4,161	13,670	14,244
Issaquena	2,473	—	4,285	3,804	—	11,325
Leflore	2,337	7,365	6,972	4,815	15,578	13,311
Quitman	2,002	6,176	6,149	3,684	10,516	10,535
Sharkey	2,327	7,279	6,368	3,220	11,637	12,002
Sunflower	2,237	6,773	6,015	4,130	12,329	12,334
Tallahatchie	2,392	5,620	5,322	3,588	9,814	10,591
Tunica	1,695	—	5,757	3,350	16,081	11,40
Washington	2,691	7,189	7,500	4,920	13,952	12,336
	Peripheral Counties					
Carroll	2,399	5,400	4,286	3,795	11,117	10,235
Grenada	2,848	6,611	7,179	5,039	12,007	12,569
Holmes	2,292	6,078	5,089	3,548	13,624	9,442
Panola	2,357	5,968	6,008	4,343	10,566	11,265
Tate	2,892	5,895	6,674	5,181	11,347	13,501
Warren	3,365	8,019	9,509	5,325	14,451	15,040
Yazoo	2,352	6,914	7,454	3,937	12,100	12,272
Mississippi	2,833	7,325	7,409	5,194	12,183	12,830
United States	4,505	7,808	10,495	8,859	15,687	18,696

Source: U.S. Census Bureau. "Labor Force Status in 1979 and Income Characteristics in 1979 by Race and Spanish Origin for Counties: 1980." *1980 Census of the Population* (Washington, DC: U.S. Department of Commerce, 1983); ibid. "Income in 1989 of Householders, Families and Persons by Race and Hispanic Origin: 1990." *1990 Census of the Population* (Washington, DC: U.S. Department of Commerce, 1993); U.S. Department of Commerce. "Counties-Civilian Labor Force and Personal Income". *City/County Data Book* (Washington, DC: Government Printing Office, 1983); ibid. "Counties- Labor Force and Personal Income". *City/County Data Book* (Washington, DC: Government Printing Office, 1994).

Table 4.6   Per Capita Incomes of Mississippi Delta Residents by Race, 1999

County	White	Black	All
Core Counties			
Bolivar	19,752	8,135	12,088
Coahoma	21,580	8,724	12,558
Humphreys	19,075	7,889	10,926
Issaquena	17,235	6,813	10,581
Leflore	21,729	8,494	12,553
Quitman	16,741	8,151	10,817
Sharkey	19,976	7,751	11,396
Sunflower	18,981	8,198	11,365
Tallahatchie	16,077	7,184	10,749
Tunica	22,715	7,929	11,978
Washington	21,782	9,010	13,430
Peripheral Counties			
Carroll	17,877	11,787	15,744
Grenada	17,017	9,091	13,786
Holmes	20,613	8,165	10,683
Panola	17,647	8,414	13,075
Tate	18,573	11,113	16,154
Warren	23,109	10,406	17,527
Yazoo	17,888	7,213	12,062
Mississippi	19,387	10,042	15,853
United States	23,918	14,437	21,587

Source: U.S. Census Bureau. "Per-Capita Incomes in 1999 (Dollars) (Black or African American Alone)". http://factfinder.census.gov/; ibid. "Per-Capita Incomes in 1999 (Dollars) (Whites Alone)". http://factfinder.census.gov/; ibid. "Per-Capita Incomes in 1999 (Dollars) (Universe: Total Population)". http://factfinder.census.gov.

According to table 4.8, individuals who once had few job opportunities in the Delta are now working. By the end of the 1990s, the number of jobs in Tunica County (approximately 13,000 in 2000) outnumbered its population (approximately 8,500 in 2000). By 1999, Tunica County's unemployment rate dropped by 11.6 percentage points from 17.2% in 1991 to 5.6%. Coahoma, Quitman, and Panola also experienced unemployment decreases from double-digit to single-digit percentages from 1991 to 1999. In fact, by the end of the 1990s, all of the Delta's counties experienced unemployment declines. Unfortunately by 2004, higher jobless rates were apparent in Delta counties—including Coahoma, Tunica, Warren, and Washington, which all have casinos.

Table 4.7 Poverty Among Individuals in the Counties of the Mississippi Delta, 1990–1999

			Core Counties			
County	1990 Rate	1993 Rate	1995 Rate	1997 Rate	1999 Rate	Change from 1990–1999
Bolivar	53.4	40.1	35.2	29.4	33.3	−20.1
Coahoma	47.6	42.2	37.4	30.0	35.9	−11.7
Humphreys	46.2	41.9	38.9	32.0	38.2	−8.0
Issaquena	45.4	40.0	39.9	33.2	33.2	−12.2
Leflore	38.6	37.6	34.7	29.1	34.8	−3.8
Quitman	46.8	40.2	37.2	31.5	33.1	−13.7
Sharkey	50.4	44.3	42.1	35.9	38.3	−12.1
Sunflower	49.9	45.9	41.6	34.3	30.0	−19.9
Tallahatchie	44.3	38.9	33.7	27.6	32.2	−12.1
Tunica	56.0	43.4	36.6	26.6	33.1	−22.9
Washington	35.7	35.8	31.8	26.0	29.2	−6.5
			Peripheral Counties			
Carroll	50.5	24.4	20.8	18.0	16.0	−34.5
Grenada	21.2	23.3	20.1	18.1	20.9	−0.3
Holmes	57.1	50.0	44.9	36.0	41.1	−16.0
Panola	29.2	29.6	25.7	21.6	25.3	−3.9
Tate	21.6	21.1	18.0	14.9	13.5	−8.1
Warren	21.0	22.9	19.2	16.9	18.7	−2.3
Yazoo	39.8	38.2	34.5	27.5	31.9	−7.9
State of MS	25.2	24.6	21.4	16.8	19.9	−5.3
U.S.	13.1	15.1	13.8	12.6	12.4	−0.7

Source: Slater and Hall, eds. "States and Counties: Labor Force and Employment," *1993 County and City Extra*; ibid. "States and Counties: Poverty, Housing, and Disability"; U.S. Census Bureau. "Poverty Status in 1999 by Age (Whites Alone Between the Ages of 18-64)" www.census.gov; ibid. "Persons and Families Below Poverty Level by Detailed Race: 1989, 1992, and 1993." *Income, Poverty, and Valuation of Noncash Benefits: 1993* (Washington, D.C.: U.S. Department of Commerce, 1995); ibid. "Poverty Status in 1989 of Families and Persons by Race and Spanish Origin for Counties: 1990." *Characteristics of the Population. General Social and Economic Characteristics. 1990 Census of the Population* (Washington, DC: U.S. Department of Commerce, 1993); ibid. "County Estimates for People of All Ages in Poverty for Mississippi: 1993." www.census.gov; ibid. "County Estimates for People of All Ages in Poverty for Mississippi: 1995." www.census.gov; ibid. "County Estimates for People of All Ages in Poverty for Mississippi: 1998". www.census.gov.; ibid. "Persons Below the Poverty Level and Below 125% of Poverty Level: 1970 to 1999." *Statistical Abstract of the U.S.: The National Data Book, 19th ed* (Washington, DC: U.S. Department of Commerce, 2001); ibid. "Profile of Selected Economic Characteristics: 2000." www.census.gov.

Table 4.8   Annual Unemployment Rates in the Counties of the Mississippi Delta, 1991–2004

			Core Counties		
Delta County	1991 Rate	1999 Rate	Percent Change 1991-1999	January 2004	Percent Change 1999-2004
Bolivar	9.9	8.3	−1.6	10.3	+2.0
Coahoma	12.2	5.3	−6.9	8.6	+3.3
Humphreys	10.9	5.9	−5.0	14.9	+9.0
Issaquena	17.4	6.4	−11.0	17.9	+11.5
Leflore	13.6	8.4	−5.2	12.6	+4.2
Quitman	15.0	4.4	−10.6	17.7	+13.3
Sharkey	18.3	8.0	−10.3	24.8	+16.8
Sunflower	10.9	5.9	−5.0	13.2	+7.3
Tallahatchie	16.4	4.9	−11.5	18.4	+13.5
Tunica	17.2	5.6	−11.6	13.4	+7.8
Washington	12.2	6.8	−5.4	12.5	+5.7
			Peripheral Counties		
Carroll	14.2	4.2	−10.0	5.6	+1.2
Grenada	9.2	3.4	−5.8	5.8	+2.4
Holmes	16.1	8.5	−7.6	17.0	+8.5
Panola	10.3	4.3	−6.0	12.9	+8.3
Tate	9.9	6.3	−3.6	7.5	+1.2
Warren	8.1	4.2	−4.1	5.6	+1.4
Yazoo	9.3	5.3	−4.0	10.3	+5.0
U.S.	6.8	3.7	−3.1	6.3	+3.4
Mississippi	8.6	4.3	−4.3	6.3	+2.0

Source: Slater and Hall, eds. "Civilian Labor Force," *1993 County and City Extra;* ibid. "States and Counties: Labor Force and Employment."

Many Delta residents believe that the area's large population of poor African Americans continue to live in poverty and are unemployed because of their unwillingness to work. One body of research observed that poverty in America wears a black face because of this assumption that African Americans live in poverty because of their unemployment status and refusal to work.[58] "The casinos are hiring everyday," one interviewee for this text stated "You can find a job now if you want one, but some people just don t want one."[59] Moreover, an analysis of the beliefs of affluent Delta residents toward its poor residents found that their perceptions ranged from a belief that "there is a job for everyone who wants one," to "You could put a factory in some people's backyard and they still wouldn't work."[60]

Table 4.9   Employed, African American, Poor Persons in States in 1989 and 1999

	1989	
State	Percent Employed	Percent of Employed African Americans Living Below the Poverty Line
Mississippi	57.0	42.9
Louisiana	57.8	42.7
Arkansas	58.5	41.4
Iowa	64.4	35.5
Wyoming	65.2	34.7
Alabama	65.3	34.6
Minnesota	65.4	34.5
Kentucky	65.9	34.0
West Virginia	66.02	33.98
Oklahoma	66.08	33.92

	1999	
State	Percent Employed	Percent of Employed African Americans Living Below the Poverty Line
Maine	75.1	24.8
Montana	77.4	22.5
Vermont	77.7	22.2
North Dakota	80.2	19.7
Louisiana	81.7	18.2
Mississippi	82.6	17.4
Iowa	82.9	17.0
West Virginia	83.6	16.3
Oklahoma	84.6	15.3
Arkansas	84.9	15.0

Source: Analysis of Public Use Microdata Files (PUMS) data from the 1990 and 2000 U.S. Census. Public Data Query (PDQ) explore software can be used with microdata from the census to obtain tabulations such as the distribution of population by state or the distribution of the national population by race, educational attainment by race, and so forth. This table shows the results of a query of the following variables to determine the percentage of employed persons in states who are African American and poor in the 2000 census: the universe/selection (esr = 1 & age>18) stands for civilians employed at work of the age of 18 and older. The row variable (state) and the column variables (poverty < = 100 & race1) denote that we are trying to determine the percentages of individuals by race in states who live below the poverty line. In the 1990 census, the following variables were used: the universe/selection (work89 & age>18) stands for civilians employed at work in 1989 of the age of 18 and older. The row variable (state) and the column variables (poverty < = 100 & race) denote that we are trying to determine the percentages of individuals by race, in states, who live below the poverty line.

Despite these stereotypical beliefs equating poverty with laziness, the state of Mississippi and the Delta region have a large concentration of employed African Americans living in poverty. Table 4.9 provides promising data about the reduction in the state of Mississippi's African American working poor population. In 1989, the state had the highest percentage of African Americans living below the poverty level in the nation. Approximately 42.9% of black workers earned incomes below the poverty level; however by 1999, the percentage had fallen to 17.4% ranking the state of Mississippi with the sixth highest population of African American working poor persons in the nation. This still is a high percentage, but is an improvement over the previous decade's.

Unfortunately in the Mississippi Delta, table 4.10 shows that a higher percentage of African Americans are members of the working poor than in the state in general. In 1999, the four Delta counties with casinos, Coahoma, Tunica, Warren, and Washington, had African American working poor populations of 75.9, 36.7, 66.2, and 52.1% respectively. Other Delta counties had black working poor populations that ranged from 40% to over 80%.

The substantial percentages of African American working poor residents of the Mississippi Delta provide evidence that black workers continue to hold jobs with the lowest wages and thus continue to be plagued by concentrated poverty. One elected official acknowledged the fact that poverty remains in part because of the low wages of many casino employees with one stating that "These are service-oriented jobs and semi-skilled jobs in the gaming industry. People are poor because the pay is not very good. The average employee makes about $7 or $8 because they have no skills for positions that pay more. We didn't have any jobs before the gaming industry. Now we have more jobs, but they don't pay a decent wage."[61]

The Effect of Casinos on Per-Capita Incomes and Unemployment in the Mississippi Delta

By the end of the 1990s, many disturbing features of the Delta's economy remained. African American incomes lagged far behind white incomes, poverty rates continued to double state and national averages, and many employed African American workers continued to live in poverty. According to the per-capita income and unemployment data previously outlined in this chapter, the residents of the Mississippi Delta have experienced some semblance of higher incomes,

Table 4.10   *Percentages of Employed, Poor Families in Delta Counties by Race in 1999

Delta County	Black Families	White Families
Bolivar	73.6	9.0
Carroll	43.5	11.6
Coahoma	75.9	12.0
Grenada	60.9	11.9
Holmes	79.0	12.2
Humphreys	81.1	7.5
Issaquena	65.5	14.7
Leflore	75.4	12.1
Panola	60.8	15.3
Quitman	68.3	17.7
Sharkey	78.6	11.4
Sunflower	64.5	6.7
Tallahatchie	71.2	17.1
Tate	36.7	9.0
Tunica	66.2	14.1
Warren	52.1	9.4
Washington	67.0	10.0
Yazoo	79.1	11.4

*Information was only available by race for families not for individuals.

Source: U.S. Bureau of the Census. "Poverty Status in 1999 of Families by Family Type by Work Experience of Householder and Spouse-Universe: Black Alone". Census 2000 Summary File Four Sample Data. http://factfinder.census.gov; ibid. "Poverty Status in 1999 of Families by Family Type by Work Experience of Householder and Spouse-Universe: White Alone". Census 2000 Summary File Four Sample Data. http://factfinder.census.gov; ibid. "Poverty Status in 1999 of Families by Family Type by Work Experience of Householder and Spouse-Universe: Families". Census 2000 Summary File Four Sample Data. http://factfinder.census.gov.

lower poverty rates, and substantially lower unemployment levels after the legalization of gaming for the first time in several decades. A key question is whether these lower rates of joblessness and higher wages resulted from the gaming industry. Linear regression analysis allows researchers to estimate the extent to which an independent variable(s) significantly accounts for change in a dependent variable. When a perfect causal relationship exists between these variables, a straight line can be drawn. This section questions whether a statistically significant relationship exists between gaming and two dependent variables (black per-capita incomes and black unemployment rates). Gaming, the independent variable, is defined on the basis of whether casinos operated in those counties. In order to observe differences in the counties with and without casinos, the counties in the state that lacked casinos in 2000 received a code of 0, while those with casinos were coded with a 1 in the data set.

Linear regression analysis also involves an analysis of the Y-intercept or constant (the value of the dependent variable when the independent variable equals zero), a description of the change in the slope of the line (b coefficient) to explain the change in the dependent variable for every one unit change in the independent variable, calculation of a Pearson's correlation coefficient (Pearson's r), and finally an observation of whether the results are statistically significant.[62] The Pearson's r ranges from -1 to $+1$ and measures the strength of the relationship among the variables. The r^2 (coefficient of determination) is a better way to ascertain whether the model is a good fit to the data. It answers the question: if you have information on the independent variable, how much of the variance in the dependent variables can you explain?

Ultimately, in regression analysis, the goal is to reject the null hypothesis that posits that no relationship exists between the variables. Because it is impossible to gage the exact relationship between the independent and dependent variables, the objective is to reject the null hypothesis with a certain level of confidence.[63] A .05 level of statistical significance means that the null hypothesis will be incorrectly rejected five times in every 100 samples. When the significance or probability (p) value is less than .05, the results are statistically significant and we can reject the null hypothesis.[64] This means that we are 95 percent confident that the relationship in the sample also exists in the larger population.[65] The null hypothesis is incorrectly rejected when a relationship is found between the variables based on analysis of data in the sample, but no such relationship exists among the population.

Table 4.11 provides the results of a multivariate regression analysis of the effect of the presence of casinos on the black per-capita incomes and unemployment rates of the residents of counties in Mississippi. The impact of a number of independent variables was examined. Although the presence of casinos resulted in higher black per-capita incomes and lower black unemployment rates, these results were not statistically significant. The percentage of black college and high school graduates and the amount of black political incorporation had a stronger impact on black per-capita incomes. We cannot reject the null hypothesis that no relationship exists between the presence of casinos and black per-capita incomes because our results are not statistically significant. Moreover, the table shows that none of

Table 4.11   The Impact of Selected Variables on 1999 Black Per-Capita Incomes and 1999 Black Unemployment Rates in Mississippi Counties

	Black Per-Capita Incomes	Black Unemployment
Presence of Casinos	77.330	−.306
% of Black College Graduates	253.193***	−.069
% of Black High School Graduates	98.562*	−.069
Political Incorporation Measure	−576.157*	.275
Constant	5407.966**	9.090***
R2	.310	.030
Adjusted R2	.274	−.020
Standard Error	1625.755	2.4429
F	8.651***	.601

* = p < .05
** = p < .01
*** = p < .001 (one-tailed tests)

Entries are unstandardized coefficients from an OLS multiple regression model.

the independent variables had a statistically significant impact on black unemployment. In addition, black per-capita incomes were approximately $576 lower in counties with greater levels of black political power. The relationship between black political incorporation, black per-capita incomes, and black unemployment rates will be discussed in further detail in chapter 5.

In summary, the changes in black per-capita incomes and the decreases in unemployment in counties with casinos are not necessarily attributable to the presence of casinos. This regression analysis failed to find a statistically significant relationship between the legalized gaming variable and the black per-capita incomes and unemployment dependent variables. Thus, the changes in these dependent variables cannot conclusively be said to have resulted from the presence of casinos. The next section examines whether legalized gaming contributed significantly to the lower poverty rates in the Mississippi Delta.

Concentrated Poverty in the Mississippi Delta

In communities with high levels of concentrated poverty, a large number of poor families live in one contiguous geographic area.

These communities are plagued by high unemployment and poverty rates as well as by high incidents of welfare dependency.[66] Scholarly research has mostly examined concentrated poverty in urban, predominantly African American communities; however, African Americans in concentrated, impoverished, rural areas experience unique and complex conditions that differ from urban residents.[67] One study of concentrated poverty distinguished urban from rural poverty in the following manner:

> In many cases, poverty is different in rural America. It is generally more dispersed, not found in the high concentrations we find in many of Americas central cities. Rural poverty is often symptomatic of a region s narrow economic base-a focus on extractive industries like mining or agriculture, for example, to the exclusion of other kinds of activity. Isolation also plays a distinct role in shaping rural poverty. Our rural communities are not only isolated from the investment capital that cities are (relatively) more successful at attracting; rural places are also more isolated from the diversity of institutions and networks that can mobilize responses to the complex problems of chronic poverty and joblessness.[68]

This characterization by William Julius Wilson in *When Work Disappears* attributes widespread concentrated poverty to an absence of industries, jobs, and decent wages.[69] Wilson's concept of social isolation posits that a lack of jobs for unskilled and uneducated African Americans, the movement of middle-class African Americans from poor neighborhoods, and high unemployment especially among males has contributed to the social isolation of the residents of neighborhoods with high rates of concentrated poverty. Moreover, the loss of the middle class from inner-city neighborhoods weakens institutions that encourage political participation and activism-churches, community organizations, and political and civic groups.[70]

Mary Corcoran's summary of the concept of social isolation in "Rags to Rags" and Cynthia M. Duncan's summary in *Worlds Apart* also attribute joblessness as the primary cause of the unwavering poverty rates of the black urban underclass. Corcoran's analysis of Wilson's concept stated that "Labor market and demographic changes have socially isolated the inner-city black poor and affected the structure and organization of family and community life. If opportunities change, then the culture will eventually respond."[71] Duncan observed that the "Restructuring of the economy has had a profound effect in rural areas where extractive and goods-producing jobs continue to decline and fewer high-end service jobs emerge at all. . . . Good jobs continue to be hard to find, and people are still leaving . . . the Delta."[72]

This literature leads to an inference that poverty in urban inner-city areas will decrease after a new industry produces jobs and higher wages and after growth occurs in the black middle class. In rural communities like the Mississippi Delta, the loss of the African American middle class has not impacted the current poverty rate because the region has never had a black middle-class. Therefore in the Delta, one must focus on the relatively new gaming industry and question whether it caused the regions lower black poverty rates. This research primarily seeks to examine the relationship between the presence of casinos and poverty in the Delta, but also considers the impact of three control variables (the percentage of black high school and college graduates and the amount of black political power) on the dependent variable. These control variables are included out of the belief that the educational levels of black county residents and the percentage of African American elected officials have an effect on the county's poverty rate. It is expected that poverty rates are lower in counties with greater percentages of black college and high school graduates and in those with stronger levels of black political incorporation.

The results in table 4.12 reveal that both the percentages of black college graduates and black political incorporation variables have statistically significant relationships on the poverty level at the .001 level. Poverty declines in counties with larger numbers of black college graduates, but increases in counties with greater numbers of black elected officials. A statistically significant relationship was not found between the presence of casinos and poverty variables.

Table 4.12   The Impact of Selected Variables on Black Poverty in Mississippi's Counties, 2000

Presence of Casinos	.962
% of Black College Graduates	−.610***
% of Black High School Graduates	2.254
Political Incorporation Measure	4.741***
Constant	41.387***
R2	.368
Adjusted R2	.335
Standard Error	5.9099***
F	11.220***

* = p < .05
** = p < .01
*** = p < .001 (one-tailed tests)

Entries are unstandardized coefficients from an OLS multiple regression model.

In the Mississippi Delta, decreased incidents of joblessness, higher incomes, and lower poverty rates have been evident after the legalization of gaming; however, this economic progress cannot be said to have resulted significantly from the gaming industry. Nevertheless, this progress has occurred in an area with nothing but escalating unemployment and poverty rates in the decades prior to the 1990s. Thus, this research supports Wilson's findings on social isolation to a large extent because poverty will decrease if poor workers receive jobs and higher wages. The decline in unemployment (growth in the number of jobs for the uneducated and unskilled populace) and increase in wages (as shown by the higher per-capita incomes) have provided opportunities for impoverished residents to get out of poverty. However, jobs and higher wages are not enough to significantly raise the overall economic status of poor African Americans in the Mississippi Delta due to the continuing legacy of elite resistance and institutional racism.

Power Relationships among Elites and Nonelites in the Gaming Era

Although a rise in incomes and a concomitant decline in unemployment and poverty have occurred in the Mississippi Delta, other aspects of Delta life, especially the inequitable power relationships among white elites and black citizens, largely remained the same. After the legalization of gaming, the Mississippi Delta continued to be a society of the powerful and the powerless. John Gaventa in *Power and the Powerless* argued that elites must lose political and economic power and nonelites must gain it in order to change a class stratification of elite wealth and nonelite poverty.[73] To some degree, the socioeconomic standing of many of the Mississippi Delta's African American population rose as exhibited by their lower unemployment rates, lower incidents of concentrated poverty, higher per-capita incomes, and reduced dependency on plantation elites for jobs. Nevertheless, African Americans have not gained economic power as a group because a sizable number still live in poverty, lack equal educational opportunities, and earn low wages. Workers with higher salaries live in Tennessee, Arkansas, and in areas of Mississippi outside of the Delta.[74]

In addition, the existing power relationships remained unchanged because of the lack of an African American presence among the highest echelon of landowners and casino executives. One study attributed the persistence of high poverty rates among African American workers to "The Tunica people, the blacks, [having] the low-pay jobs, the kitchen jobs, while the dealers hail from Memphis. This is still a county where locals refer to the 11 millionaires who own most of the land."[75] Most of the land in Tunica County is owned by the members of the Flowers, Leatherman, Owen, and Parker families. Moreover, African Americans own insignificant portions of land in all of the counties of the Mississippi Delta. Table 4.13 provides a listing of the owners of the highest land acreage in the Mississippi Delta according to reports of the Delta Council and Delta Farmers Advocating Resource Management (FARM).[76]

Many, however, object to blaming the Delta's current landowning elite class for the continuing lack of black economic power because of their provision of land and overall acceptance of the gaming industry from its earliest inception. Despite a long history of elite attempts to dominate local industries to the detriment of the black majority, the members of the current landowning families have not attempted to control the governance and management of casinos.[77] Should these actions of the present-day members of the plantation bloc lead to an inference that elite and nonelite relationships have improved in the Delta? Also, is the depiction of elites as unitary actors who promote their interests to the detriment of others false?

In a sense, these relationships are not as strained as in the past because of the lack of glaring, conspicuous elite opposition to the relatively new gaming industry; however, the legacy of their historical resistance to the black community's advancement and of a political and economic system purposely designed to marginalize African Americans continues to affect the well-being of black Deltans. According to one scholar, the plantation bloc's acceptance of new economic growth initiatives and lack of opposition to black employment opportunities does not erase the legacy of the plantation elite's economic and political power structure:

> After years of blocking all industry, several farmers have recently begun efforts to promote development that will bring new jobs: a retirement home, casino gambling, other service industry businesses-investments that are in their interests and that no longer jeopardize finding and keeping field workers. But remnants of old plantation-style dependency linger-the rent-free homes for tractor drivers and their families, wage garnishing for loans during the off-season or to pay creditors who might come to the bossman rather than directly to the borrower, furnishing of advances or help with health care expenses when the worker has no income in the winter months.[78]

The status of the Deltas prevailing plantation elite class is consistent with the finding of elite theorists. The Mississippi Delta continues to be a society in which the ruling elite are a small population of white

Table 4.13   The Most Powerful Landowners in the Delta

Name of Landowner	City and County of Residence
Fred Ballard	Greenville (Leflore)
Dan Branton	Leland (Washington)
Bruce Brumfield	Inverness (Sunflower)
Bobby Carson	Marks (Quitman)
James R. (Jimmie Dick) Carter	Rolling Fork (Sharkey)
Laurence Carter	Rolling Fork (Sharkey)
Kenneth Hood	Perthshire (Bolivar)
Shea Leatherman	Tunica (Tunica)
Harley Metcalf III	Greenville (Leflore)
Frank Mitchener	Sumner (Tallahatchie)
Chip Morgan	Stoneville (Washington)
Lester Myers	Indianola (Sunflower)
Griffin Norquist	Yazoo City (Yazoo)
C. Penn Owen	Tunica (Tunica)
William A. Percy II	Greenville (Leflore)
Tom Robertson	Holly Ridge (Sunflower)
Travis Satterfield	Benoit (Bolivar)
Mike Sturdivant	Glendora (Tallahatchie)
Ellis Trigg Woolfolk	Tunica (Tunica)

Source: BF Smith Foundation, "Farmers Advocating Resource Management: Delta F.A.R.M. Final Report," Unpublished paper (Stoneville, MS: BF Smith Foundation, 2004); ibid., "1998 Delta Council Annual Report," Unpublished paper. www.deltacouncil.org; ibid., "2000 Delta Council Annual Report," Unpublished paper. www.deltacouncil.org; ibid., "2001 Delta Council Annual Report," Unpublished paper. www.deltacouncil.org; ibid., "2002 Delta Council Annual Report," Unpublished paper. www.deltacouncil.org.

landowners who use various leadership and governing styles to control the amount of resources groups receive in local areas; determine the way in which their society will be governed; have their interests served; and live in a separate world of wealth, power, and privilege.[79] In today's Mississippi, the sizable African American population poses no political or economic threat to plantation elites because of their lack of representation in countywide political offices, lack of economic power as a group, and consequently their inability to impact the welfare of landowning families.

Conclusion

This chapter examined the following questions: Has one of the poorest areas in the nation become an entrepreneurial state? Is there any evidence that the elites were threatened by outsiders-casino executives and owners whose industry resulted in numerous changes in a society that had traditionally resisted change? Has the gaming industry markedly changed the economic power relationships among white elites and African American nonelites?

Essentially, the gaming windfall and influx of new casinos failed to uplift the poor as expected. The analysis of data in this chapter has discovered that the presence of casinos in Delta counties failed conclusively to cause higher black per-capita incomes, lower unemployment rates, or lower poverty levels. The region experienced lower poverty rates because the percentages of poor individuals in the Delta declined by several percentage points after 1992; however, the eighteen counties in the Mississippi Delta region continue to rank among the poorest in the nation and white landowners still reap the highest profits from the industry. Thus, gaming has yet to bring about the desired economic transformation in the Delta because it failed to substantially alter the economic power relationships among white elites and black nonelites.

This chapter argued that even after overt elite resistance to black political and economic advancement is less apparent, the legacy of this resistance continues to have a negative impact. This legacy has resulted in a large concentration of unskilled and uneducated workers in the Delta. Many African American residents uplifted their economic status and now hold the major elective offices in many Delta towns, but are still poor. Chapter 5 questions why the combination of economic growth and an increase in political power among African Americans failed to eliminate disproportionately high poverty rates in some Delta communities.

CHAPTER 5

THE TRANSFORMATION OF
DELTA PLANTATION POLITICS

Introduction

During the heyday of the traditionalistic plantation political era, elected officials lived by the motto, "What's good for the planter is good for the Delta."[1] Beginning in the 1960s, the first major changes to the Delta's political structure occurred after the Voting Rights Act and political mobilization tactics resulted in substantial increase in black voter registration and officeholding. Currently, Mississippi has more black elected officials than any other state.

In most of the Delta's towns, however, the shift in power from white to black politicians has not significantly improved the economic well-being of African American residents. Moreover they hold few countywide offices in all of the Delta's eighteen counties. The typical experience of the African American citizenry during the transitional and modern periods has been strong political incorporation in rural towns, but few or no African American representatives in powerful at-large elected positions and high incidents of black poverty everywhere in the region.

According to scholarly literature, an increase in black economic and political power results in a decrease in black poverty. The concept of social isolation hypothesized that individuals and families remained in poverty because of their "social isolation" from jobs and economic institutions while the political incorporation theory concluded that a rise in black officeholding eventually results in substantive benefits in black communities. It can be inferred from these concepts that the combination of an improved African American economic standing and a rise in black political power should lead to substantial declines in black poverty rates. Why has this not happened in the Mississippi Delta?

This chapter examines the significant changes in the Mississippi Delta during the transitional and modern phases of its political development as black voters established and expanded their political incorporation. The chapter then seeks to ascertain the current amount of political power African Americans possess in the towns and counties of the Mississippi Delta. The main inquiry is whether a lack of black political power contributes to the remaining incidents of black poverty in the region.

The Political Incorporation Theoretical Framework

In *Protest Is Not Enough*, Rufus Browning, Dale Rogers Marshall, and David Tabb analyzed the reasons why African Americans and Latinos mobilized successfully in some cities but not in others; why mobilization resulted in significant minority representation in some cities but not in others; and why minority representation resulted in responsive policies in some areas but not in others.[2] Their framework found that most African American and Latino political efforts involved group mobilization, electoral activity, group representation, incorporation, and finally "governmental responsiveness."[3] Minority voters mobilize their communities by registering them to vote. On election day, they had a large turnout so that their preferred candidates would win. After these victories, minority officeholders delivered benefits to those who elected them. The ultimate goal was to achieve political incorporation-an equal or leading role in the local governing coalition. Browning, Marshall, and Tabb's definition in *Racial Politics in American Cities*, African Americans have political power in their communities when they have elected African American mayors, City Council members, aldermen, and when other political representatives are committed to serving the interests of African Americans.[4] They defined political power as

> People who have long been excluded from holding office or from any significant influence over city government . . . have achieved power when they wrest concessions from an unwilling city hall; when they win office against determined opposition; when they succeed in forming a coalition that defeats an incumbent group; when their coalition is able to change the politics and personnel of city government; and when they are able over a period of years to institutionalize the changes they sought.[5]

Political incorporation comes in three forms-weak, moderate, and strong. A minority group has weak incorporation when it has not elected any of its group members in political offices and did not

participate in a coalition that controlled city government on the issues of greatest concern to it.[6] Moderate incorporation involves a
group having elected a few minority representatives in cities and
counties, but has a coalition that is resistant to minority interests.[7] Finally, a group possesses strong political incorporation or political
equality when it has an equal or dominant role in a local governing
coalition that is strongly committed to minority interests and an
equal ability to influence local decision-making.[8] Most of the African
American residents of small, predominantly black Delta counties
achieved weak levels of political incorporation countywide in the aftermath of the Voting Rights Act and strong incorporation in predominantly black Delta towns.

During the modern era, the Delta's political incorporation has
been "fragmented" because of separate and distinct white and black
political structures. One analysis of Mississippi politics explained
that Delta counties have "had fragmented leadership structures, particularly along racial lines. Resources which are necessary for the
well being of the community remain stuck in racial enclaves."[9] Power
in the white structure, which dominates Delta counties, has been
based on elite rule. Members of the plantation bloc have been "the
ones most likely to get what they want in the community" because of
their ownership of land and control of banking, wholesale, retail,
and legal institutions.[10]

The black structure, on the other hand, has been pluralistic in
nature because several individuals rather than a few elites hold political offices and make decisions on behalf of the larger community. In
order to promote their community's interests, black politicians from
small towns have had numerous conflicts with white elites. In addition, these politicians have remained dependent on plantation elites
because of the latter's possession of the preponderance of political
influence, economic influence, and land.[11]

The subsequent sections of this chapter will explain the fact that
the African American residents of all of the region's counties have
continued to pursue stronger levels of political incorporation since
the 1960s. Until recently, these efforts seemed almost futile and continue to remain so in some largely African American populated Delta
counties. After the ratification of the Voting Rights Act of 1965,
Africans registered to vote and mobilized their bloc vote in support of
black candidates, but were disappointed with their inability to elect
black representatives in proportion to their numbers in the population and with the successful tactics imposed by plantation elites to
maintain the latters' dominance of major county political offices.

The Voting Rights Act of 1965, the Transitional Era, and the
Realization Gap

Probably the most significant contributor to African American political development in Mississippi was the ratification of the Voting Rights Act of 1965. After its passage, African Americans in several Southern states witnessed a transition from political ostracism to political inclusion. The intent of the Civil Rights Acts of 1957 and 1960 had been to end suffrage discrimination on the basis of race, color, or national origin; to stipulate that local registrars maintain voter registration records; and to appoint referees to monitor elections where evidence of discrimination existed.[12]

Neither of these federal statutes had resulted in a significant increase in black voter registration by the mid 1960s, however, because of laws enacted by the Mississippi legislature after their ratification such as the requirement that voters and electors be of "good moral character," and the stipulation that the names of applicants for registration be published in local newspapers so that their qualifications can be challenged by state residents if necessary (see chapter 3).[13] In Mayersville, Mississippi, a small town in Issaquena County, African Americans constituted 68% of the voting-age population in 1965. While 100% of the town's white residents were registered to vote, none of the African Americans were.[14] In Humphreys County, the black voting-age population numbered 66% in 1965. Not only were no African Americans registered to vote during that year, but none had attempted to register between 1955, when one African American was shot to death and another wounded when attempting to register, and August 1964 when a massive voter registration drive began.[15]

Unlike the Civil Rights acts of 1957, 1960, and 1964, the Voting Rights Act provided for the enforcement of its provisions. Section 3 stipulated that the U.S. Civil Service Commission appoint federal examiners to list the persons who were qualified to vote in forty counties in North Carolina and in six Southern states-Alabama, Georgia, Louisiana, Mississippi, South Carolina, and Virginia.[16] These areas were targeted because of decades of dismally low rates of African American voter registration and political participation historically. Section 4 of the act also prohibited the use of literacy tests and "good moral character" clauses. The Preclearance Requirement in section 5 prohibited states from enacting new voting laws, prerequisites, or procedures without the authorization of the U.S. District Court in the District of Columbia or in the U.S. Attorney General's office. In addition, section 8 authorized federal examiners to monitor elections in the targeted counties by observing whether eligible voters were actually being permitted to vote. Section 10 prohibited states from requiring the payment of poll taxes as a precondition for voting.[17] Section 11 prohibited individuals from practicing other forms of intimidation, threats, or coercion against voters and for refusing to tabulate votes from black citizens.

Substantial increases in black voter registration occurred in the immediate aftermath of the Voting Rights Act. The largest gain was in Mississippi, where black voter registration increased from 6.7% in 1965, to 59.8% in 1967, and to 66.3% in 1970.[18] In addition, Mississippi voters elected Robert Clarke as their first black legislator since Reconstruction and twenty-one other African American political figures in 1967.[19] Black candidates also won offices in Delta counties where white resistance had always been strongest such as Bolivar, Holmes, and Issaquena. From the turn of the century to 1965, the only voters in Mississippi who had elected black politicians lived in the all-black Delta town of Mound Bayou.[20]

African American elected officials increased their political leverage in areas where they constituted the majority population in a manner consistent with the political incorporation framework-mobilizing a core base of support through increased voter registration and turnout drives, drafting candidates to run for offices, and electing their preferred candidates.[21] In "Preconditions for Afro-American Leadership," Minion KC Morrison discovered that impoverished black voters in Bolton, Mayersville, Tchula, and other Mississippi Delta towns were able to elect black mayors and other representatives during the late 1960s and early 1970s because young, charismatic activists developed leadership and mobilization skills during the civil rights movement and later won political offices.[22] Morrison's research found that "a strong and independent personality [became] the symbol necessary to inspire mass participation."[23] Through their work in political groups, churches, social groups, and campus organizations at historically black colleges and universities, these activists registered a large number of black voters after the passage of the Voting Rights Act, drafted candidates or ran for office themselves, and won elections.[24]

In Holmes County, a small number of poor African American farmers boldly fought for the integration of schools, expanded job opportunities, and suffrage rights during the transitional era. Holmes was an anomaly in the Delta because the "dirt farmers" who initiated the civil and political rights battle were landowners and thus less dependent on white elites for subsistence than black sharecroppers.[25] Also, a small black middle-class group of ministers, teachers, and business-people lived in the same segregated areas of the county as the dirt farmers. Beginning in the early 1960s, the farmers regularly visited the local registrar's office in unsuccessful attempts to register to vote and later filed the landmark U.S. Supreme Court lawsuit, *Alexander v. Holmes County.* When the farmers first challenged the county's practice of disfranchisement, segregation, and racism, black middle-class residents refused to assist them because of legitimate fears of economic and physical reprisals from whites. Two years after the ratification of the Voting Rights Act in 1967, African Americans from all class backgrounds worked together in the battle for civil and political rights.[26]

During the year's primary and general elections, black candidates in Holmes County (which included a few of the dirt farmers but mostly middle class black candidates) improved their political status from weak to moderate political incorporation. During the traditionalistic era, African Americans had completely lacked the right to engage in any political activities, had no African American representatives, and had been ignored by the elite-dominated governing coalition. By the late 1960s, moderate political incorporation became a reality after thousands of black Deltans registered to vote and elected black candidates for the first time since Reconstruction. In the 1967 primary, twelve African American candidates ran for district and at-large offices that had not held by an African American since Reconstruction.[27] Among those elected were Howard Taft Bailey as County Election commissioner and Robert Clarke in the legislature.[28] In many Delta towns, strong political incorporation followed in the immediate years after 1967 as black voters registered and voted on election day for candidates drafted by the community.

Considering Mississippi's history of disfranchisement and intimidation, the higher black registration rates and victories of black contenders were very impressive during the transitional era. In a succession of the largest towns in core Delta counties, a transition from white elite to African American political rule transpired. During the transitional and modern eras, African Americans achieved strong incorporation in small Delta towns like Belzoni (Humphreys County), Clarksdale (Coahoma County), Cleveland (Bolivar County), Greenville (Washington County), Greenwood (Leflore County), Indianola (Sunflower County), Jonestown (Coahoma County), Marks (Quitman County), Mayersville (Issaquena County), Rolling Fork (Sharkey County), Sumner (Tallahatchie County), and Tchula (Holmes County); as a result whites abandoned their aspirations to hold local elective offices because "It [didn't] do them any good to run for anything anymore."[29] One study painted a demographic profile of black representatives in Mississippi's counties and found that black political success was directly related to the proportionate size of the county's black voting-age population, a younger population (between the ages of 23 and 31), smaller increases in population size than other counties, poor economic conditions (high poverty and low incomes), low educational levels, and high unemployment.[30]

In spite of the gains made after the Voting Rights Act, African Americans in the Mississippi Delta and in other Southern states soon experienced a "realization gap" because

> . . . The dramatic increase in black voter registration after the passage of the Voting Rights Act did not immediately result in a commensurate increase in the number of black elected officials. The expectation that Mississippi's newly enfranchised black voters would now be able to elect their fair share of black officeholders was not realized. . . . In the first statewide elections after the Voting Rights Act became law, held in 1967, despite the fact that blacks had population majorities in 28 counties and that black voters constituted 28 percent of the statewide electorate, and other off-year elections, there were only 29 black elected officials in the entire state, or only 0.6 percent of the total number of elected officials.[31]

After the ratification of the Voting Rights Act of 1965, black voters expected to use their voting power to elect black representatives in proportion to their numbers in the population and to transform their status from access to empowerment. After they gained "access"—the right to participate fully in the political process, they would elect percentages of black candidates in proportion to their numbers in the population. African American political empowerment was defined in a study of political mobilization efforts in three predominantly black rural counties in Georgia as "(1) blacks holding office in proportion to their numbers in the population; (2) the enactment of public policies favorable to the black community; and (3) the rise in the socioeconomic status of the black community."[32]

Despite the increased rates of black political participation and officeholding, however, racial polarization, elite resistance, and a low African American socioeconomic status continued to be the norm during the transitional era. African American political development in the Mississippi Delta had advanced to new levels by the late 1960s, but the remnants of the old traditionalistic political culture remained in place. After the end of the traditionalistic order, Delta residents expected a new political order where blacks and whites voted without obstructions and lived in counties governed by coalitions of black and white politicians. These optimistic expectations soon wavered as reality set in during the transitional, post-Voting Rights Act years. While African Americans attempted to elect politicians who would bring prosperity to them, the elite members of society sought to preserve their economic status and to prevent any kind of wealth redistribution.[33]

Instead of disfranchising African American voters, white elites resolved to maintain their dominance of legislative, aldermanic, county commissions, and boards of supervisors' offices in the state during the transitional and modern eras. The plantation bloc practiced ingenious methods to dilute the black vote during the transitional and modern eras of Mississippi's political development. These included changing elective offices to appointed offices, changing the qualifying requirements for candidates, combining predominantly black and predominantly white counties for the purpose of maintaining a white voting majority, creating multimember districts, instituting at-large elections, and gerrymandering district lines along racial lines.[34] In the 1966 regular and special sessions of the Mississippi legislature, state representatives introduced approximately thirty bills for the purpose of changing the election process in the state, especially in predominantly black counties. Twelve of these bills became law.[35]

Counties in the Delta region were divided into five congressional districts with predominantly white voting-age populations and none with a predominantly black population. In an article in the *Jackson Daily News*, one state representative admitted that the purpose of this division was to dilute the black vote. Referring to three of the new congressional districts, State Representative Thompson McClellan of Clay County, Mississippi concluded, "This patently was drawn in a manner to devalue the vote of a certain group of people."[36]

Black activists immediately filed lawsuits questioning the legality of these electoral changes. In the case of *Connor v. Johnson*, the Mississippi Freedom Democratic Party and several other black plaintiffs filed a class-action suit in a federal district court that challenged the constitutionality of the state's congressional districts and the apportionment of the seats in both houses of the state legislature.[37] Their complaint alleged that African Americans in Mississippi were entitled to be represented by a black Congress-person since they constituted 43 percent of the state's population. Before a federal district court was convened to hear the case, the legislature enacted a bill redrawing the boundaries of its five congressional districts.[38] In addition, the legislature combined state legislative districts in which black citizens constituted both the majority population and the majority of the registered voters, with those with predominantly white populations and voting majorities. A federal district court found that these actions were unconstitutional and struck down several of these legislative and congressional districts.[39] On appeal, the U.S. Supreme Court affirmed the district court's decision; however, an African American Congress-person would not again serve until 1986 when Mike Espy became the first black congressional representative from Mississippi and from the rural South since the 1880s.[40] Also, after State Representative Robert Clarke's election in 1967, twelve years passed before the election of another African American legislator. In 1979, Dr. Aaron Henry, president of the Mississippi State Conference of the National Associate for the Advancement of Colored People (NAACP), Clarksdale pharmacist, and one of the state's most visible civil rights activists, won election to the Mississippi legislature.[41]

Perhaps the most enduring changes to the election process lay in the change of board of supervisors' elections from district to at-large. During the 1966 legislative session, Mississippi legislators introduced four bills to switch the elections for members of the county boards of supervisors and county boards of education from district to countywide.[42] House Bill 223, introduced by Representative Charles Deaton of Leflore County and eleven other representatives from Delta counties or from predominantly white counties with majority black county supervisor's districts, dealt specifically with the replacement of district with at-large county supervisor elections. After the change, supervisors would be elected countywide, but fulfill duties in their district of residence.[43]

For almost a century, five supervisors had been elected in separate districts or beats. The members of these boards have always been the most powerful elected officials in Mississippi counties because of their complete control of the county budget and county departments. They also maintain the county's roads, bridges, courthouses and jails, hospitals, health departments, libraries, and garbage disposal.[44] Once elected, they have almost total control within their districts and cannot be removed from office because the state constitution lacks provisions for a recall vote or for public referenda.[45] Because of their sizable population in the Delta, African Americans could increase their representation on supervisory boards from zero to five in many counties. Countywide elections, however, could prohibit this possibility if black voters formed a majority in one or a few districts, but not countywide.

After ratification of House Bill 223 in 1966, at least fourteen Mississippi counties instituted at-large elections for county supervisors during the 1967 and 1971 county elections. All but four of these counties had at least one predominantly black supervisor's district.[46] Only three African American contenders ran for a seat on the board of supervisors in these counties, but all were defeated.[47]

The NAACP, on behalf of black voters in Adams and Forest counties in Mississippi, filed two class-action lawsuits, *Fairley v. Patterson* and *Marsaw v. Patterson* (which was later consolidated in *Fairley v. Patterson*) to challenge the change to countywide board of supervisors' races. In *Fairley*, the plaintiffs alleged that the 1966 law violated the Fourteenth-and Fifteenth-Amendment rights of African American voters and also should be struck down because of the legislature's failure to comply with the section 5 preclearance requirement of the Voting Rights Act.[48]

Fairley was later consolidated with four other cases questioning the legality of the law's other provisions. *Ballard v. Patterson, Bunton v. Patterson,* and *Griffin v. Patterson* each objected to a new requirement that the county superintendent of education be appointed rather than elected in eleven counties.[49] *Whitley v. Johnson* challenged the new qualifying requirements that imposed significant barriers for independent candidates in local and state elections.[50] The plaintiffs in these lawsuits appealed to the U.S. Supreme Court after a federal court found no evidence of racial discrimination, concluded that the law was not subject to the section 5 provision, and dismissed their complaints.

These cases were then consolidated with a Virginia case, *Allen v. State Board of Elections.* In *Allen,* the plaintiffs objected to a stipulation that an illiterate voter add the names of write-in candidates on ballots "in his own handwriting."[51] Although blind and disabled voters received assistance from election workers or from other "persons of their choice," no provision was made for the assistance of illiterate voters.[52] The ballots of the plaintiffs in the *Allen* case were discarded after they voted for 1966 write-in candidates by placing labels printed with the name of their candidate on the ballot.

In *Allen,* the Court had to determine whether section 5 of the Voting Rights Act stipulated that all of the respective changes should have been examined by the U.S. Attorney General's Office or by the District Court of the District of Columbia before being implemented. After years of litigation, the plaintiffs received a favorable ruling when the Court found that

> . . . The Voting Rights Act was aimed at the subtle, as well as the obvious, state regulations which have the effect of denying citizens their right to vote because of their race. Moreover, compatible with the decisions of this Court, the Act gives a broad interpretation to the right to vote, recognizing that voting includes "all action necessary to make a vote effective". . . . Indicative of an intention to give the Act the broadest possible scope, Congress expanded the language in the final version to include any "voting qualifications or prerequisites to voting, or standard, practice, or procedure."[53]

Because of this ruling, each of the provisions of these new statutes had to adhere to the section 5 requirement. In each of Mississippi's eighty-two counties, the earlier practice of selecting five supervisors in each respective county through district elections was reinstated.[54] However, the representatives in the most powerful county offices in the Mississippi Delta remained disproportionately white, male, wealthy, and unconcerned with the problems of the underclass both during and after the transitional phase.[55] Moreover, black and white politicians served in areas populated mostly by the members of their racial group and seldom participated in biracial alliances to accomplish their goals. During the transitional era, the transition from weak and moderate to strong black political incorporation, as impressive as it was, failed to diminish the elite's stronghold on the Delta's political and economic affairs. In many small towns, strong black political incorporation materialized; yet, African Americans continued to possess weak incorporation countywide. The next section assesses the current amount of black political incorporation in the Mississippi Delta's towns and counties.

The Continuing Search for Governmental Responsiveness in the Modern Era

Since the 1960s, black Deltans have successfully mobilized their bloc vote and increased their political leverage, but until recently failed to dominate countywide governing coalitions in most counties throughout the Delta region and throughout the entire state of Mississippi. In Delta counties, the lack of governmental responsiveness during the modern era has resulted mostly from the lack of African American proportional representation in the region's most powerful positions. One observation that "The political transformation, i.e., the change from all white elected officials to black proportional representation, which was supposed to have been facilitated by the Voting Rights Act of 1965 is still a dream-not a reality," is applicable to the Mississippi Delta and many other Southern rural counties.[56]

The number of African American elected officials in Mississippi increased from 57 in 1970, to 254 in 1980, to 897 in 2000, making Mississippi the state with the largest number of black elected officials, but African Americans as a group continue to lack county representation in proportion to their population in the entire state. Even in counties with black voting-age populations of 40% and above, African American contenders have won few county and countywide elections.[57] In the twelve Delta counties where African Americans constituted over half of the population in 1980, the percentage of African Americans in countywide elected and appointed positions was far less than 50%; Bolivar 7%; Coahoma 16%; Holmes 44%; Humphreys 25%; Issaquena 5%; Leflore 13%; Quitman 11%;

Sharkey 8.3%; Sunflower 0%; Tallahatchie 4%; Tunica 12.5%; and Washington 3.6%.[58] Moreover, African Americans have remained severely underrepresented on county boards of supervisors. By 1989, 68 of the 410 county supervisors in the entire state (16.6%) were African American and only 1 African American served on a county board in each of the Delta's eighteen counties.[59]

The plantation bloc maintained control of these boards before the 1990s for several reasons. Many white supervisors elected in at-large races continued to serve in later years. Also, the Mississippi Constitution still stipulates supervisors to own land.[60] An even greater obstacle for some African American supervisory candidates has been election fraud. Operation Pretense was a 1980s federal probe that resulted in the arrests of fifty-seven supervisors in twenty-six Mississippi counties. Several precinct officials throughout the state had failed to record the names of all individuals who voted, that allowed the ballot boxes to be stuffed.[61] At other times, black voters claimed that they were forced to work overtime on election day by plantation owners and firms such as Baldwin Piano, Vlassic Pickle, and local catfish factories.[62]

Table 5.1 indicates the degree to which African Americans remained underrepresented in county political offices during the modern era. One study of Delta politics found that "By the late 1980s, even with a considerable number of African Americans in office in Mississippi, the African American community was still without a strong voice. There were not enough black elected officials to exercise real power."[63] With the exception of Holmes and Humphreys counties, African Americans failed to constitute the majority of members on county boards of supervisors in majority African American Delta counties by 1991. Moreover, African American contenders served in no other countywide elective offices in the region, but successfully competed for municipal offices in the small predominantly black towns of the Mississippi Delta.

The commission form of government has also disadvantaged African American City Council candidates in many towns and cities. This governmental system was utilized in large cities more frequently than in small towns. Even when black voters composed 40% or more of the local populace, the at-large elections of commissioners usually resulted in white candidate victories. Faced with court challenges by numerous African American groups, many cities and counties later chose their commissioners through the use of district rather than countywide elections. These district or ward elections greatly increased the prospects of victory for African American candidates, especially in majority black areas.[64]

Table 5.1 **African American Political Power in the Mississippi Delta's Towns and Cities, 1991**

Delta Town (County)	Population by Race, Poverty Rates, Federal, and State Elected Officials						
	Total Population	Black Population	White Population	Poverty Rate	*U.S. Rep.	State Senators	State Rep.
Alligator (Bolivar)	187	77.3	20.9	47.2	1	0	0
Anguilla (Sharkey)	883	77.0	22.0	47.5	1	0	0
Arcola (Washington)	564	95.0	48.0	49.7	1	0	1
Belzoni (Humphreys)	2,536	68.0	30.5	35.0	1	0	0
Benoit (Bolivar)	641	76.3	21.3	49.3	1	0	0
Beulah (Bolivar)	460	95.9	21.5	33.8	1	0	0
Cary (Sharkey)	392	64.4	34.6	36.7	1	0	0
Clarksdale (Coahoma)	19,717	68.5	29.9	36.2	1	0	1
Coahoma (Coahoma)	254	98.1	1.5	55.3	1	0	1
Coldwater (Tate)	1,502	69.7	29.4	23.5	0	0	0
Como (Panola)	1,387	71.8	26.8	37.5	0	0	0
Cruger (Holmes)	548	74.2	25.6	44.7	1	0	1
Dickens (Holmes)	149	87.7	11.9	40.2	1	0	1
Doddsville (Sunflower)		61.6	32.4	30.7	1	0	0
Drew (Sunflower)	2,349	73.6	25.3	40.5	1	0	0
Duncan (Bolivar)	578	77.5	19.5	58.6	1	0	0
Durant (Holmes)	2,838	70.2	28.8	35.1	1	0	1
Falcon (Quitman)	167	99.7	0.3	39.0	1	0	0
Friars Point (Coahoma)	1,334	93.9	5.9	44.0	1	0	0
Glendora (Tallahatchie)	165	92.3	4.6	62.6	1	0	0
Goodman (Holmes)	1,256	65.8	33.2	45.6	1	0	1

(continued)

Table 5.1 (*continued*)

	Population by Race, Poverty Rates, Federal, and State Elected Officials						
Delta Town (County)	Total Population	Black Population	White Population	Poverty Rate	*U.S. Rep.	State Senators	State Rep.
Greenville (Washington)	45,226	69.6	28.9	29.6	1	0	1
Greenwood (Leflore)	18,906	65.4	32.8	33.9	1	0	0
Gunnison (Bolivar)	611	86.7	12.6	47.9	1	0	0
Hollandale (Washington)	3,576	83.2	16.0	38.6	1	0	1
Indianola (Sunflower)	11,809	73.4	25.7	27.4	1	0	0
Isola (Humphreys)	732	63.7	32.7	25.1	1	0	0
Itta Bena (Leflore)	2,377	81.3	18.1	34.5	1	0	0
Jonestown (Coahoma)	1,467	96.3	2.6	49.6	1	0	0
Lambert (Quitman)	1,131	82.8	15.6	39.9	1	0	0
Leland (Washington)	6,366	67.0	32.0	27.5	1	0	1
Lexington (Holmes)	2,227	67.2	31.3	37.2	1	0	1
Lula (Coahoma)	224	77.3	19.7	39.3	1	0	0
Marks (Quitman)	1,758	64.7	34.6	30.3	1	0	0
Mayersville (Issaquena)	329	88.0	11.9	49.9	1	0	0
Metcalfe (Washington)	1,092	97.6	1.2	47.4	1	0	1
Moorhead (Sunflower)	2,417	71.2	27.9	39.5	1	0	0
Morgan City (Leflore)	139	83.2	16.4	42.6	1	0	0
Mound Bayou (Bolivar)	2,222	98.4	0.81	45.6	1	0	0
*North Tunica (Tunica)	1,314	94.9	4.7	50.7	1	0	1
Pace (Bolivar)	354	82.7	13.7	26.0	1	0	0
Renova (Bolivar)	636	95.9	2.6	34.5	1	0	0

				Elected Judges	Election Commission	Mayors
Rolling Fork (Sharkey)	2,444	69.2	29.7	37.1	1	0	0
Rosedale (Bolivar)	2,595	82.0	16.7	46.0	1	0	0
Ruleville (Sunflower)	3,245	80.7	18.6	36.0	1	0	0
Schlater (Leflore)	404	60.6	38.9	44.3	1	0	0
Shaw (Bolivar)	2,349	92.1	7.3	41.6	1	0	0
Shelby (Bolivar)	2,806	91.1	7.9	44.5	1	0	0
Sidon (Leflore)	596	83.3	14.8	56.9	1	0	0
Silver City (Humphreys)	348	78.3	21.6	49.3	1	0	0
Sledge (Quitman)	577	75.9	23.2	24.7	1	0	0
Sunflower (Sunflower)	729	71.2	27.9	39.5	1	0	0
Tchula (Holmes)	2,186	95.9	93.4	54.4	1	0	1
Tutwiler (Tallahatchie)	1,391	87.3	11.8	38.5	1	0	0
Vaiden (Carroll)	789	71.0	28.4	32.9	0	0	0
Vicksburg (Warren)	20,908	58.9	40.5	32.7	1	0	1
Webb (Tallahatchie)	605	61.3	35.1	26.6	1	0	0
Winstonville (Bolivar)	277	97.8	1.9	45.6	1	0	0
Yazoo City (Yazoo)	12,427	69.7	28.7	40.2	1	0	0

Countywide and Municipal Positions

	Aldermen/Vice Mayor Council/Commission	Board of Supervisors	**Other Countywide Officials	Elected Judges	Election Commission	Mayors
Alligator (Bolivar)	2	1	0	0	3	0
Anguilla (Sharkey)	0	1	0	0	0	0
Arcola (Washington)	4	1	0	0	0	1
Belzoni (Humphreys)	3	3	0	0	4	0
Benoit (Bolivar)	0	1	0	0	3	0

(continued)

Table 5.1 (*continued*)

	Countywide and Municipal Positions					
	Aldermen/Vice Mayor Council/Commission	Board of Supervisors	**Other Countywide Officials	Elected Judges	Election Commission	Mayors
Beulah (Bolivar)	4	1	0	0	3	1
Cary (Sharkey)	0	1	0	0	0	0
Clarksdale (Coahoma)	2	1	0	1	1	1
Coahoma (Coahoma)	5	1	0	0	1	1
Coldwater (Tate)	0	0	0	0	0	0
Como (Panola)	0	1	0	0	0	0
Cruger (Holmes)	0	3	0	0	4	0
Dickens (Holmes)	0	3	0	0	4	0
Doddsville (Sunflower)	3	1	0	0	0	0
Drew (Sunflower)	2	1	0	0	0	0
Duncan (Bolivar)	1	1	0	0	3	0
Durant (Holmes)	3	3	0	0	4	0
Falcon (Quitman)	4	2	0	0	3	1
Friars Point (Coahoma)	5	1	0	0	1	1
Glendora (Tallahatchie)	3	0	0	0	1	1
Goodman (Holmes)	4	3	0	0	4	0
Greenville (Washington)	2	1	0	0	0	0
Greenwood (Leflore)	4	1	0	2	3	0
Gunnison (Bolivar)	5	1	0	0	3	1
Hollandale (Washington)	4	1	0	0	0	1
Indianola (Sunflower)	3	1	0	0	0	0

City (County)					
Isola (Humphreys)	0	1	0	0	4	0
Itta Bena (Leflore)	4	1	0	0	3	0
Jonestown (Coahoma)	5	1	0	0	1	1
Lambert (Quitman)	2	2	0	0	0	1
Leland (Washington)	2	1	0	2	0	0
Lexington (Holmes)	0	3	0	0	4	0
Lula (Coahoma)	1	1	0	0	1	0
Marks (Quitman)	0	2	0	0	3	0
Mayersville (Issaquena)	5	2	0	0	0	1
Metcalfe (Washington)	5	1	0	0	0	1
Moorhead (Sunflower)	1	1	0	0	0	0
Morgan City (Leflore)	0	1	0	0	3	0
Mound Bayou (Bolivar)	5	1	0	2	3	1
*North Tunica (Tunica)	0	2	0	0	3	0
Pace (Bolivar)	5	1	0	0	3	1
Renova (Bolivar)	5	1	0	0	3	1
Rolling Fork (Sharkey)	0	1	0	0	0	0
Rosedale (Bolivar)	4	1	0	0	3	1
Ruleville (Sunflower)	2	1	0	0	0	0
Schlater (Leflore)	1	1	0	0	3	0
Shaw (Bolivar)	5	1	0	0	3	1
Shelby (Bolivar)	2	1	0	0	3	1
Sidon (Leflore)	1	1	0	0	3	0
Silver City (Humphreys)	0	3	0	0	4	0
Sledge (Quitman)	2	2	0	0	3	0
Sunflower (Sunflower)	0	1	0	0	0	0
Tchula (Holmes)	3	3	0	0	4	1

(continued)

Table 5.1 (continued)

	Countywide and Municipal Positions					
	Aldermen/Vice Mayor Council/Commission	Board of Supervisors	**Other Countywide Officials	Elected Judges	Election Commission	Mayors
Tutwiler (Tallahatchie)	0	0	0	0	1	0
Vaiden (Carroll)	0	0	0	0	0	0
Vicksburg (Warren)	1	2	0	1	2	1
Webb (Tallahatchie)	0	0	0	0	0	0
Winstonville (Bolivar)	5	1	0	0	3	1
Yazoo City (Yazoo)	2	2	0	1	0	0

*North Tunica County is not a formally incorporated town, and includes the town of Robinsonville, but excludes Tunica City.
**These positions include coroner, county attorney, and tax assessor-collector.

Source: Joint Center for Political and Economic Studies. *Black Elected Officials: A National Roster, 1991, 20th ed.* (Washington, DC: Joint Center for Political and Economic Studies, 1992); University of Mississippi Center for Population Studies. "Population Changes for Mississippi Places 1980, 1990, and 2000. www.olemiss.edu/depts/sdc/citychg.pdf.

Another obstacle for African American candidates during the modern period involved their persistent inability to establish biracial coalitions. According to the political incorporation framework, minorities must participate in coalitions that control city government in order to gain benefits in their communities. African Americans in many of the region's small towns did not have to establish electoral coalitions with whites because their populations are large enough for them to elect African American politicians without use of the white vote; however, black politicians must develop governing coalitions with white elite landowners and business-people who possess important fiscal resources. Attempts to develop coalitions among wealthy conservative white elites, poor and working-class whites, and liberal African Americans have been futile during the modern political era, however.[65] Candidates have struggled to construct winning coalitions among these factions, but life in the Delta still consists of

> . . . Two distinct worlds-one black, one white. And like the railroad tracks that often separate white and black communities, poor race relations is the dividing line that kept those worlds from uniting. Some here say it's up to the power brokers-preachers, politicians and business people-to help erase that line. Others shake their heads and wonder whether even they can change things.[66]

The experience of the African American residents of Tunica County and the town of Tunica, Mississippi, demonstrates the fragmented politics of the Delta and the lack of governmental responsiveness to the African American community's interests. Tunica County's government, like that of most Delta counties, consists of a county administrator and a five-member county board of supervisors. Board members hold elective positions and then appoint an administrator to set the budget and coordinate the operation of various governmental agencies. Several of the county's governmental agencies report to the board rather than to a chief executive. No African American has ever served as county administrator and only five have served on the county board of supervisors since the election of its first black supervisor, James Dunn, in 1984.[67] During the 2004 local election, Tunica County voters elected its first predominantly African American board of supervisors and its first African American board president, Cedric Burnette. Three African American representatives-James Dunn, Cedric Burnette, and Curtis Jackson-now hold positions on the board.

The small number of black supervisors and other officeholders in majority African American Tunica County resulted from several factors. The lack of funding to mount successful campaigns against incumbents has been cited as a primary reason, "Blacks are qualified to run. Blacks are motivated to vote, but the black candidates don't have the finances to run for office."[68] Even when black contenders possessed funds, their campaigns were hampered by the complex race relations in Tunica County. Black voters supported white candidates in the predominantly black district; however, white voters rarely supported black supervisory candidates, "Every district is majority African American, but they couldn't elect a majority black board until this year [2004] and support their own. Curtis Jackson won this year in part because of a split white vote. In the past, blacks either voted for white candidates or didn't vote at all. Black leaders endorsed white candidates over black candidates because they received benefits like jobs and money."[69]

In Tunica County, African Americans have achieved a limited degree of political incorporation, but in the town of Tunica, or Tunica City, they remain absent from political offices. The predominantly white and separately annexed town of Tunica has a 75 percent white population and a mayor-alderman governmental system. Most of the town's white families have lived in the "white sub," an impeccable residential area with manicured lawns and beautiful homes, while most black families still live in the "black sub" outside the city limits.[70] No African American has ever seriously campaigned for, or served as, mayor of Tunica City. The current mayor, Bobby E. Williams, is the chief executive official and governs the town with the assistance of five aldermen. No African American has ever been elected to an aldermanic post and no visible black political organizations have ever existed in the town or county. Tunica has a "black county [and a] white city [because] whites kept blacks out [of the town of Tunica in the past]."[71] In addition, the lack of black officeholding in the town of Tunica has occurred "because most of the population is white. Blacks haven't run there."[72] Moreover, the amount of racial polarization that has always existed in the county has precluded the formation of biracial electoral and governing coalitions.

Scholarly research has touted the state of Mississippi's transition from a traditionalistic plantation political society to one with the highest number of black elected officials in the nation; however, these studies have exaggerated the degree of political power possessed by black Mississippians, especially in the predominantly black Delta region. Black political power is defined in this book as the ability of black voters to elect political representatives from their racial group and the power to demand that these representatives implement their preferred policies.[73] In rural areas especially, individuals with political power also possess "power's second face"-the ability to

maintain the "quiescence of the powerless" through the "mobilization of bias"-implement initiatives favored by elites, to exclude those
preferred by nonelites from the decision-making process, and to mit-
igate opposition from nonelites.[74] This facet of elite political power in
the Delta will be discussed further.

One can infer from the Delta experience that a significant rise in
black officeholding does not always lead to a growth in political
power. African Americans can only gain governmental responsiveness when they hold the majority of the most powerful offices in rural
counties rather than in towns. Otherwise, they gain symbolic rather
than substantive political power-feelings of pride from having black
representatives, but no actual power to serve the interests of the people who put them in office. Moreover, the absence of adequate
African American representation in most county offices means that
the plantation bloc has not lost power because it still controls the
most powerful political as well as economic institutions. As mentioned in chapter 4, elites must lose power and African Americans
must gain power for real political and economic advancements to
occur among the nonelite class.[75]

Black candidates in Tallahatchie County, Mississippi won
at-large elective offices and positions on local boards of supervisors
after an arduous battle to alter county district lines in accordance
with racial demographic shifts. Because of the distrust and divisions
both across and within racial lines, Southern Echo was confronted
with a formidable task when attempting to galvanize black voters to
increase their countywide political power. No African American
had ever been elected as a member of the Tallahatchie County
Board of Supervisors or in any other countywide office despite the
county's majority black population. In addition, Tallahatchie
County was one of the ten poorest counties in the nation. The
plantation bloc solidly controlled the board of supervisors, but
white elite opposition was not the only contributor to black officeholding since black voters failed to cast a cohesive bloc vote for
black candidates:

> These conditions [the majority black population, but the small number
> of black elected officials] were in part due to the intransigence of the
> white minority, but they were also the product of internal strife, turf bat-
> tles, and unaccountable leadership within the black community. The
> unity of purpose achieved in the civil rights movement had dissipated
> into "mischiefs of faction" during the 1970s and 1980s, as a multitude of
> organizations, clubs, and networks pursued their own divergent agen-
> das. The prevailing opinion in the county was that it was impossible to
> unite the black candidates around any issue of importance.[76]

In 1990, the organization began a campaign culminating three years later with the swearing in of the first black members of the Tallahatchie County Board of Supervisors in the county's history. The work of the Jackson, Mississippi-based Southern Echo community organizing group was crucial for attacking the dilution of the black vote in countywide Delta elections. As chapter 6 will detail, the group has been instrumental in providing assistance to many Delta communities. With the aid of Southern Echo, the residents of poor Delta neighborhoods targeted their most pressing problems, found solutions, and successfully challenged elite rule. The redistricting fight was probably the most significant contributor to the growth of black political power in Tallahatchie County since ratification of the Voting Rights Act of 1965 and the filing of the federal lawsuits of the 1960s and 1970s. The group's two primary objectives were to train individuals for leadership roles within their communities and to convince local voters that their efforts toward an expansion of black political power would not be a waste of time.[77] Beginning in 1990, meetings were held in Delta neighborhoods to prepare county residents for public hearings of the Joint Standing Committee on Legislative and Congressional Reapportionment.[78]

In addition, an alliance of organizations-Southern Echo, the Mississippi Redistricting Coalition (MRC), an organization established solely to redistrict lines so that marginalized communities could elect representation; the Rural Organizing and Cultural Center of Holmes County; and the Mississippi Action for Community Education (MACE)-conducted workshops in 1991 to educate voters about the redistricting process, obstacles to African American candidate victories, laws requiring the drawing of district lines according to the "one-person, one-vote principle," and about the Voting Rights Act's provisions.[79] Role-playing sessions in which participants played roles as white supervisors were crucial components of the workshops because they allowed the participants to envision the arguments the latter would make against redistricting and to construct arguments in response.[80]

Also in 1991, The Tallahatchie County Redistricting Committee (TCRC) was founded to solely address the issue of redistricting and to oversee a federal voting discrimination lawsuit, filed in September 1991. Representatives from TCRC met with the all-white members of the board to request that district lines be drawn in accordance with the county's racial demographics. They argued that African Americans constituted the majority population in three of five districts and thus that three majority black districts should be created. After the board members refused their request, African American citizens packed their meetings for six consecutive months demanding that they meet with TCRC. Eventually, the board agreed to negotiate with the committee and to create the three majority black districts. This was the first time the white members of the county's board of supervisors agreed to negotiate with a black organization. The board, however, withdrew the agreement after the county's plantation bloc objected to the possibility of a majority African American board. Eventually, three new districts with majority black populations were created after a federal court ordered a new plan for supervisory districts and a November 1992 special election.[81] African American candidates won two of these elections. A third candidate for the third predominantly black district seat lost by only nineteen votes.[82] During the same special election, African Americans won a majority of seats on the County Election Commission and one of two County Justice Court seats.

During the 1995 elections, black representatives on local boards of supervisors increased to 30 percent statewide. Soon thereafter, Mississippi legislators recommended a referendum to reduce the numbers of supervisors' districts from five districts with small populations to three with large populations.[83] Such a referendum, which was eventually defeated, would have imposed more difficulties on African American contenders in supervisory elections. The next section examines the most recent occurrences of African American officeholding in the Mississippi Delta and whether the persistence of black poverty results from a lack of African American political power.

Concentrated Poverty and the Paradox of Political Power

A few studies have found that most of the marginalized groups in America have improved their socioeconomic status after first gaining political power. The political incorporation framework and others have stipulated that underclass communities must mobilize their constituencies and elect representatives in order to alleviate their social and economic problems.[84] In one of the few books analyzing the relationship between race, politics, and economic development, James B. Jennings concluded, "Political mobilization is a requisite condition for improving significantly the quality of social and economic life in the Black community. . . . Without political mobilization and community consciousness the social and economic problems of Black America will continue to worsen."[85] Even with strong black political incorporation, significant reductions in poverty may not take place; yet, communities that lack such incorporation will not experience any significant economic benefits especially in racially polarized rural areas. Without political power in rural areas where elites have successfully denied them of political and economic influence for years, black citizens will forever be locked in a cycle of poverty.

Over the years, African Americans throughout the United States achieved varying levels of political success, but made less headway when attempting to improve their economic plight. Even when their racial group earned higher incomes, wide economic disparities remained along racial lines and among the black middle class and black poor. Some black families joined the ranks of the middle class, but others remained in poverty.[86]

During the modern era of Mississippi's political development, many Delta residents enjoyed superior working conditions and other advantages from their casino jobs that were superior to any they ever could have gotten through farm labor. African Americans also made an impressive transition from complete political exclusion to varying degrees of incorporation during the transitional and modern political eras. Despite the benefits that African Americans gained after the legalization of gaming and the increased amount of black political power in the Mississippi Delta, substantial numbers continue to grapple with high rates of concentrated poverty.

The data in table 5.2 reveal the percentages of families living in poverty, racial populations, and the number of black political figures in Delta towns with at least 60% black populations. This information indicates that Greenville in Washington County, Greenwood in Leflore County, and Tchula in Holmes County have the greatest amounts of black political incorporation in the Mississippi Delta. In Greenville, African Americans are among the representatives in all major political offices including one African American Congress person, one state senator, one state representative, four aldermen, four members of the board of supervisors, three other black countywide officials, one African American mayor, and several African American elected judges and election commissioners. Greenville, with a 69.9% black population, has an almost 30% poverty rate despite its political power. In Greenwood, African Americans serve in Congress, the state senate, and the state legislature. In addition, the town has a black alderman, two members of the board of supervisors, two other African American countywide officials, as well as elected judges and election commissioners, but has a 33.9% poverty rate. Poverty is lower in both Greenville and Greenwood than in most other Delta towns, but nevertheless is substantial. In addition, Tchula has five black aldermen, two members of the board of supervisors, four countywide officials, one African American mayor, and an African American election commissioner, but over half of the residents of this 95.9% black town live in poverty.

Table 5.2 African American Political Power in the Mississippi Delta's Towns and Cities, 2004

| Delta Town (County) | Population by Race, Poverty Rates, Federal, and State Elected Officials | | | | | | |
	Total Population	Black Population	White Population	Poverty Rate	*U.S. Reps.	State Senators	State Reps.
Alligator (Bolivar)	220	77.3	20.9	47.2	1	2	2
Anguilla (Sharkey)	907	77.0	22.0	47.5	1	0	1
Arcola (Washington)	563	95.0	48.0	49.7	1	1	3
Belzoni (Humphreys)	2,663	68.0	30.5	35.0	1	1	1
Benoit (Bolivar)	611	76.3	21.3	49.3	1	2	2
Beulah (Bolivar)	473	95.9	21.5	33.8	1	2	2
Cary (Sharkey)	427	64.4	34.6	36.7	1	0	1
Clarksdale (Coahoma)	20,645	68.5	29.9	36.2	1	1	2
Coahoma (Coahoma)	325	98.1	1.5	55.3	1	1	2
Coldwater (Tate)	1,674	69.7	29.4	23.5	0	1	2
Como (Panola)	1,310	71.8	26.8	37.5	0	0	2
Cruger (Holmes)	449	74.2	25.6	44.7	1	2	1
Dickens (Holmes)	1,325	87.7	11.9	40.2	1	2	1
Doddsville (Sunflower)	108	61.6	32.4	30.7	1	1	2
Drew (Sunflower)	2,434	73.6	25.3	40.5	1	1	2
Duncan (Bolivar)	578	77.5	19.5	58.6	1	2	2
Durant (Holmes)	2,932	70.2	28.8	35.1	1	2	1
Falcon (Quitman)	317	99.7	0.3	39.0	1	1	2
Friars Point (Coahoma)	1,480	93.9	5.9	44.0	1	1	2
Glendora (Tallahatchie)	285	92.3	4.6	62.6	1	1	1
Goodman (Holmes)	1,252	65.8	33.2	45.6	1	2	1

(continued)

Table 5.2 (*continued*)

	Population by Race, Poverty Rates, Federal, and State Elected Officials						
Delta Town (County)	Total Population	Black Population	White Population	Poverty Rate	*U.S. Reps.	State Senators	State Reps.
Greenville (Washington)	41,633	69.6	28.9	29.6	1	1	3
Greenwood (Leflore)	18,425	65.4	32.8	33.9	1	1	2
Gunnison (Bolivar)	633	86.7	12.6	47.9	1	2	2
Hollandale (Washington)	3,437	83.2	16.0	38.6	1	1	3
Indianola (Sunflower)	12,066	73.4	25.7	27.4	1	1	2
Isola (Humphreys)	768	63.7	32.7	25.1	1	1	1
Itta Bena (Leflore)	2,208	81.3	18.1	34.5	1	1	2
Jonestown (Coahoma)	1,701	96.3	2.6	49.6	1	1	2
Lambert (Quitman)	1,967	82.8	15.6	39.9	1	1	2
Leland (Washington)	5,502	67.0	32.0	27.5	1	1	3
Lexington (Holmes)	2,025	67.2	31.3	37.2	1	2	1
Lula (Coahoma)	370	77.3	19.7	39.3	1	1	2
Marks (Quitman)	1,551	64.7	34.6	30.3	1	1	2
Mayersville (Issaquena)	795	88.0	11.9	49.9	1	0	1
Metcalfe (Washington)	1,109	97.6	1.2	47.4	1	1	3
Moorhead (Sunflower)	696	71.2	27.9	39.5	1	1	2
Morgan City (Leflore)	305	83.2	16.4	42.6	1	1	2
Mound Bayou (Bolivar)	2,102	98.4	0.81	45.6	1	2	2
North Tunica (Tunica)	1,450	94.9	4.7	50.7	1	1	1
Pace (Bolivar)	364	82.7	13.7	26.0	1	2	2
Renova (Bolivar)	623	95.9	2.6	34.5	1	2	2

Rolling Fork (Sharkey)	2,486	69.2	29.7	37.1	1	0	1
Rosedale (Bolivar)	2,414	82.0	16.7	46.0	1	2	2
Ruleville (Sunflower)	3,234	80.7	18.6	36.0	1	1	2
Schlater (Leflore)	388	60.6	38.9	44.3	1	1	2
Shaw (Bolivar)	2,312	92.1	7.3	41.6	1	2	2
Shelby (Bolivar)	2,926	91.1	7.9	44.5	1	2	2
Sidon (Leflore)	672	83.3	14.8	56.9	1	1	2
Silver City (Humphreys)	337	78.3	21.6	49.3	1	1	1
Sledge (Quitman)	529	75.9	23.2	24.7	1	1	0
Sunflower (Sunflower)	696	71.2	27.9	39.5	1	1	2
Tchula (Holmes)	2,332	95.9	93.4	54.4	1	2	1
Tutwiler (Tallahatchie)	1,364	87.3	11.8	38.5	1	1	1
Vaiden (Carroll)	840	71.0	28.4	32.9	0	0	0
Vicksburg (Warren)	26,407	60.4	37.8	19.3	1	0	1
Webb (Tallahatchie)	587	61.3	35.1	26.6	1	1	1
Winstonville (Bolivar)	319	97.8	1.9	45.6	1	2	2
Yazoo City (Yazoo)	14,550	69.7	28.7	40.2	1	1	2

Countywide and Municipal Positions

	Aldermen/Vice Mayor Council/Commission	Board of Supervisors	Countywide Officials	Elected Judges	Election Commission	Mayors
Alligator (Bolivar)	2	0	0	0	0	0
Anguilla (Sharkey)	0	1	0	0	0	0
Arcola (Washington)	4	0	0	0	0	1
Belzoni (Humphreys)	2	2	1	0	2	1
Benoit (Bolivar)	0	0	0	0	0	0

(continued)

Table 5.2 (*continued*)

Countywide and Municipal Positions

	Aldermen/Vice Mayor Council/Commission	Board of Supervisors	Countywide Officials	Elected Judges	Election Commission	Mayors
Beulah (Bolivar)	5	0	0	0	0	0
Cary (Sharkey)	0	1	0	0	0	0
Clarksdale (Coahoma)	2	2	0	1	0	0
Coahoma (Coahoma)	5	0	0	0	0	1
Coldwater (Tate)	3	0	0	2	1	1
Como (Panola)	3	1	0	0	0	1
Cruger (Holmes)	4	2	4	0	0	1
Dickens (Holmes)	0	2	4	0	0	0
Doddsville (Sunflower)	4	2	0	0	0	1
Drew (Sunflower)	2	2	0	0	0	1
Duncan (Bolivar)	2	2	0	0	0	1
Durant (Holmes)	3	2	4	0	0	1
Falcon (Quitman)	5	1	0	0	0	1
Friars Point (Coahoma)	4	0	0	0	0	1
Glendora (Tallahatchie)	5	3	0	0	0	1
Goodman (Holmes)	1	2	4	0	0	0
Greenville (Washington)	4	4	3	3	2	1
Greenwood (Leflore)	4	2	2	3	2	0
Gunnison (Bolivar)	4	0	0	0	0	3
Hollandale (Washington)	4	4	0	0	0	0
Indianola (Sunflower)	3	2	1	0	0	0

Isola (Humphreys)	3	2	1	0	0	1
Itta Bena (Leflore)	3	2	0	0	0	1
Jonestown (Coahoma)	4	0	0	0	0	1
Lambert (Quitman)	4	0	1	0	0	1
Leland (Washington)	3	0	0	4	3	0
Lexington (Holmes)	1	2	4	0	0	0
Lula (Coahoma)	1	0	0	0	3	0
Marks (Quitman)	3	1	0	0	0	1
Mayersville (Issaquena)	5	1	0	0	0	1
Metcalfe (Washington)	5	4	0	0	0	1
Moorhead (Sunflower)	2	2	1	0	0	1
Morgan City (Leflore)	0	2	0	0	0	0
Mound Bayou (Bolivar)	5	0	0	1	4	1
**North Tunica (Tunica)	0	2	1	0	1	0
Pace (Bolivar)	5	0	0	0	0	1
Renova (Bolivar)	6	0	0	0	1	1
Rolling Fork (Sharkey)	0	1	0	0	0	0
Rosedale (Bolivar)	0	0	0	0	0	1
Ruleville (Sunflower)	5	2	1	0	0	1
Schlater (Leflore)	2	2	0	0	0	0
Shaw (Bolivar)	4	0	0	0	0	1
Shelby (Bolivar)	3	1	0	0	0	1
Sidon (Leflore)	1	0	0	0	0	1
Silver City (Humphreys)	0	2	1	0	0	0
Sledge (Quitman)	3	1	0	0	0	1
Sunflower (Sunflower)	0	2	1	0	0	0
Tchula (Holmes)	5	2	4	0	1	1
Tutwiler (Tallahatchie)	4	3	0	0	0	1

(continued)

Table 5.2 (*continued*)

Countywide and Municipal Positions

	Aldermen/Vice Mayor Council/Commission	Board of Supervisors	Countywide Officials	Elected Judges	Election Commission	Mayors
Vaiden (Carroll)	0	0	0	0	0	0
Vicksburg (Warren)	1	2	1	3	2	1
Webb (Tallahatchie)	0	3	0	0	0	0
Winstonville (Bolivar)	5	0	0	0	0	1
Yazoo City (Yazoo)	3	2	0	1	2	1

*Representative Bennie Thompson represents all of the Delta's counties with the exception of Carroll, Grenada, Panola, and Tate.
**North Tunica County is not a formally incorporated town, but includes the town of Robinsonville.

Source: http://encyclopedia.thefreedictionary.com; Joint Center for Political and Economic Studies. "Black Elected Officials Roster of Mississippi Black Elected Officials - Latest Data - May 2004 - Joint Ceter.xls," Unpublished report (Washington, DC, 2004).

African Americans have the weakest amount of political incorporation in Vaiden (Carroll County). According to data collected by the Joint Center for Political and Economic Studies, no African American political figures hold elective offices in this 71% black town that has a 32.9% poverty rate. These poverty levels are higher than those in Greenville and Greenwood, the towns with the most black political power. Thus, an argument that poverty rates are greater in towns with less black political power would not be accurate because substantial rates of concentrated poverty are prevalent in all of the Mississippi Delta's predominantly black towns, including those with weak, moderate, and strong political incorporation.

The presence of black elected officials had little positive impact on the socioeconomic status of black residents in most of the Delta's towns as indicated by the persistence of concentrated poverty. The regression analysis in chapter 4 has shown that black per-capita incomes were lower and black poverty rates were higher in counties with stronger levels of black political incorporation. Ironically, this means that the higher-paying jobs produced by the gaming industry and the growth in black political power failed to cause higher black per-capita incomes and lower black poverty rates in the Mississippi Delta. In these counties, black politicians have inherited a "hollow prize" because they hold more political offices, but lack the fiscal resources to aid the people who put them in office.[87] For example, almost all of the residents and elected officials in Jonestown, Mississippi (Coahoma County) are African American; three-fourths of the town's adult population are women; and nearly every household received some form of public assistance (food stamps, housing assistance, or Medicaid). Also, the county's 30% poverty rate in 1997 and 49.6% rate in 2002 were the seventh highest in the state in both 1997 and 2002.

As indicated in chapter 1, African American political power is defined by the number of African American landowners because of the power that Delta landowners possessed historically, but African Americans are not listed among the most influential members of the landowning elite class. Also, political power is not only defined by the number of black elected officials, but also by the power of their positions. The most powerful county positions are the board of supervisors and countywide officials followed by municipal position officeholders. Therefore, counties with the greatest number of African American members of the board of supervisors and countywide officials as well as those with the most municipalities with powerful black elected officials have the strongest degrees of political incorporation. Other factors in this definition of political incorporation are the number of African American Congress-people, state senators, and state representatives. Counties that have black representatives in some of the major political offices have moderate political incorporation, and those with few or no African American representatives in these offices have weak incorporation.

Table 5.3 provides a summary of the number of black elected officials in Delta counties. According to the table, the counties with the strongest measures of black political incorporation in 2004 were Holmes, Humphreys, Leflore, Quitman, Sharkey, Tallahatchie, and Washington. The counties of Bolivar, Coahoma, Issaquena, Panola, Tunica, Warren, and Yazoo had moderate political incorporation and the counties of Carroll, Grenada, Sunflower, and Tate had weak incorporation.

Table 5.4 compares the mean poverty rates in Delta counties according to their measures of black political incorporation. According to this information, poverty rates have decreased in all of the counties since 1970, but the greatest reductions have been in counties with less black political power-Carroll County (a 26.6%), Tunica County (22.5%), and Tate County (19.5%). The counties with the lowest poverty levels in the Delta in 1999 (20% or less)-Tate, Carroll, Warren, and Grenada-also have the weakest amounts of black political incorporation. The finding that poverty is higher in counties with higher levels of black political power is consistent with those of the regression analysis in chapter 4.

A "paradox of political power" has existed for black Deltans during the modern era. One analysis of Mississippi Delta politics summarized the current state of the African American experience in Delta politics:

> Blacks' success in the long, hard struggle to become a part of the political process in the South may be no guarantee that, in itself, newfound political power will lead to significantly improved conditions-especially in the economic arena. . . . While black political success . . . has resulted in some symbolic and economic benefits-these communities have been able to secure external financial assistance (mainly from the federal government) more successfully than before the election of black officials-there has been relatively little change in the fundamental economic status of the black population, and persistent racial inequalities remain obstacles to improvement.[88]

In many of the Delta's towns and counties, African Americans serve in major elective offices, but failed to translate their political influence into black economic power. For example, in the town and county of Tunica, African Americans have held few political offices and few community empowerment organizations existed until

Table 5.3 Delta Counties with Strongest and Weakest Amounts of Black Political Incorporation: Numbers of African American Elected Officials in National, State, Countywide, and Municipal Offices

Delta County	U.S. Representatives	State Senators	State Representatives	Board of Supervisors	Aldermen, Vice Mayors, Councilmen
Bolivar	1	2	2	2	4
Carroll	1	0	0	1	1
Coahoma	1	1	1	2	17
Grenada	0	0	0	2	4
Holmes	1	2	1	3	21
Humphreys	1	1	1	3	4
Issaquena	1	0	1	2	5
Leflore	1	1	2	3	10
Panola	0	0	2	2	9
Quitman	1	1	2	3	18
Sharkey	1	0	1	3	1
Sunflower	1	1	2	0	17
Tallahatchie	1	1	1	5	7
Tate	0	1	2	0	3
Tunica	1	1	1	2	0
Warren	1	0	0	2	5
Washington	1	1	4	4	15
Yazoo	0	1	3	2	5

Delta County	Election Commissioners	Countywide Officials	Elected Judges	Municipal Mayors	*Political Incorporation Measure
Bolivar	2	0	3	9	2
Carroll	1	0	0	0	1
Coahoma	3	0	1	3	2
Grenada	0	0	1	0	1
Holmes	5	3	4	4	3
Humphreys	3	0	0	1	3
Issaquena	0	0	0	1	2
Leflore	2	2	3	2	3
Panola	0	0	0	1	2
Quitman	3	0	1	4	3
Sharkey	0	0	0	0	3
Sunflower	0	1	0	3	1
Tallahatchie	2	1	0	2	3
Tate	0	0	0	1	1
Tunica	4	0	0	0	2
Warren	2	0	3	1	2
Washington	2	1	0	3	3
Yazoo	2	0	1	0	2

*Counties with weak levels of black political incorporation received a 1, with moderate incorporation a 2, and with strong incorporation a 3.

Source: Joint Center for Political and Economic Studies. "Black Elected Officials Roster of Mississippi Black Elected Officials-Latest Data-May 2004-Joint Center.xls." Unpublished report. (Washington, DC, 2004).

Table 5.4 Black Poverty Rates in Delta Counties with Strong, Moderate, and Weak Black Political Incorporation

Delta County	1970 Poverty	1980 Poverty	1990 Poverty	1993 Poverty	1995 Poverty	1997 Poverty	1999 Poverty	Change from 1970–1999
			Poverty in Delta Counties with Strong Black Political Incorporation					
Holmes	53.0	39.1	57.1	50.0	44.9	36.0	41.1	−11.9
Humphreys	53.8	35.1	46.2	41.9	38.9	32.0	38.2	−15.6
Leflore	36.3	27.0	38.6	37.6	34.7	29.1	34.8	−1.5
Quitman	49.8	30.9	46.8	40.2	37.2	31.5	33.1	−16.7
Tallahatchie	49.9	34.4	44.3	38.9	33.7	27.6	32.2	−17.7
Washington	34.1	26.3	35.7	35.8	31.8	26.0	29.2	−4.9
			Poverty in Delta Counties with Moderate Black Political Incorporation					
Bolivar	44.3	31.8	53.4	40.1	35.2	29.4	33.3	−11.0
Coahoma	42.8	30.6	47.6	42.2	37.4	30.0	35.9	−6.9
Issaquena	42.0	27.8	45.4	40.0	39.9	33.2	33.2	−8.8
Panola	38.3	35.0	29.2	29.6	25.7	21.6	25.3	−13.0
Tunica	55.6	44.8	56.0	43.4	36.6	26.6	33.1	−22.5
Warren	22.2	13.9	21.0	22.9	19.2	16.9	18.7	−3.5
Yazoo	—	—	39.8	38.2	34.5	27.5	31.9	—

Poverty in Delta Counties with Weak Black Political Incorporation

Carroll	42.6	25.0	24.4	20.8	18.0	16.0	−26.6
Grenada	27.9	25.1	23.3	20.1	18.1	20.9	−7.0
Sharkey	47.2	37.0	44.3	42.1	35.9	38.3	−8.9
Sunflower	46.2	30.0	45.9	41.6	34.3	30.0	−16.2
Tate	33.0	20.8	21.1	18.0	14.9	13.5	−19.5

Poverty in the State of Mississippi and the United States

State of MS	28.9	10.1	20.2	24.6	21.4	16.8	12.4	−16.5
U.S.	12.6	13.0	12.1	12.2	12.3	12.6	19.9	+7.3

Source: U.S. Census Bureau. "Poverty Status in 1969 of Families and Persons by Race and Spanish Origin for Counties: 1970." *Characteristics of the Population. General Social and Economic Characteristics. 1970 Census of the Population* (Washington, DC: U.S. Department of Commerce, 1970); ibid. "Poverty Status in 1979 of Families and Persons by Race and Spanish Origin for Counties: 1980." *Characteristics of the Population. General Social and Economic Characteristics. 1980 Census of the Population* (Washington, DC: U.S. Department of Commerce, 1980); U.S. Census Bureau. "Poverty Status in 1989 of Families and Persons by Race and Spanish Origin for Counties: 1990." *Characteristics of the Population. General Social and Economic Characteristics. 1990 Census of the Population* (Washington, DC: U.S. Department of Commerce, 1990); ibid. "Persons Below the Poverty Level and Below 125% of Poverty Level." *Statistical Abstract of the U.S.: The National Data Book, 19th ed.* (Washington, DC: U.S. Department of Commerce, 1999); and www.census.gov.

recently. The abundant gaming revenues revitalized the local and state economies to some degree, but failed to substantially trickle down to the Delta's poorest communities. Even if African Americans in Tunica County possessed a stronger degree of political power, the experience of other black-led cities and counties demonstrates that black politicians may have no more of a commitment to the poor than white politicians or may have the same constraints as black politicians in other Delta counties-a lack of financial capital, an inability to attract new industries, and a large population of uneducated and unskilled residents. Thus as chapter 6 will explain, the Delta experience shows the need for political, human, financial, and social capital to transform the economic plight of the poor.

Political incorporation is strong in some Delta communities because they are governed by black politicians. It is moderate in others because African Americans may not constitute the dominant governing coalition, but hold many positions. The lack of countywide black political power, however, means that politics in the Mississippi Delta has not undergone the kind of progressive transformation as is thought. Despite the influx of gaming jobs in Tunica County, high rates of concentrated poverty remain. William Julius Wilson in *The Truly Disadvantaged* argued that the residents of neighborhoods with high unemployment, low incomes, and high poverty rates experience a "social isolation"-a lack of access to the employment opportunities found in more prosperous neighborhoods.[89] Moreover, the cycle of concentrated poverty will decrease when their social isolation ends. In Tunica County, the record low unemployment rates mentioned in chapter 4 provides clear evidence of a lower amount of social isolation, but the substantial black poverty rates remain in part because of the continuation of plantation politics in the region-that is, elite control of countywide offices and county boards of supervisors. Moreover, the legacy of elite resistance to African American educational and employment gains left a populace of poor uneducated, and unskilled workers.

Conclusion

During the transitional and modern periods, legalized gaming delivered many economic benefits to the state of Mississippi and African Americans gained an important political voice. During the transitional periods, the number of African American voters increased and the first black elected officials since Reconstruction were sworn in. In the modern era, the state of Mississippi elected more African American political figures than other states as African Americans established a strong political base in many cities and towns.

In spite of these gains, the legacies of the plantation political culture continued to affect African American political development. Few African Americans won at-large elected positions in Delta counties before the late 1990s and African Americans remain generally underrepresented in county offices. The current lack of black political empowerment in many counties of the Mississippi Delta results in large part from the political disfranchisement of African Americans by white elites before the 1960s, black vote dilution tactics in subsequent decades, and racial polarization among black politicians and white elites.

The case of Tunica County instructs us that black poverty will remain unchanged in a financially prosperous county unless African Americans have a combination of a strong countywide political base, active community empowerment groups, and assistance from external actors. In Tunica County, where casino gaming has been most profitable, African American citizens have had weak and moderate amounts of political incorporation in the state with almost no minority representatives before the 1980s. During the 1980s and 1990s, Tunica's black residents had moderate incorporation because of the token black representation that exists, but the interests of the black community were ignored by a majority white political establishment. Therefore, despite the majority black voting-age population, the black citizenry of Tunica County remains excluded and the poor have not reaped all of the benefits from legalized gaming as expected.

An analysis of Tunica's neighboring Delta counties demonstrates the limitations of African American political officeholding. Black elected officials dominate local politics in small, predominant black towns, but lack the fiscal resources necessary for improving the plight of the poorest Delta residents. Plantation elites still control most of the wealth, land, and institutions in these towns and in their surrounding counties and refuse to share these resources with black politicians. Thus, concentrated poverty has remained a staple of Delta life in the region's counties regardless of the extent of black political power. It will take many years for the Delta's nonelites to improve their socioeconomic status because of the legacy of the plantation culture and the paradox of political power. Chapter 6 will explain the need for community empowerment groups, continued bids for elective office, and enhanced social capital activities so that African Americans can enjoy a better standard of living in the Mississippi Delta.

CHAPTER 6

BUILDING BLACK AND INTERGROUP SOCIAL CAPITAL TIES IN THE DELTA

Introduction

The concept of social capital assesses the relationships developed among the residents of neighborhoods and communities. By improving these relationships, these individuals learn to work collectively, establish trusting relationships, mobilize resources for political action, and improve conditions in the areas in which they live. In both urban and rural neighborhoods, efforts are taking place in churches, schools, and social and civic organizations to develop new leaders, inform local residents of dilemmas that should be addressed, and create an agenda for addressing them.

This chapter examines the origin and development of the concept of social capital and the distinction between black and intergroup social capital. It examines in particular the tactics utilized by poor Mississippi Delta communities to get what they want from elites through the development of social capital. More specifically, this chapter analyzes the way in which the residents of communities with abundant financial capital, but moderate political incorporation (Tunica County) and the residents of communities with a sizable degree of political power, but little financial capital seek substantive benefits through the development of social capital. The efforts of black Deltans to utilize their black social capital to improve their communities and the challenges they face when attempting to develop intergroup social capital indicate that biracial relationships are more difficult to develop than black social capital relationships. In addition, they are even more complex in rural counties with histories of conflicts among elites and nonelites.

The Concept of Social Capital

As early as 1835, scholars wrote of the important role of civic and social associations in communities. In the classic book, *Democracy in America*, the political theorist Alexis de Tocqueville found that memberships within groups fostered a sense of unity and concern for their community's welfare and an interest in civic engagement-all of which were vital elements of a participatory democracy. De Tocqueville conducted a study of Nineteenth century America and wanted to determine why American society supported a democratic form of government while France used a central political authority. According to de Tocqueville, the healthy American democracy resulted from the involvement of citizens in churches, town meetings, political associations, and other voluntary associations. Through their work in these associations, Americans benefited from working for the collective good, participated in groups to achieve their goals, and engaged in political activism.[1] By participating, citizens learned that it was better to collaborate with others for their own personal gain, for the good of the community, and for the well-being of the nation.

De Tocqueville's research became the origin for the concept of social capital as scholars sought explanations for the decline in associational memberships and the lack of public interest in politics. The research of the sociologist James S. Coleman and the economist Glenn C. Loury laid the groundwork for latter research by Robert D. Putnam.[2] Putnam's conceptualization defined social capital as "features of social organization, such as trust, norms, and networks, that can improve the efficiency of society by facilitating coordinated actions."[3] It reveals, among other things, the relationships among people in their communities, the amount of time and energy they have for each other, the time parents devote to their children, the concern of neighbors for each other's families, and the relationships among church members.

Social capital relationships can be "strong" or "weak." Communities have strong ties when their residents interact with each other on an almost daily basis and weak relationships when they associate less frequently with their neighbors and with individuals residing outside their communities.[4] A number of studies have found that communities with strong social capital ties have experienced greater economic, political, and/or social advancement. Therefore, the residents of low-income areas must build their social capital by interacting with each other in order to accomplish their goals and by subordinating their individual interests in favor of group interests to empower their communities.

Putnam's research found that most American communities have had weak social capital ties during recent decades because of their increasingly impersonal, individualistic, and antisocial behavior. In the award-winning book, *Making Democracy Work*, Putnam not only explained the fact that the decline in social capital led to "civic disengagement," shown most evidently in the lack of interest in politics, but also to a "coarsening of societal discourse"—colder, isolated, and unfriendlier relationships in society. Unlike the era of activism outlined by de Tocqueville, Americans in recent decades were less concerned with interacting with their neighbors, voting, joining political organizations, working in labor unions, participating in church functions, attending parent-teacher association meetings, and becoming members of other civic and social groups.[5] Putnam characterized the growing tendency of Americans to be individualistic as "bowling alone" or

> ... [living] in splendid isolation, relating to friends but paying little attention to our community. We live in a society where the town square has been replaced by the mall, cable television, and the internet. Yet, Americans claim they want to be more involved in working together with their neighbors on civic problems, that they want to have more of a voice in the political process, and that we ought to have smaller government and more voluntarism by rank and file citizens.[6]

For Putnam, these impersonal social relationships led to a decline in community, civic, religious, political, and social activism. He found that the absence of social capital among Americans for more than a quarter-century was shown in the 25 to 50 percent declining memberships in social and political organizations, labor unions, and bowling leagues. In addition, community residents have had more impersonal relationships with their neighbors and friends since 1965 and lacked interest in political activities such as attending rallies and speeches, town hall meetings, and joining political parties. Finally, Putnam found a similar level of disinterest in American participation in sports clubs, literary discussion groups, labor unions, and churches.[7]

According to his research, the erosion of social capital has affected Americans from varied racial, economic, and educational backgrounds. Although African Americans belonged to more religious and civic associations than whites, a decline of social capital was evident in their communities as well.[8] Moreover, neither individuals with higher educational levels nor those with higher incomes have had stronger social capital ties over the last twenty-five years than other Americans.[9] In fact, Putnam discovered that the decline in social interaction and civic activism was more widespread among more affluent community residents than among poor and middle-class Americans.[10]

Putnam attributed the erosion of social capital to several factors. His research discounted explanations such as the pressures of time and money (working longer hours), residential mobility, and the increased numbers of women in the workforce as being the cause for weak social capital ties in America.[11] However, the decreasing numbers of successful marriages and the lack of participation in "face-to-face political activities" that require neighbors to interact with each other, discuss important social and political issues, and solicit financial assistance for their activities were a significant cause of these weak relationships.[12] In order to build social capital local community residents must work together in neighborhood associations such as issue-based citizen organizations; neighborhood crime watch organizations; and social, civic, self-help, and service organizations to identify the problems in their neighborhoods and to find the resources to help them address them.[13]

Critics of Putnam's research have argued that its findings about the decline in social capital, civic engagement, and political participation in white middle-class areas have been incorrectly generalized to communities of color. It has been assumed that less social capital exists in poor, black, rural areas because of its decline in white middle-class neighborhoods.[14] The study, "Social Capital, Intervening Institutions, and Political Power" found little evidence of an absence of social capital in poor communities populated largely by people of color, but a lack of financial, intergroup, and other forms of capital.[15] In recent years, a body of research has distinguished black social capital from intergroup social capital and concluded that healthy social capital relationships exist among African Americans, but their ability to gain the resources necessary to improve their communities is limited by their lack of social capital with white elites.

Black and Intergroup Social Capital

Why is black social capital crucial to the political and economic advancement of African American communities and what does it consist of? One study defined a primary benefit of black social capital in the following way, "[It] enables African American leaders to mobilize and cooperate to gain social ends . . . and to address racial injustice."[16] African Americans have enhanced their social capital ties in churches; civil rights organizations; community development organizations; fraternities; historically black colleges and universities; and social, civic, and political groups.[17] These institutions have allowed them to socialize with each other, address community problems, and educate each other both during and after their formal exclusion from white institutions.

In addition, viable social capital ties must exist in African American communities because of the limitations of black political office-holding. Chapter 5 explained how voters in many Delta towns elected black political figures in most local offices, but received symbolic rather than substantive representation. Because of the inability of black politicians to deliver tangible benefits to their constituents, black voters have attempted to improve their communities by working together in community development organizations while continuing to enhance their political influence.

In recent years, a few studies have been added to the growing literature examining the challenges that minority activists encounter when attempting to develop and sustain bonding and bridging social capital relationships. Bonding social capital ties are those that are present among the residents of communities. In *Black Social*, Marion E. Orr referred to bonding social capital in African American neighborhoods as black social capital that refers to the predominantly black organizations, businesses, colleges, and churches that served the needs of African Americans during a time of exclusion from white institutions. After the end of state-sanctioned segregation, these black institutions continued to promote solidarity among African Americans.[18] Intergroup or bridging social capital, on the other hand, involves a system of cooperation and negotiation among individuals of different races.

Most black social capital research discovered that African American neighborhood activists increased their bonding social capital ties first, then improved their bridging social capital relationships when attempting to address their communities' ills. Moreover, these activists used similar strategies. After mobilizing themselves in local organizations and in institutions to find solutions to their problems, they networked with regional and national community empowerment groups for financial assistance.[19] Especially in urban cities with large black populations, the members of neighborhood associations and community development organizations recruited members, mobilized them to work for change, developed a strategy for revitalizing their neighborhoods, and sought to enhance their political power.[20] When local activists combined their existing social capital with resources from outside actors, they magnified their ability to economically revitalize their communities, challenge elites, and combat poverty.

The New Haven, Connecticut, experience provides an example of minority neighborhood residents building their bonding and later their bridging ties while also seeking to enhance their political influence. In 1989, a coalition of African Americans and Latinos utilized their bonding social capital to mobilize voters in black, Latino, and racially mixed neighborhoods on behalf of the mayoral campaign of the African American candidate John Daniels. Coalition members informed Daniels about the issues they were most concerned with especially that of police abuse and the need for community policing-an issue that then became a focal point of his platform.[21] They then focused on bridging social capital by attracting enough whites into their coalition to secure Daniels's victory and to assist him as he sought the backing of white politicians for Community Policing Management Teams (CPMT) or Community Management Teams (CMT) in most city neighborhoods.[22] Thus, the multiracial coalition that engineered Daniels's victory and that had historically possessed a limited amount of political power, later received prominent roles in the city's community policing efforts after attracting white voters into their coalition and negotiating with white politicians.

After using their newly amassed political influence to implement community policing, they sought to economically revitalize poor neighborhoods through the use of grants from an Empowerment Zone/Enterprise Community (EZ/EC) program. During the Clinton administration, the EZ/EC Initiative was designed to financially assist impoverished rural and urban areas. In 1993, New Haven was one of sixty-six cities that was designated an enterprise community and was to receive $3 million in federal aid, eligibility for certain tax breaks, and a preference when applying for federal grants.[23] Although many conflicts emerged among neighborhoods competing for enterprise community funds, New Haven's poorest communities enhanced their bonding social capital to develop proposals explaining why they needed these funds and improved their bridging social capital by taking these proposal to white politicians and eventually received assistance.[24]

Mark R.Warren's book, *Dry Bones*, provides another example of minority communities improving their bonding and bridging relationships. In the cities under analysis in this study, local residents strengthened their bonding social capital in neighborhoods, churches, and schools to pinpoint problems and to develop an agenda for addressing them, and engaged in political activism through their work in religious or "faith-based" groups. They later developed multiracial coalitions as a way to strengthen their bridging social capital. The Texas Industrial Areas Foundation (IAF), an interfaith and multiracial group of community organizers, revitalized many of the nation's most impoverished communities by utilizing the relational organizing strategy. Using the slogan "no permanent allies, no permanent enemies," the IAF strategy used the strong bonding social capital relationships in minority areas to its advantage, equipped local activists with better leadership skills, and allowed them to make the primary decisions in leading their own communities. It also created bridging social capital by allowing a multiracial group of leaders from various religious communities to assist these low-income communities with financial resources and to advocate their needs with whites.[25]

Almost universally, the research on black social capital concluded that most communities were more successful when attempting to strengthen their bonding rather than their bridging social capital relationships. For example, Orr's study of school reform in Baltimore found that conflicts existed among the African American members of educational organizations, parents, clergy, elected officials, and community activists, but all eventually agreed about the problems that existed and their possible solutions. On the other hand, these individuals found it more difficult to gain the cooperation of white business elites, suburban legislators, and state education officials when implementing school reform.[26]

Eventually, intergroup social capital relationships improved in Baltimore because of the growth of African American political power, strong black social capital ties, and financial capital from the African American middle class. The efforts of the city's first African American mayor, Kurt Schmoke, were also pivotal in the improved intergroup ties because his work as a liaison allowed black residents to gain the necessary resources from white political leaders and business-people to reform the local public school system.[27] Schmoke held a number of meetings in African American communities to determine their preferred reforms and convinced the predominantly white business establishment to provide financial assistance.[28]

Cynthia M. Duncan in "Social Capital in America's Poor Rural Communities" found that the economic progress of African Americans in the Mississippi Delta was hampered by weak bridging or intergroup social capital relationships among white elites and black nonelites, but were also hampered by an absence of black social capital. According to Duncan's article, an almost complete lack of black social capital still exists in the Delta due to the divisions among black political leaders, a sense of apathy among black community residents for community empowerment projects, and competition among Delta towns for scarce economic resources. Her research attributed the absence of strong social capital ties in the Delta to the divisive tactics of plantation elites, "Powerful landowners deliberately created divided, unequal social systems in which the poor were vulnerable, dependent and suspicious. . . . The lack of trust and cooperation persists today, rooted in the insecurity and even jealousy that prevail when resources are scarce, and fanned by political corruption and arbitrary power in fundamentally undemocratic communities."[29]

This book argues that black social capital ties in the rural Mississippi Delta region have been weaker than those in many majority African American cities, but are not as scarce as Duncan found. Her definition of social capital mostly relied on the inability of rural churches to adequately serve as institutions for community change for poor families. Conditions in Southern rural communities have made it difficult for African Americans to mobilize themselves in independent churches and in community empowerment groups that existed in cities.

The information received from the interviewees for this book, however, indicated that African Americans in the Delta have maintained healthy social capital relationships due to the role of churches, schools, and neighborhood residents. Churches were owned and controlled by plantation elites, but "helped local residents cope with conditions, provided assistance to needy families in the form of food and clothes during poor harvest seasons and provided spiritual guidance."[30] "Plantation schools" and historically black colleges and universities served an important role in the development of black social capital when African Americans were excluded from white schools. Moreover, black neighborhoods fostered social capital relationships because their residents lived in close proximity to each other, attended church together, worked together, and assisted each other.[31] Thus, segregated churches, schools, and neighborhoods were vital institutions for fostering solidarity and trust among African Americans in the Mississippi Delta.

As chapters 3 and 5 explained, despite the depth of black social capital in many Delta counties during civil rights and political movements, intergroup social capital ties remained strained among white elites and black nonelites. Impoverished African American residents of rural counties have been confronted with unique challenges when attempting to translate their bonding social capital ties into community improvements and when attempting to gain white elite support for their efforts. To improve their schools and to economically revitalize the region, Delta residents have followed the model used in other communities for enhancing their bonding social capital to develop a plan for addressing their problems and later their bridging social capital to secure financial resources from white elites.

"We Can't Save these Little Towns": Black Social Capital in the Delta

A statement by one Mississippi Delta resident summarized the prevailing belief that the region's economic conditions are beyond help,
"The future of the Delta's economy is not in its small towns. Compa-
nies are not going to put a manufacturing plant in a town where one
third of the population is over 60 years old, and one-third under 18.
We can't save these little towns. The economy is not there."[32] Despite
this pessimistic view expressed by one individual but shared by many,
black Deltans are attempting to use their bonding social capital to attack poverty and the given substantive economic benefits from elites.
A recent report found that "The Delta region has tremendous human
resources: people with a strong work ethic, and rekindled hopes for
the future. The Delta people are trying to help themselves."[33]

Despite the finding of scholarly articles of an absence of strong
black social capital relationships in the Delta, viable relationships were
evident during the "listening sessions" conducted by the Lower Mississippi Delta Development Commission (LMDDC) beginning in April
1988. Representative Mike Espy (D-MS) and Senator Dale Bumpers
(D-AR) developed the LMDDC to produce a comprehensive strategy
for improving conditions in 219 Delta counties in the states of Arkansas, Illinois, Kentucky, Louisiana, Mississippi, Missouri, and Tennessee
within ten years (see figure 6.1).[34] The commission's main goal was "to
make the Delta and its people a full partner in America's future . . . [by]
giving every person in the Delta the chance to be a part of the American
Dream" by reducing illiteracy, poverty, and unemployment; improving
housing; providing educational and job-training courses; giving relocation incentives to industries; and securing federal funds.[35]

Like neighborhood activists in cities like Baltimore and New
Haven, the African American residents of the Mississippi Delta's
poorest counties identified the region's most pressing problems and
developed potential solutions. Before attending the listening sessions, local politicians and empowerment group representatives from
MACE (Mississippi Action for Community Education), a non profit
community empowerment organization founded during the 1960s,
and the National Association for the Advancement of Colored People
(NAACP) assisted local residents in preparing an agenda to present
to the commission's members. Eventually, over four hundred recommendations were offered to solve the Delta's economic, educational,
and social dilemmas. A report, "The Delta Initiatives Realizing the
Dream," summarized these suggestions and pledged to make a serous
effort to implement them over the next decade.[36]

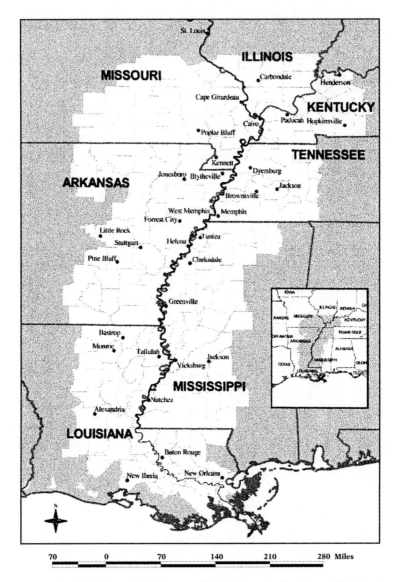

Figure 6.1 Delta Counties in Arkansas, Illinois, Kentucky, Louisiana, Mississippi, Missouri, and Tennessee

Source: Bureau of Transportation Statistics

The LMDDC was an ambitious attempt to change a seemingly unchangeable society of hopelessness, but its progress was inhibited by the lack of intergroup social capital in the Delta. Although most residents of the targeted counties were African Americans and women, wealthy white elites, rather than local residents, served on the commission.[37] By 1990, approximately three-fourths of adult Mississippi Delta residents were women; however, no African Americans and only a few women were appointed to serve by the governors from each of the seven states that had counties that were targeted by the commission.[38]

Moreover, many white members of the commission allegedly wanted it to fail. One examination of the LMDDC found that Mississippi's plantation bloc opposed the commission and "felt threatened by any discussion of their role in intensifying economic monopoly, ethnic conflict, and poverty. . . . Those operating from the dominant plantation bloc tradition objected to any serious discussion of how to address poverty and ethnic relations outside a discussion of what they saw as the region's principal problem, the crisis affecting agriculture."[39] The LMDDC experience shows a chronic absence of intergroup social capital. Poor minority communities with strong levels of bonding social capital but a lack of bridging social capital possess the capability to address and combat their problems, but are unable to convince individuals on the opposite racial and/or economic spectrum that they should assist them.

In 1994, Delta residents again followed the model of utilizing their black social capital to develop a plan for addressing their problems and later appealing to white elites for fiscal resources after then Secretary of agriculture Mike Espy designated his former Mississippi Delta congressional district as an empowerment zone. Espy established the Mid-Delta Mississippi Empowerment Zone (MDEZA) program to pursue "sustainable development, economic opportunity, and community-based partnerships" in the Delta region.[40] Local community residents were involved in all aspects of the program as consultants, staff members, and directors. Strong social capital ties were crucial to apply for up to $40 million in block grants and to convince businesses to relocate into Delta counties. The businesses were then offered tax credits to pay wages and training expenses for their employees.[41] Small towns and grassroots organizations also had to meet a matching fund requirement. Before receiving assistance from the MDEZA, an applicant needed to already possess 65 percent of the requested funds.[42] For example, a group in need of $50,000 for a youth program would have to already have secured at least $125,000 from state, county, and local governmental agencies, private businesses, or nonprofit organizations before receiving any funding.[43]

Despite the fact that black social capital resulted in community residents working together to assess their needs, complete EZ/EC applications, apply for block grants, and open MDEZA offices, the program had mixed results. On a positive end, the MDEZA provided evidence that some Delta residents were able to improve their communities by working collectively. For example, local politicians, after receiving input from community residents, convinced the MDEZA to provide tax credits and $900,000 in federal funds for a Dollar General Regional Distribution Center in Indianola (Sunflower County), Mississippi.[44] Public and private investment in the project exceeded $38 million for the facility; the Mississippi Department of Community and Economic Development provided $2 million in matching funds; enterprise zone tax credits provided up to $3,000 for every resident hired; and Dollar General invested more then $25 million for a center that provided hundreds of mostly low-wage jobs.[45]

On a negative end, like with the LMDDC, the tense intergroup social capital relationships among white elites and black nonelites remained a barrier to the success of the MDEZA program. Although the Mississippi Department of Community and Economic Development contributed funds to the Dollar General endeavor, community empowerment organizations in the Delta usually found the matching fund requirement to be an insurmountable burden because of the absence of intergroup social capital and the low socioeconomic status of most Delta residents. The Dollar General project, despite its successes, was not the norm.

The economic status of Mound Bayou, a small Delta town in Bolivar County, Mississippi, provided an example of the disappointments associated with the MDEZA program. Founded by former slaves, Mound Bayou was once one of few Delta towns with black-owned businesses and a small but stable black working class community in the early 1900s. In subsequent years, Mound Bayou experienced population declines and job losses. After the occurrence of this "brain drain," abandoned buildings and substandard housing replaced an oil mill, Hostess bread factory, hospital, and black-owned bank.

No economic revitalization resulted from MDEZA funds in Mound Bayou or in Bolivar County. After the program's implementation, the number of local businesses decreased. Also, tax incentives failed to draw any new industries into the county and only two applications for enterprise zone funds were approved.[46]

The lack of intergroup social capital in the immediate area was one causal factor for Mound Bayou's inability to profit from the MDEZA's goals. Unsuccessful applicants for funds found the 65 percent matching fund requirement to be a "problem for small municipalities because [they don't] even have 65 cents."[47] Few local organizations received the necessary matching funds from agencies, businesses, other organizations, or from the small, polarized landowning elite class that had no interest in the program. One Bolivar County resident believed that the matching fund requirement was purposely designed to disadvantage black organizations, "In Indianola, the Dollar General Center was seen as a benefit to everyone because of its new jobs and revenues. Plus, the landowners made money off of selling their land, but they [the landowning elites] couldn't see that they would profit from giving money for community empowerment efforts. They [the elite class] didn't care about youth centers, educational programs, and other things because their kids would never step foot in those places. It was almost as if the matching fund requirement was put there to purposely keep poor black organizations from being able to get funds for community development projects because the people who put the requirement in place had to have known that our organizations wouldn't have been able to get the funding for projects and that the rich people wouldn't help us."[48] The town is now thought of as "a tragedy . . . [with] a rich and compelling history [that is] . . . moving backward, not forward."[49]

The absence of intergroup social capital was not the sole cause of the MDEZA's shortcomings in Delta towns and counties, however. The residents of neighboring towns and counties failed to establish collaborative bonding social capital relationships with each other. Glenn Brown, executive director of the North Delta Planning and Development District found that "Each county is a county to itself. Every time I go to a meeting it's always 'We' and it's never 'why not let's hook up together and see if we can do something?' I've seen what has been going on for the past 20 years. It will continue on because of the same leadership they have."[50]

The program was also plagued by poor management, corruption, and fraud on the part of its leadership. First, many of its board members possessed little or no experience in this kind of endeavor.[51] High turnover resulted because many executive directors and board members were removed from their positions because of their ineptness.[52] Also, because the decision of who gets funding was handled internally, MDEZA members awarded funds on the basis of patronage rather than who was most qualified.[53] Eventually, independent reviewers were sent to the Delta from Washington, DC, to award funds to potential applicants. An African American elected official in the Delta believed that the empowerment zone failed mainly because of the lack of intergroup cooperation and because of patronage:

> We received funding [for the empowerment zone] in 1993. It was supposed to make a tremendous effort, but didn't work out that way. . . . I was hoping that blacks and whites could look back on this as a success. . . . The empowerment zone would have been an example of blacks and whites

working together, but people got funds who didn't deserve them. Other people didn't get funds who should have. As African Americans, we must empower ourselves first, then deal with the elites. We must have a vision and a mission.[54]

The MDEZA experience, and to a lesser extent the LMDDC experience, reinforced a finding that "poor communities lack the resources to address their needs, no matter how strong they become internally."[55] Individuals may have strong social capital ties in the towns and counties in which they reside, but must compromise with the residents of adjacent towns and counties to receive federal funds. Most importantly, all of the Delta's communities must strive to develop cooperative intergroup social capital relationships with white elites to enhance their communities.

Until recently, Tunica's elites possessed two facets of political power mentioned in chapter 1-the ability to dominate the local governing coalition and to marginalize the issues and needs of subordinate groups. On one hand, local elites held the most influential positions in the county's only incorporated town, Tunica, and in the entire county despite its majority African American population. Before the 2004 local elections, Tunica County had a weak amount of political incorporation. According to the data in chapter 5, African Americans occupied a significant number of political offices in at least one town in other Delta counties, but held none in Tunica and few in Tunica County. Because of this African American political subordination, the elites dominated the local political arena and always had their interests served. On the other hand, the elites possessed power's "second face" because of their ability to maintain the "quiescence of the powerless"—ignore the interests of nonelites and prevent them from successfully challenging elite rule.[56] Starting in 1992, the year that the Delta received the first gaming revenues, to December 2003, Tunica County's board of supervisors introduced no proposals for low-income housing, job-training programs, or other incentives to benefit the poor.[57] According to the board's longest-serving African American board member, James Dunn, because only one or two African Americans typically served on the board in one election cycle, they possessed a limited ability to promote the black community's interests, "It was just two of us [supervisors] for so many years. There were things we couldn't do because we simply didn't have the resources to fight the power structure."[58]

Until recently, Tunica County's elite class also mitigated dissension among nonelites. Traditionally, African Americas in Tunica County declined participation in civil rights or in community empowerment protests. Evidence exists, however, that the elites have lost this aspect of power because of African American protests for superior schools. Despite the lack of intergroup social capital, how have the African American residents of Tunica County pressured political and landowning elites for parity through the development of black social capital?

The Complex Legacy of Plantation Schools and the Dual
Public School System in Tunica County

Many of the recent conflicts among black nonelites and white elites in Tunica County stem from the historical existence of a dual public school system for black and white children in the rural South. Since the 1970s, the county's public school system has had a virtually all-black enrollment and its only private school, the Tunica Institute for Learning (TIL), has maintained an all-white enrollment. Historically, the families of poor white children have received donations to cover tuition fees and the parents of private school students have opposed tax or land incentives to improve the public school system.[59] By the late 1990s, less than forty white students attended the county's four public schools and no black students attended the TIL.[60] In the Mississippi Delta, public and private schools have provided a completely different quality of education for black and white students.

For much of the Delta's history, black children attended "plantation schools"-one-room churches or houses with a large black heater in the center of the room, wooden desks, damaged textbooks, and a high student-teacher ratio. In a 1949 report, white school officials indicated that they were fully aware of the negative impact of its plantation schools on black students, "The low enrollment and average daily attendance [of African American students] is the result of the type of school available to the Negro-uncomfortable school buildings with little or no equipment, an inadequate course of study, and poorly-trained teachers."[61] These children of sharecroppers attended school sporadically during the cotton industry's off-season from December through March of each year because they often had to work in the fields if weather conditions permitted it. After a federal court ruling, Delta counties implemented a mandatory rule that all children under the age of sixteen had to attend school regularly from September through June of each year.[62] In 1953, the Tunica County Colored High School (later renamed the Tunica Vocational School and the Rosa Forte High School) opened in North Tunica as the first public high school for black students. Before its opening, Tunica was the only county in Mississippi that lacked a high school for black students.

Three public elementary schools and one public high school were reserved for whites.[63] In the summer of 1954, when the landmark *Brown
v. Board of Education* decision ruled that segregated public schools
were unconstitutional, one in four white children in Mississippi graduated from high school while only one out of forty black children
graduated.[64] Because white Mississippians staunchly refused to abide
by the *Brown* decision, voters approved a constitutional amendment to
abolish the state's public schools rather than desegregate them.[65]
However, this action never took place because the 1955 *Brown II* decision held that public schools be desegregated "with all deliberate
speed" and thus allowed Mississippians to delay the integration of public schools indefinitely.[66]

Conditions for black teachers were no better than those for their
students because of their low salaries and demeaning treatment. Although teachers were supposed to be paid every twenty days, they
would not be paid for months at a time especially during the "peak"
months for harvesting cotton. From the middle to the end of August,
September, October, and November of each year, black schools
closed while both students and teachers worked in cotton fields.[67]
After the schools reopened, one study described the actions that
black teachers had to "perform" before receiving their pay:

> On payday, when the black teachers gathered at the courthouse to col-
> lect their checks, the white officials asked them to sing Negro spiritu-
> als before the checks were handed out. To the whites, these little
> impromptu concerts were evidence of the good will between the races
> because they showed how much the whites were interested in "their"
> blacks and their music. The blacks saw it as having to sing for their
> paychecks.[68]

The year 1969 would be a pivotal year for the public school system
in the South. The U.S. Supreme Court held, in *Alexander v. Holmes
County*, that public schools be desegregated "at once."[69] As a result,
local school boards could no longer avoid the Brown decision.
Approximately 3,000 African American and 430 white students were
enrolled in Tunica County's black and white public schools, respectively. In 1969 and 1970, a federal judge ordered the rezoning of public schools giving students the option of attending any public school in
their zone. After Tunica County High School closed, Rosa Fort and
Dundee were the only public schools in the county.[70] When faced with
the prospect of having their children attend federally court-ordered
desegregated schools with black children, white parents either withdrew their children from public schools altogether or enrolled them
in "makeshift" schools in local churches created by white teachers who

had also abandoned the public school system by Christmas 1969, but who were still being paid by the local school board.[71]

White opponents of school integration advocated their right to "freedom of choice" when selecting schools for their children. After a 1970 federal court decision rejected this argument, all of Tunica County's white families transferred their children to a new private academy-the Tunica Institute for Learning on a street later renamed Academy Road.[72] One observer pointed out in later years, "[After] noticing that the word 'Academy' doesn't appear in the name of the Tunica Institute for Learning. I wonder why they didn't name the street "Segregated Academy Road.""[73]

The historically racially polarized nature of public and private schools is another sign of the lack of intergroup social capital among African Americans and whites in Tunica County. By the 1980s, the legacy of the dual school system resulted in substandard public schools with a majority black enrollment in Tunica and in the other counties of the Mississippi Delta. According to the data in table 6.1, the dismally low 14.8 percent high school graduate rate in Tunica County was the lowest in the Delta in 1980. Moreover, white Delta residents were four times more likely to graduate from high school than African Americans. Almost a decade later, the Tunica County school district was ranked 145th among Mississippi's 153 school districts because of its low test scores and was placed on academic probation.[74]

Seemingly, the dilemmas of Tunica County's public schools could not possibly worsen, but the local school board, parents, activists, and political elites were overwhelmed in later years. The local school district is currently under the supervision of the State Department of Education (SDE) because of the inability of local officials to improve student educational achievement and to reduce the high dropout rates. Since the 1988-1989 school year, SDE has consistently assigned the Tunica County School District one of the lowest accreditation ratings in the state due primarily to the low test scores and to the high failure rates of its students. On December 12, 1996, the district lost its accreditation for having met less than 70 percent of the accreditation performance standards of the State Board of Education. The board upheld the decision on February 21, 1997. As a result, on March 14, 1997, the governor of Mississippi declared a "state of emergency" in the school district.[75]

Before the legalization of gaming, its proponents argued that casino revenues could assist the failing Tunica County public school system; however, the African American residents of Tunica County soon found this to be a false promise. By the mid-1990s, casino revenues flooded in, but the board of supervisors refused to allocate any

Table 6.1   Percentage of Whites and Blacks Ages 25 or More Completing High School in the U.S., the State of Mississippi, and in Mississippi Delta Counties in 1980

Area	Whites	Blacks	Blacks as a % of Whites
U.S.	68.6	51.2	74.4
Mississippi	60.9	32.7	53.7
Mississippi Delta	61.4	23.8	38.1
Core Delta Counties			
Bolivar	67.4	27.8	41.2
Coahoma	63.8	26.2	39.8
Grenada	—	—	—
Humphreys	—	23.1	—
Issaquena	—	20.1	—
Leflore	64.0	24.5	38.3
Quitman	51.3	19.4	37.8
Sharkey	61.5	26.4	42.9
Sunflower	62.6	22.1	35.3
Tallahatchie	53.0	18.6	35.1
Tunica-	—	14.8	—
Washington	67.4	31.8	47.2
Peripheral Delta Counties			
Carroll	50.6	23.9	47.2
Holmes	64.4	25.2	39.1
Panola	54.7	20.7	37.8
Tate	62.1	22.8	36.7
Warren	72.8	33.2	45.6
Yazoo	63.8	24.7	38.7

Source: U.S. Census of Population, 1980, General Social and Economic Characteristics, table 53, and Detailed Population Characteristics, U.S. Summary, table 262 (Washington, DC: U.S. Government Printing Office, 1983). John Saunders, "A Demography of the Delta." In A Social and Economic Portrait of the Mississippi Delta, eds. Arthur G. Cosby, Mitchell W. Brackin, T. David Mason, Eunice R. McCulloch (Mississippi: Mississippi State University Social Science Research Center, Mississippi Agricultural and Forestry Experiment Station, 1992), 55-56.

of these moneys for the renovation and enhancement of public schools until black residents threatened to sue.[76] In 1996, the predominantly white board of supervisors denied a $15 million request from the all-black county school board to erect new elementary and middle schools and to renovate other public schools. The Concerned

Citizens for a Better Tunica County organization, created in 1993 to improve the quality of public schools, held neighborhood meetings to inform community residents about the board's refusal to allocate funds to public schools.[77] These meetings became strategy sessions whose goal was to mobilize neighborhood residents to fight elites. This battle never took place because members of Concerned Citizens and the local school board eventually obtained 20 percent of the revenues so that the school district could reduce its debt, renovate and expand existing schools, and improve student test scores.[78]

Although community residents gained public school funding without having to seek additional aid, their struggle provided evidence that political and landowning elites had little intention of using revenues for schools as had been promised. Instead, elites planned to either cater to the interests of elite families or attract additional upper-income white families into the counties.[79] By the late 1990s, African American nonelites in Tunica County had to engage in more aggressive mobilization through the development of social capital to fight elites for superior schools.

The Battle for Governmental Responsiveness through the Development of Black Social Capital

During the late 1990s, the school location protest was probably the most significant example of community empowerment activism in Tunica County. In 1999, a wealthy landowner, C. Penn Owen Jr. rezoned his farmland in North Tunica County for an upscale subdivision consisting of 250 homes priced from $100,000 to $120,000.[80] In addition, a portion of this land was reserved for a new elementary school. The county bought the tract and the board of supervisors allocated $8 million for the school's construction. Political and landowning elites in Tunica County planned to build the school in the fastest-growing area of Tunica County as an attempt to make North Tunica County an extended suburb or "exurb" of Memphis, Tennessee, attract middle-class families, increase the county's tax base, and transform its image. As indicated in the previous section, the lack of adequate schools discouraged families from moving to Tunica County in previous years. For example, a 1996 housing study revealed that white families living in the immediate area would not move to North Tunica County unless they had alternatives to majority black public schools.[81]

On the surface, the contribution of land by a wealthy member of the plantation bloc and plans for a state-of-the-art elementary school showed signs of progress in intergroup relationships; however, every issue is a black versus white, elite versus nonelite matter in the counties of the Mississippi Delta. Because the county only had two substandard all-black elementary schools, residents welcomed the idea of a new school, but objected to its planned location near a subdivision that had not yet been built rather than in a midway point between the subdivision and predominantly black neighborhoods. The homes in the subdivision were unaffordable to almost all of the county's black residents whose median earnings were $18,000 or less.[82] They perceived the new school as a "publicly funded segregated academy"— a racially exclusive public school for children from middle and upper-income white families. One report expressed the belief of many that the school would become a "new, virtually all-white public school in an affluent pocket and an affront to longtime residents left with substandard schools."[83] Local political elites refused to choose another location and were so confident that black nonelites would not challenge their decision about the location that they had already bought the land, developed plans for the new houses, and laid waterlines.

In order to receive redress, Tunica's black parents sought governmental responsiveness according to the political incorporation framework. The Tunica County experience proves that the residents of rural counties often pursue governmental responsiveness in a different fashion than the situation in the cities. According to the political incorporation model, African American activists in cities usually mobilized their bloc vote, elected African American political representatives, achieved varying degrees of political power, and eventually received governmental responsiveness from their elected leaders (see chapter 5).[84]

Because of their weak political incorporation, the black citizens of Tunica County mobilized themselves to receive governmental responsiveness from elites by mostly working in relatively new local community empowerment groups and from regional and national community development organizations. Historically, Tunica County's African American citizenry believed that they lacked the resources to fight elites because of their lack of financial resources and political power. By the late 1990s, however, they found that they possessed valuable resources for achieving governmental responsiveness in local community empowerment organizations such as Concerned Citizens, the local chapter of the NAACP, as well as from their few African American elected officials. African American voters did not abandon their efforts to elect black representatives, but felt they could accomplish their goals more effectively through organizations because of their lack of black political power.[85] First, these groups held several neighborhood meetings to inform the community that plantation elites and the white members of the board of supervisors adamantly refused to compromise on the school's location issue.

Regional community empowerment organizations, Representative Bennie Thompson (D-MS), and the U.S. Justice Department were crucial allies of Tunica County's disadvantaged population in their fight against local landowning and political elites. Community development organizations such as Southern Echo and the Mississippi Education Working Group (MEWG) organized a coalition of separate and distinct local community development groups in Delta towns.[86] These groups contacted the members of a national advocacy organization, the Advancement Project, to advance their cause. Reasoning that building the school in the subdivision would violate a 1970 school desegregation order, the Justice Department ruled in September 1999 against the school's planned location.[87]

The battle of elites and nonelites over the location of the new school indicates that after years of political powerlessness and later by a governing agenda that failed to benefit the poor, Tunica County's African American citizenry strengthened their social capital ties, mobilized themselves, and demanded that casino revenues benefit their families by providing better educational opportunities to African American children. This is very significant considering the fact that they rejected attempts to mobilize themselves and to protest unjust conditions in earlier years. Their previously underdeveloped black social capital gave them the capacity to battle wealthy local elites despite their lack of money. The mobilization in black neighborhoods to identify problems and needs was spurred mostly by local, relatively new community empowerment groups rather than by politicians. The members of these groups solicited assistance from others to battle elites so that they could achieve governmental responsiveness. This is consistent with literature that has pointed out the importance of community organizations for building social capital and for meeting the needs of nonelites, especially women and people of color.[88]

Some scholars have disagreed with the finding of an overall absence of social capital in poor, majority African American communities, but have attributed the persistence of poverty to a lack of financial resources and intergroup social capital in these neighborhoods. In Tunica County, the lack of established black political power and of stable working relationships across racial lines continues to hamper the ability of black nonelites to improve their quality of life. But, what about communities with a greater amount of political power? How do the residents of politically empowered communities, but little financial capital receive governmental responsiveness from elites? Tunica's neighboring Delta counties have many small towns governed mostly by African Americans and evidence of strong black social capital ties, but lack a human capital base of educated workers, financial capital, and intergroup social capital ties. The only real indication of viable intergroup cooperation in Tunica's neighboring counties has been exhibited in the approval of black nonelites and white elites of the region's burgeoning prison industry; yet, intergroup cooperation has been elusive on issues of concern to African Americans like educational equity and the development of low and moderate-income housing.

Building Black Social Capital after the Growth of Black
Countywide Power

After the Voting Rights Act of 1965, the percentages of black registered voters and black elected officials in Mississippi grew substantially, but African American candidates failed to win countywide elections before the 1990s. After these victories, black voters strategized about the best way to take advantage of their enhanced political position in the wake of remaining elite opposition. This section examines the manner in which African Americans utilized their expanded political base when confronting plantation elites for improved conditions in their communities.

Through their work in organizations, black Deltans are proving that they will no longer be subjected to a quiescence of the powerless and are pressuring the plantation bloc to address issues they usually ignored. During the 1960s, protest groups such as the Council of Federated Organizations (COFO), the Mississippi Freedom Democratic Party (MFDP), and the Student Nonviolent Coordinating Committee (SNCC) formed and accomplished many goals, but were short-lived. After the growth in the number of countywide officeholders, new organizations formed in the Delta. In Tallahatchie Housing Incorporated (THI), the Tallahatchie Education and Redistricting Committee (TERC), the Citizens for Quality Education (CQE), and the Drew Community Voter's League (DCVL), African American communities enhanced their existing social capital relationships to address a multitude of issues, especially the need for a higher caliber of schools and superior housing conditions.

THI and the TERC were organized in the county after the elections of its first African American countywide officials. Community residents had already addressed issues plaguing their neighborhoods that were never seriously addressed by the county's white political establishment, during meetings and public hearings on the redistricting process. By the late 1990s, both the board of aldermen and the election commission had African American majorities and two African American representatives served on the board of supervisors.

Tallahatchie County's African American citizenry considered the substandard conditions of local housing units and the dismal quality of the 90 percent black public school system to be the county's most serious problems. THI, founded in 1992, had a number of goals, but primarily wanted to address the county's housing shortages, lack of affordable housing, and unfit housing.[89] Almost half of Tallahatchie County's black families lived in housing units with safety hazards or a lack of basic amenities.[90] Moreover, several generations of families lived in small substandard houses because of the lack of housing for low-income families. One analysis of Tallahatchie County's housing conditions found that "Families suffered from three-generational living arrangements where one home would house a fifty-something year old woman, her twenty-something year old children and their children. It was also very common to see a household with ten or more family members crammed into a two or three bedroom house."[91]

The THI worked with the board of supervisors and aldermen to gain approval for the first new low-income housing unit in almost two decades, a loan assistance program for first-time homeowners, and the condemnation of several houses and buildings. Initially, the board of supervisors' votes on the housing units split along racial lines because the three white supervisors believed that the county's funds should be devoted to more pressing causes such as tourism and the erection of middle-class housing subdivisions.[92] Eventually, the new units won approval by the five-member board because three supervisors (two African American and one white) voted favorably. After a meeting of local political figures and THI representatives to discuss housing needs, a black elected official described the attitude of the white supervisors as follows:

At first, I guess they [white members of the board of supervisors] just didn't care about black people living like rats in slums. We had to make them understand that the entire county would suffer if they [the board of supervisors] didn't make it possible for new apartments and houses to be built. Our county still had an image of being the place where Emmett Till was lynched in 1955. No tourist would want to visit a place if they drove past people living like savages. Once, we made that argument, one of the white supervisors voted yes on the proposal to make it possible to build new housing. The shameful thing is that we don't have money for very many things, but the money was there for decent housing and they [white members of the board] didn't want to build anything because they knew that black people would benefit from new housing unless it was real expensive.[93]

Many THI members founded TERC in 1998 as an organization solely devoted to achieving educational parity among the county's public and private schools. Tallahatchie County's public school students performed at the lowest levels on required state standardized tests, had one of the lowest retention rates, and one of the highest suspension and expulsion rates in the state.[94] These parents knew that public schools would never rise to the quality of private schools because of their lack of resources, but wanted to raise student achievement and retention rates by "maximizing the opportunities presented by having an overwhelmingly African American board of supervisors. . . [identifying] and [developing] strategies to address issues around education and [ensuring] that community people would maintain their present political power and continue to enhance it."[95]

Decades before TERC's founding, Tallahatchie County's all-white school board made decisions on behalf of an all-white student body. The children of plantation elites attended public schools before the explosion of private academies in the rural South during the 1960s. African American parents, whose children attended plantation schools, had no input in the operation of schools because of their fears of elite retaliation.[96] In later years, the school board became one of the first elected bodies with African American representation in Tallahatchie County. As white students accelerated their exodus from public schools and as the quality of these schools declined, white parents abandoned their desire to control school decisions.[97] In most of the more recent school board elections, few or no white candidates have run for office. By 1998, Tallahatchie County had a black superintendent and a predominantly black school board. The parents of schoolchildren believed that the black school superintendent, school board members, and supervisors would be more amenable to their demands for better schools.[98]

The members of TERC presented several demands to the superintendent during a private meeting. They had already met with the black members of the board of supervisors and black school board members for recommendations on how to proceed with the meeting with the superintendent. First, the parents sought a review and reconsideration of zero tolerance policies that resulted in high student suspension and expulsion rates.[99] Second, the school district needed to commit itself to the consideration of qualified African American candidates for teaching and administration positions in a county with an approximately 70 percent teaching and administrative staff.[100] Third, the physical and verbal abuse of black students by their teachers had to end immediately. Eventually, TERC accomplished the firing of a high school teacher for openly addressing students as "niggers."[101] Fourth, a committee of parents with input over all major school decisions needed to be established. Fifth, new buses were needed to relieve overcrowding.

After the superintendent agreed to meet their demands and conditions improved, one TERC member observed, "The schools still need work, but they're not nearly as bad as they were before we founded TERC and started making demands. If we hadn't said anything, nothing would ever have changed."[102] Because the members of TERC realized that nonelites would never receive attention as long as they remained silent, they used "direct action" and "strategic planning" when confronting local elites. The rationale behind these strategies was expressed by one member as follows: ". . . Because of the 'hands off' approach that the teachers and administrators take when approached with community problems, . . . it is not until [we] hold large meetings, interrupt school board meetings with large numbers of people and march into the offices of officials who have ignored or avoided [us] that the power structure takes [us] seriously."[103]

By the late 1990s, Holmes County, Mississippi, a peripheral Delta county of over 20,000 residents, had an approximately 76 percent black population and a public school system with a 100 percent black enrollment. Like most other Delta public school systems, low achievement, teacher shortages, a lack of resources such as adequate textbooks and extracurricular activities, and high dropout, suspension, and expulsion rates were the norm in Holmes County's public schools. After a series of meetings, a group of parents in Holmes County developed CQE as "a leadership development, education and training organization working to develop new grassroots leaders and organizers to empower the African American community in Holmes County, Mississippi. Their vision is based on the principle that all children can learn and have the right to learn."[104]

This organization interacted with local and state elected officials to address the poor conditions of their schools. Unlike other relatively new Delta organizations, CQE solicited the active participation of public school students in their organizing work and decision-making. Its Youth Governance initiative equipped local youths with the skills to participate in decision-making in civic activities, in the formation of public policy, and in the building of an effective organization and community.[105] The role of students were crucial for pinpointing the problems in schools. Eventually, a third-grade teacher was fired for degrading students, criticizing their parents in class, and bruising them when administering corporal punishment.[106] The group has also secured additional funding from the Mississippi legislature for books, supplies, extracurricular activities, higher teacher salaries, and more remedial classes.[107]

The DCVL of Sunflower County was founded in 1996 because its public schools experienced dilemmas similar to those in Holmes and Tallahatchie counties. Delta representative Robert Huddleston, Tallahatchie County's first black county supervisor Jerome Little, and the members of Southern Echo who had worked in Tallahatchie County redistricting workshops assisted approximately forty parents and students to assemble a list of goals and timetables for the organization. After the DCVL became a formal organization with a more sizable membership, they addressed two primary issues-complaints of unfair disciplinary practices at all of Drew's public schools and approximately 40 percent withdrawal, suspension and expulsion rates of students annually.[108]

After forming this organization, establishing goals, and developing strategies for the accomplishment of their goals, the DCVL voiced its concerns to the City Council. Only one African American school board member had been appointed to serve on the five-member board and complaints of inappropriate disciplinary practices had been made by several students against a high school principle and teacher. Both were eventually fired. Another teacher and administrator were reprimanded for harsh disciplinary practices and for ignoring complaints from parents and students, respectively.

After these actions by the school board, parents and teachers were the targets of retaliation from school officials. In 2000, several parents who were outspoken critics of the school system or members of the DCVL were arrested for visiting school grounds to see their children.[109] The Voters League provided support and defense for parents and for some students who had been suspended. As a result, many of these students remained in school and avoided further punishment and parents received the right to attend school functions.[110]

The work of THI, TERC, CQE, and the DCVL have important implications for the concept of social capital. First, each used direct action protests to attack their community's problems and enlisted the aid of black politicians before negotiating with white elites. The literature summarized in an earlier section of this chapter stipulated that African Americans followed a similar pattern when using their existing social capital relationships to address their problems. These included networking with regional and national community empowerment groups for financial and other assistance; recruiting the members of community development organizations and equipping

them to work for change; developing strategies for improving housing conditions and schools; and continuing efforts to enhance their
political power.[111]

Second, the Tallahatchie County redistricting battle was a catalyst
for activism by each group. After black elected officials won more
powerful positions countywide, black communities formed new organizations to use their political representation to their advantage.
Small groups had already met and pinpointed problems that were
prevalent in the Mississippi Delta-inadequate housing and ineffective
schools in poor neighborhoods that had been neglected for years by
elites. The regional community empowerment group, Southern
Echo, aided each in order to establish formal groups and solicited resources from other individuals and organizations. In the Mississippi
Delta, the work of Southern Echo proves that African American communities could not have mobilized themselves to confront local elites
successfully or gained financial support without the assistance of community development associations.

Third, the research of de Tocqueville discussed the contribution
of neighborhood associations, community development groups,
churches, political organizations, and other voluntary associations for
improving a community's well-being. These groups allowed individuals with common goals to meet, find ways to attack their community's
problems, and make their political leaders accountable.[112] The Delta
has few neighborhood and community development associations, but
those that do exist indicate the important role of these groups for revitalizing communities with both weak and strong amounts of political
power. It was only through the work of these groups that any substantive change took place in housing and schools. After the expansion of
black countywide political influence, new empowerment groups
formed in many majority African American counties of the Mississippi
Delta, but the mobilization of Tunica County's residents occurred in
existing groups long before the growth in black political power.

Fourth, the social capital relationships should not be defined by
the number of members in organizations and associations, but by the
willingness of individuals to downplay their interests for the benefit of
the entire community. Putnam's research stated that a decline in social capital ties was evident because of the lower rates of memberships
in civic, political, neighborhood, and social organizations.[113] Few
neighborhood associations and community development organizations exist in the counties of the Mississippi Delta and those that do
have had few members; however, the social capital ties of African
Americans should not be defined as "weak." Small numbers of

individuals first met informally, then in organizations. After the formation of an organization and a strategy to attack their problems, others in the community supported causes furthered by these groups. Some conflicts within black communities made it difficult for them to gain the resources necessary to improve their neighborhoods such as the corruption in MDEZA and allegations that white candidates paid African American community leaders for endorsements in Tunica County. These, however, are typical of any community. Black social capital is strong in the sense that they know how to identify problems and to subvert interests for the common good when need be.

Finally, the ability of African Americans to use their political power to their advantage remains inhibited by the lack of intergroup social capital in the Mississippi Delta, especially on issues involving schools. Although white teachers and administrators have been blamed for some problems, the main dilemma that African Americans encounter with white elites concerns their lack of interest in the Delta's majority or all-black public schools.[114] Black parents, teachers, and administrators, school board members, and other elected officials have to rely on their social capital relationships to address the schools' problems because of the noninvolvement of white elites and the belief that white teachers and administrators impede rather than contribute to progress in schools.[115]

Using Black Social Capital for Economic Revitalization in Tunica's Neighboring Counties

Although the agricultural, catfish, and gaming industries are the primary sources of economic revenue in the Delta, the prison industry has become one of the most heavily recruited in many counties. During the 1990s, sixteen new correctional facilities, including six for-profit prisons opened in the state of Mississippi that left Mississippi with the third highest incarceration rate behind the states of Texas and Louisiana.[116] In Mississippi and in other states generally, communities with large populations of poor people of color recruit from prisons out of desperation for economic growth, jobs, and revenues. Because of the lack of a human capital base of educated, middle-class citizens, an abundance of cheap land in rural areas, industrial redlining, and a massive loss of manufacturing jobs, Delta elites and nonelites have placed a high priority on the erection of new prisons because "It's an industry that is more inclined to locate in the Mississippi Delta than other upscale industries. The Delta is trying to pursue any industry it can get. We're not going to get a A-1 top-notch industry, but will get the industry no one else wants."[117] Bolivar County, for example, lost 1,000 manufacturing jobs and Leflore County lost 3,000 industrial jobs from 1999 to 2002.[118] According to table 6.2, Mississippi's prisons are among the primary sources of revenue in predominantly black counties with poverty rates in the 30 percentile range and high school completion rates in the 50 and 60 percentile range.

In addition, Tunica's neighboring counties are relying on prisons as a strategy for economic development because they have not received the expected "spillover benefits" from legalized gaming and also lack the ability to open casinos within their borders. State law required that casinos only operate in counties adjacent to the Mississippi River and only counties with casinos receive gaming revenues (see chapter 4). Delta counties without casinos have had to find alternative ways to pursue economic growth.

Ironically, the reliance on prisons as a strategy for economic growth has resulted in biracial collaboration among the Delta's elites and nonelites because of the profits gained by both groups. Moreover, both black and white politicians have solicited prisons in the towns, counties, and districts they govern.[119] The acceptance of individuals from diverse racial and class groups of the prison industry proves that intergroup cooperation can be achieved in racially polarized rural areas when both elites and nonelites receive economic benefits. Landowning elites sell and lease their land in exchange for funds. Legislators lure new prisons into their districts because the increase in revenues and jobs helps them fulfill promises to bring economic growth and therefore improves their prospects for reelection.[120] Town and county officials receive revenues from the regional prisons located within their boundaries and possess an almost autonomous right to operate them. In some cases, local sheriffs are compensated for housing inmates from overcrowded state penitentiaries in local jails. Also, private prison owners, such as Wackenhut Corrections Corporation of Palm Beach Gardens, Florida; Corrections Corporation of America (CCA) of Nashville Tennessee; and Tuscolameta Incorporated of Walnut Grove, Mississippi, finance their own building costs and pay for the right to operate in the counties.[121] Thus, private and regional prisons that depend on inmates for revenue create jobs and are perceived as a guaranteed source of revenue in areas desperate for a new industry. One Delta elected official provided the rationale behind the recruitment of new correctional facilities, "Crops are not good. Industry is not moving in. Prisons are helping the economy of the towns they're coming into, so what would you do? With the crime rate growing as it is, you're never going to run out of customers."[122]

Table 6.2 Racial Population, Poverty, and Educational Levels of Delta Counties with Prisons in 1999

Delta County	White Population	Black Population	Poverty Rate	% Completing High School	% Completing College
*Bolivar	33.2	65.1	33.3	65.3	18.8
*Carroll	62.6	36.6	16.0	66.6	10.9
Coahoma	29.8	69.2	35.9	62.2	16.2
Grenada	57.9	40.9	20.9	63.8	13.5
*Holmes	20.5	78.6	41.1	59.7	11.2
Humphreys	27.1	71.5	38.2	53.7	11.6
*Issaquena	36.3	62.8	33.2	58.8	7.1
*Leflore	30.0	67.7	34.8	61.9	15.9
Panola	50.4	48.4	25.3	63.5	10.8
**Quitman	30.4	68.6	33.1	55.1	10.6
Sharkey	29.3	69.3	38.3	60.6	12.6
*Sunflower	28.9	69.7	30.0	59.3	12.0
*Tallahatchie	39.6	59.4	32.3	54.4	10.9
Tate	67.8	31.0	13.5	71.7	12.3
Tunica	27.5	70.2	33.1	60.5	9.1
Warren	54.9	43.2	18.7	77.0	20.8
**Washington	33.9	64.6	29.2	66.5	16.4
*Yazoo	44.7	53.9	31.9	65.0	11.8
U.S.	75.1	12.3	12.4	80.4	24.4
Mississippi	61.4	36.3	19.9	72.9	16.9

*These counties have correctional facilities, penitentiaries, or prisons.

**These counties sought, but were denied legislative approval for, correctional facilities, penitentiaries, or prisons.

Source: U.S. Census Bureau. "County Estimates for People of All Ages in Poverty for Mississippi: 1998." www.census.gov.; ibid. "Mississippi Map Stats." www.fedstats.gov.; ibid. "Persons Below the Poverty Level and Below 125% of Poverty Level: 1970 to 1999." *Statistical Abstract of the U.S.: The National Data Book, 19th ed.* (Washington, DC: U.S. Department of Commerce, 2001); ibid. "Profile of Selected Economic Characteristics: 2000." www.census.gov.; ibid. "U.S.A." www.fedstats.gov.

The elites and nonelites of various Delta communities have followed similar patterns to enhance their black and intergroup social capital ties in pursuit of new prisons. In all of the predominantly black, low-income Delta communities with prisons, local residents provided the initial impetus by demanding that their elected officials attract new industries. Most cited the decline in manufacturing jobs and the closure of factories to bolster their argument that industries were more needed now than during any previous time in the region's history.[123]

Next, local mayors, municipal officials, and county officeholders encouraged state legislators to introduce bills for legislative approval and for funds to build prisons. Although the Mississippi legislature denied the requests of local officials in Quitman and Washington counties, for new prisons, other counties won necessary approval even after the state's inmate population started to decline.[124] During the 1990s, additional prisons were necessary because the nation's prison population had increased substantially after revised state and federal laws required the incarceration of nonviolent criminals, reduced opportunities for parole, and imposed longer sentences.[125] By 2000, however, the numbers of inmates began to decline and private correctional facilities struggled for profits, but new prisons continued to be built in Mississippi as sources for economic revenue and jobs.

The experience of Tallahatchie County, Mississippi, indicates the commitment of elites, nonelites, and state legislators to the erection and maintenance of new prisons. The attempt to win approval for The Tallahatchie County Correctional Facility of Tutwiler, Mississippi was a "joint effort. Everyone worked together because we really needed the economic and tax revenues and jobs. Politicians, businessmen, local citizens, and churches all wanted it."[126] Unlike the steadfast elite opposition to the redistricting of board of supervisors seats, all segments of the county favored the prison industry. The local citizenry, the Tallahatchie County Ministerial Alliance, an association of African American Baptist ministers; local politicians; and the members of the county's Industrial Development Authority wanted the facility because of the potential financial benefits for the county and for the debt-ridden town of Tutwiler. During its first year of operation in 1999 as a private prison owned and managed by the CCA, Tutwiler received $5,350 a month for water fees from the CCA and the county received $600,000 a year, new jobs, and a slight reduction in property taxes.[127] The $34 million facility currently employs 353 workers and delivers over $500 million in tax revenue annually.[128]

Industrial Development Authority President Otey Sherman, a prominent businessman, led the effort to convince the CCA to build the private prison in Tutwiler. The town paid for the prison's water-and sewage-lines while the state and county paid half the costs of training the prison's employees.[129] In Tallahatchie County, the prison industry has been profitable and was necessary because "It didn't cost us one red cent to do this [open a prison]. It doesn't cost us a thing. . . . It's been a windfall for us. The downside is that it's a prison and we face the possibility of escapes, but the chance of that happening is very slim."[130]

Despite the commitment of black ministers, black elected officials in Tutwiler, local elites, and state legislators, the facility was on the verge of closing because of a lack of prisoners. The members of the state House and Senate approved a bill cosponsored by Senator David Jordan (D-Greenwood), whose district includes the prison, to allow the Tallahatchie County prison to accept inmates from other states and to avoid losing approximately 282 jobs in the county. This legislation passed by a wide margin in both the state Senate and House and was signed by Governor Haley Barbour in January 2004.[131] Thus, Mississippi's political elites not only allocated funds for the building of prisons, but also allowed privately owned prisons to house inmates from other states as a way to support a successful albeit controversial new industry.

The prison industry, and the support it received from political figures and plantation elites, provides an example of a profitable economic development project that was implemented through the development of black social capital and later through intergroup cooperation. However, the acceptance of the prison industry should not be perceived as a sign of improved relationships among white elites and black nonelites because the Mississippi legislature allotted additional funds for the building and maintenance of prisons while reducing the state budget for public schools, community colleges, and universities.[132] According to Governor Ronnie Musgrove, a celebration of the universal support for the prison industry remains unwarranted because "Rather than invest in education for the rural workforce and positive economic development for poor communities, the state is undertaking a backwards approach to budgeting in which they spend a great deal of taxpayer money on corrections and then shop for the inmates to validate these expenditures after the fact."[133]

Conclusion

This chapter examined the tactics utilized by poor Mississippi Delta communities to gain substantive economic benefits from elites through the development of social capital. More specifically, it examined the question: how have the African American residents of communities with abundant revenues, but moderate political incorporation (Tunica County) and those of politically empowered communities, but few financial resources gain substantive benefits from plantation elites through the development of social capital? In poor rural communities, social capital must be generated through community organizing because of a lack of fiscal resources and opposition from white elites. Since the legalization of gaming, Tunica County has had an enormous amount of revenue, but high poverty rates remained even after local unemployment rates plummeted to record low levels. The new elementary school was supposed to benefit the African American neighborhoods because of the county's history of providing substandard "plantation" public schools for African American students. African Americans, under the direction of the Concerned Citizens for a Better Tunica County, waged and won a confrontation with elites over the location of the new school. In spite of their lack of political power in the town and county of Tunica during the late 1990s, African Americans received assistance from regional and national organizations in their efforts to mobilize, from their few black elected officials, and from the U.S. Justice Department.

Because other counties of the Mississippi Delta, with the exception of Coahoma, received none of the revenues from legalized gaming, an almost complete absence of financial capital exists. Most of these counties have a greater amount of black political power than Tunica County, but have had difficulty attracting industries, lost thousands of manufacturing jobs, and were populated disproportionately by impoverished residents. As is the case with Tunica County, a region with a historically weak level of black political incorporation, the African American residents of counties like Holmes, Sunflower, and Tallahatchie relied heavily on community development organizations to find solutions to their problems and to negotiate with local elites. Black elected officials, especially those in countywide offices, were able to promote the black community's interests through their votes on key issues. Despite the gains of the 1990s, black Deltans still have more power in towns than in entire counties. Thus, African Americans in counties with higher levels of political incorporation must still solicit outside assistance to gain benefits from elites.

PART FOUR

LESSONS LEARNED

CHAPTER 7

CONCENTRATED POVERTY, POLITICAL POWER, AND SOCIAL CAPITAL IN THE MISSISSIPPI DELTA

Introduction

This book has examined the "transformations" and "legacies" of political and economic institutions established for the profit and dominance of white landowning elites. Although racial polarization and wide disparities between the rich and poor have remained over the years, African Americans rather than whites now hold most of the major political offices in many communities and legalized gaming has created jobs, higher wages, and superior working conditions for many. Although the exclusion of the region's majority African American populace from political participation and educational opportunities has ended, white wealth, black poverty, and a lack of collaboration along racial lies continue to be vestiges of the Delta's old "cotton-obsessed, Negro-obsessed" culture.

Neither the rise in the socioeconomic status of African American workers, growth of black political officeholding, or the decreasing evidence of blatant elite resistance brought about a desired transformation among white elites and black nonelites in the Mississippi Delta. In addition to jobs and higher wages, the gaming industry was supposed to revitalize the Delta's economy and, more importantly, break the dependency of nonelites on elites for jobs. Eventually, the combination of economic and political power among African Americans was, and still is, expected to end the cycle of black poverty. Such a transformation has yet to occur, however, despite the positive changes associated with legalized gaming-that is, higher incomes, lower unemployment levels, and lower poverty rates. Double-digit poverty rates typify the economic circumstances of many African Americans, especially in predominantly black core Delta counties. Why is this so? Do the remaining poverty levels result from current elite resistance or from a lack of African American political power? Also, what measures have black Deltans taken to address poverty and their community's ills? This chapter will summarize the major findings of this book that significantly contribute to a better understanding of theories on the relationships among elites and nonelites, concentrated poverty, political power, and social capital.

The Evolution of Elite-Nonelite Relationships in the Mississippi Delta

Most of the findings of elite theories adequately depicted the relationships in the counties of the Mississippi Delta. Small groups of individuals promoted their interests to the detriment of the masses; they always had their interests served and were wealthy white men; yet, the elite and nonelite relationships in the Delta differed from those in the literature in many ways. First, Floyd Hunter found that business-people had more power than political figures. Business-people controlled the city's agenda because of the desire for growth. In the Delta, landowners rather than business-people possessed the most wealth and power because most of the businesses in the region were small, family-owned businesses. Few industries and no corporations were located in the area. Thus, throughout the Delta's history, the families who owned the most land, not the owners of local businesses or the political officeholders, possessed the most wealth, power, and influence.

Albert B. Nylander III's analysis of leadership structures in the small towns of the Mississippi Delta found that black citizens failed to break a cycle of dependency on white elites because of the latter's wealth and ownership of land. Unlike in other parts of Mississippi and the South, few African American Delta residents own significant portions of land. Currently, the political power that African Americans hold in the Delta's towns results mostly from the elective offices they have won. Because the majority of black Delta families have never own of the powerful landowning elite class.[1]

Second, Richard I. Zweigenhaft and G. William Domhoff found that in recent years members of the most elite families were from more diverse socioeconomic backgrounds and were more diverse in terms of gender, race, ethnicity, and sexual orientation.[2] Most of the Delta's elites, however, continued to be wealthy white males. Even after the increase in the number of black elected officials, wealthy landowners excluded them from the circle of elites. In counties with majority black governing coalitions, the landowners withdrew into a separate society in the towns in which they lived. The withdrawal of the wealthiest class meant that African Americans inherited the same "hollow prize"-proportional representation but few economic re-sources-in rural towns that were governed by African Americans.[3] Thus, the Delta's plantation bloc continues to consist of a small num-ber of wealthy white landowners.

Third, elite theorists almost universally agreed that the most pow-erful individuals oftentimes disagreed about the manner in which cities should be run. C. Wright Mills was one of many theorists who found that local elites have not been monolithic: "To say there are ob-vious gradations of power and of opportunities to decide within mod-ern society is not to say that the powerful are united, that they fully know what they do, or that they are consciously joined in conspiracy."[4]

Historically, white elites in the Mississippi Delta, however, have had identical views on all matters involving race. Not only were African American citizens excluded from the Delta's landowning and political elite class, but they were also disfranchised and denied eco-nomic opportunities for several decades. In later years, federal laws such as the Voting Rights Act of 1965 ended African American dis-franchisement and federal lawsuits filed by African American plain-tiffs with the assistance of civil rights organizations attacked measures designed to dilute the African American vote.

Eventually in Mississippi, an evolution occurred in the relation-ships among white elites and black nonelites because African Ameri-cans voted, attended public schools, and got jobs without overt interference from plantation elites. In fact during the post civil rights movement era, the plantation bloc had welcomed new industries because they were profitable. Progress in race relations has occurred because wealthy white elites in the Mississippi Delta no longer exhibit straightforward opposition to African American economic and polit-ical advancement. The sharecropping system, elite opposition to in-dustries capable of providing African American workers with higher wages, and laws stipulating the disfranchisement of black voters and the exclusion of black officeholders no longer exist. A more progres-sive Mississippi Delta has emerged because of the rise in black office-holding and in the socioeconomic status of many African Americans.

This book argues that elite resistance continues in many subtle forms, however. In many ways, elite families continue to have mono-lithic views on racial issues because of their desire to protect and pro-mote their interests. The Tallahatchie County redistricting struggle exemplified the fact that plantation elites still oppose the election of African American political representatives in more influential local and countywide offices. It was not until the 1990s that the first African

American countywide officials and members of the board of supervisors were elected after a vicious battle among elites and nonelites.

Perhaps the most complex examples of continued elite resistance and of a lack of intergroup social capital involved the region's predominantly black public schools. After the court-ordered end of the dual school system of black "plantation" and white public schools, white families withdrew their children from public schools and enrolled them in private academies. In subsequent years, public schools fell into disarray because of the low educational achievement of students and the loss of qualified teachers. Although white elites imposed no apparent barriers against public schools, they refused to participate in coalitions to improve schools because their children attended private schools. Essentially, the noninvolvement of white elites meant that African American parents, teachers, and administrators have had to address the problems of public schools without the assistance of wealthy whites.

Even when white elites seemed to be concerned about public schools, conflicts along racial and class lines emerged. In Tunica County, a wealthy landowner contributed land for the construction of a new elementary school as a way to attract middle-class families. The disagreements of black and white community residents over the school's location resulted in a highly publicized lawsuit. Elite resistance to the school's location was due to their opposition to its close proximity to African American neighborhoods. The elites feared that an influx of African American students would lower the quality of the school and discourage white parents from enrolling their children. Eventually, the two opposing sides reached a compromise; yet, the support of white elites for a new school resulted from a desire to attract middle and upper-income families to enhance their county's reputation and economic base, not out of a concern to provide a superior educational institution for both black and white students. This conflict in Tunica County provided additional evidence of the desire of local elites to protect their interests even if at the expense of the black majority.

The Limitations of African American Political Incorporation

According to the political incorporation theoretical framework, minority groups that increase their degree of political power from weak to moderate and strong have a higher likelihood of raising their socioeconomic standing. These groups, which have traditionally been locked out the political process, have achieved strong political incorporation, after electing candidates from their racial group in major political offices and after gaining tangible benefits from these representatives for several years.[5] In rural towns and counties and to a some extent in urban cities, African American politicians have found it impossible to reduce economic disparities among the privileged and the powerless.[6] In the counties of the Mississippi Delta, the rise in the political standing of African Americans was supposed to empower this traditionally marginalized community; yet, this book has argued that the wealthiest class has retained most of the region's political and economic power.[7] In addition, the typical degree of African Americans political incorporation has been either moderate or strong in most predominantly black towns of the Mississippi Delta. The poverty rates in all of the Delta's predominantly African American communities, however, including those with high amounts of black political power, usually doubled and tripled state and national averages.

The persistence of concentrated poverty in the region's small towns and cities points out the limited ability of African American political officeholders to uplift the socioeconomic status of their constituents. In Delta towns, African American politicians have failed to raise the economic standing of their constituents for several reasons. First, industrial redlining has resulted in the loss of industries with the refusal of others to move into the region. The prison industry has been one of few industries with a desire to relocate to the Mississippi Delta in recent decades (see chapter 5). Second, the low educational achievement levels of black Delta residents make it difficult for them to transcend out of poverty. For example, Tunica County had more jobs than residents at one time, but high poverty rates remained because African American workers lacked the educational backgrounds to take the higher-paying jobs that would lift them out of poverty.

Third, until recently, African American politicians have not had as much political power in the Delta as was thought. Mississippi's reputation as a haven for black officeholding has been somewhat exaggerated. The state has the highest number of black elected officials in the nation. Also, African Americans hold impressive amounts of political offices in majority African American towns, but have won few countywide positions or positions on influential county boards of supervisors. Before the 1990s, few African Americans had been elected as members of these boards and even fewer had won at-large elections in predominantly black counties. As of 2003, Holmes, Humphreys, Tallahatchie, and Washington were the only predominantly African American counties ever to have black majorities on boards of supervisors. By 2004, Tunica County elected its first majority African American board. It remains to be seen there whether the increase in black political representation on the county's most important political board and the abundant gaming revenues will finally result in a decrease in black poverty and a transformation of the economic and political relationships among elites and nonelites.

Political power also involves more than officeholding. To gain strong political incorporation, African American communities needed to elect a majority black political establishment for several years and demand that their preferred policies be implemented. In poor rural communities especially, politically powerful groups and individuals have a "second face"-the ability to avoid certain issues and to prevent nonelites from protesting the neglect of these issues.[8] In the Mississippi Delta, wealthy landowners determined the issues that would be furthered in counties while black elected officials controlled issues in the towns in which they governed.

Plantation elites possessed power's second face in the counties of the Delta before these residents protested inadequate housing conditions, the neglect of schools, and other issues. Over the years, the ability of plantation elites to avoid issues of concern to African American citizens and to maintain their quiescence has waned. In Tunica County, the challenge to elites over the location of a new elementary school occurred before a significant rise in African American political power. In the counties of Holmes, Sunflower, Tallahatchie, and Washington, measures for better schools and housing occurred after an institutionalization of black political power had already taken place. Nevertheless, the control of the wealthy white elite minority of at-large positions and local boards of supervisors still equips them with the most political power in the region. Moreover, legalized gaming failed to transform the economic power relationships among elites and nonelites because counties lacking casinos have received no direct revenues from gaming. Local landowners and the casinos' owners, none of whom are African American, have received the greatest financial benefits. Although unemployment and poverty rates have declined in the Mississippi Delta, the rates of African American poverty continue to rank among the highest in the nation. The African American members of the region's nonelite class have waged a war on poverty by continuing to increase their political representation, but also by developing their communitywide social capital in community development organizations.

Social Capital in the Mississippi Delta

As mentioned previously, the Delta experience points out the need for political, human, financial, black, and intergroup social capital to raise the economic plight of the poor. These concepts can be defined as follows: political capital is the control of countywide offices or the ability to determine decisions in counties and in towns; human capital consists of a population of educated and skilled workers; financial capital refers to jobs and economic resources; black social capital is the willingness of African Americans to collaboratively pinpoint problems and to find solutions; and intergroup social capital requires compromise and interaction among black nonelites and white elites.

Despite cleavages among African Americans in their communities, a strong sense of black social capital has always been evident in the Delta. Because of strained race relations, however, intergroup social capital has been lacking among black and white Delta residents. The members of the African American nonelite class have rarely been able to cooperate with white elites in order to have their needs met. Usually, us versus them, rich versus poor, and black versus white attitudes mar viable interracial relationships in the entire Delta region. The occurrences of interracial cooperation that do exist occur when racially mixed regional and national organizations such as Southern Echo assist neighborhood residents with their community mobilization and empowerment efforts.

The African American residents of Tunica County have always had a strong sense of black social capital ties and now have financial capital as a result of legalized gaming, but lack human and political capital because of the unskilled workforce and small number of countywide black officeholders and political groups. In addition, they lack intergroup social capital because of their continued inability to negotiate with white elites. Nevertheless, Tunica County has more financial capital than any other Delta county because of the profitable gaming industry.

Most African American residents of the Mississippi Delta almost completely lack financial capital in the form of jobs, decent wages, and other fiscal resources and countywide political power. Black social capital and moderate to strong black political incorporation exists in Tunica's neighboring counties, but not human, financial, or intergroup social capital. The black residents of Tunica's neighboring counties are worse off than those in Tunica County because their counties are still plagued by industrial redlining. Although the African American residents of many of Tunica's neighboring counties have more political power because of their greater number of black elected officials, these individuals still must find ways to assist large populations of permanently low-income residents.

In addition, the prospects for improved intergroup social capital remain unlikely in all of the Delta's counties because white elites live

in their own sheltered world and have no interest in addressing problems that disproportionately plague African Americans. The Lower
Mississippi Delta Development Commission (LMDDC) and the Mid-
Delta Mississippi Empowerment Zone (MDEZA) program provided
two examples of this absence of intergroup social capital. Wealthy
whites who refused to acknowledge the problems associated with the
legacy of elite rule served on the LMDDC rather than African Americans and women. Moreover, the plantation bloc refused to devote
funds so that community groups could meet an MDEZA matching
fund requirement.9 This kind of opposition compelled African
American citizens throughout the Delta to create new political and
community empowerment groups with the objective of strengthening
their black social capital and to develop strategies for dealing with
white elites. Thus, African Americans have had to enhance their social capital in communities with both weak and strong political incorporation to address the ills stemming from the legacy of elite
resistance, lack of funds, poverty, and illiteracy among the masses, as
well as an absence of countywide resources.

Conclusion

The high rates of poverty among African Americans in the Mississippi Delta have been a product of several factors. Little evidence exists of a conspiracy among elites to trap African American citizens in
poverty. The legacy of their blatant opposition to African American
political and economic advancement in the past, however, continues
to affect the current quality of life of African American residents.

African Americans in the Mississippi Delta appear to be in a no-
win situation. The rise in political power in Delta towns has failed to
abolish a cycle of concentrated poverty. On the same end, the influx
of gaming revenues and the rise in the economic standing of African
Americans in Tunica County also failed to significantly decrease the
poverty rate. Before the 2004 election of a majority African American
board of supervisors in Tunica County, no Delta county had both
black political power and economic prosperity. With the recent elections of majority African American boards of supervisors in the counties of Tallahatchie, Tunica, and Washington, conditions for the
black poor may improve, but only if these representatives are re-
elected for several consecutive years and if the problems of industrial
redlining and low educational achievement are addressed. Despite
the many positive political and economic transformations in Mississippi, some problems continue to be insurmountable.

NOTES

Chapter 1

1. James C. Cobb, *The Most Southern Place on Earth: The Mississippi Delta and the Roots of Regional Identity* (New York: Oxford University Press, 1992).

2. Frederick M. Wirt, *The Politics of Southern Equality* (Chicago: Aldine, 1970); Wirt, *We Ain't What We Was: Civil Rights in the New South* (Durham, NC: Duke University Press, 1997).

3. Lawrence J. Hanks, *The Struggle for Black Political Empowerment in Three Georgia Counties* (Knoxville: University of Tennessee Press, 1987); Minion KC Morrison, *Black Political Mobilization* (Albany: State University of New York Press, 1987).

4. Clyde Woods, *Development Arrested: The Blues and Plantation Power in the Mississippi Delta* (New York: Verso Press, 1998), 4.

5. Ibid., 225.

6. Ibid., 12.

7. Robert A. Dahl, *Who Governs: Democracy and Power in an American City* (New Haven: Yale University Press, 1961).

8. David Judge, "Pluralism," in *Theories of Urban Politics, eds. Judge, Gerry Stoker, and Harold Wolman* (Thousand Oaks, CA: Sage Publications, 1995), 16, 20.

9. Steven P. Erie, "Big-City Rainbow Politics: Machines Revividus?" in *The Politics of Urban America: A Reader,* eds. Dennis R. Judd and Paul P. Kantor (Needham Heights, MA: Allyn and Bacon, 1998), 106–121.

10. William E. Nelson Jr., *Black Atlantic Politics: Dilemmas of Political Empowerment in Boston and Liverpool* (Albany: State University of New York Press, 2000); Dianne M. Pinderhughes, *Race and Ethnicity in Chicago Politics: A Re-Examination of Pluralist Theory* (Urbana: University of Illinois Press, 1987); EE Schattschneider, *The Semi-Sovereign People: A Realist's View of Democracy in America* (New York: Holt, 1960).

11. James H. Meisel, *The Myth of the Ruling Class: Gaetano Mosca and the 'Elite': With the First English Translation of the Final Version of the Theory of the Ruling Class* (Ann Arbor: University of Michigan Press, 1962).

12. Social elites gained influence because of their prominent social standing. G. William Domhoff called them "the jet set" and "rich playboys and movie stars." See Domhoff, *The Higher Circles* (New York: Vintage Books, 1971).

13. Specialized elites affected the aspirations, values, and behavior patterns of the mass population.

14. Governing elites are appointed or elected political officials.

15. Siegfried Frederick (SF) Nadel distinguished between social elites, specialized elites, and governing elites. See Nadel, "The Concept of Social Elites," *International Social Science Bulletin* 8, 3 (1956): 413–424.

16. Gaetano Mosca, *The Ruling Class* (New York: McGraw-Hill, 1939); Roberto Michels, *Political Parties: A Sociological Study of the Oligarchical Tradition of Modern Democracy* (New York: Dover, 1959); V. Pareto, *The Mind and Society* (London: Cape, 1935).

17. Dahl, "A Critique of the Ruling Elite Model," *American Political Science Review* 52 (June 1958): 463; Domhoff, *Who Rules America?* (Englewood Cliffs, NJ: Prentice-Hall, 1992).

18. Domhoff, *Who Rules America?*

19. C. Wright Mills, *The Power Elite* (London: Oxford University Press, 1956), 3–4.

20. Ibid., 8.

21. Floyd Hunter, *Community Power Structure* (Chapel Hill: University of North Carolina Press, 1953).

22. Ibid.

23. Alan Harding, "Elite Theory and Growth Machines," in *Theories of Urban Politics*, eds. David Judge, Gerry Stoker, and Harold Wolman (Thousand Oaks, CA: Sage Publications, 1995), 36.

24. George Moyser and Margaret Wagstaffe, "Studying Elites: Theoretical and Methodological Issues," in *Research Methods for Elite Studies, eds. Moyser and Wagstaffe* (London: Allen and Unwin, 1987), 5.

25. Clarence N. Stone, *Regime Politics: Governing Atlanta, 1946–1988* (Lawrence: University of Kansas Press, 1989), 6.

26. Stone and Carol Pierannunzi, "Atlanta and the Limited Reach of Electoral Control," in *Racial Politics in American Cities, 2d ed.*, eds. Rufus Browning, Dale Rogers Marshall, and David Tabb (New York: Longman, 1997), 166.

27. H. Paul Friesema, "Black Control of Central Cities: The Hollow Prize," *American Institute of Planners Journal* 35 (March 1969): 75–79.

28. Browning, Marshall, and Tabb, "Can People of Color Achieve Power in City Government? The Setting and the Issues," in *Racial Politics in American Cities*, 9.

29. Ibid.

30. Ibid., 28.

31. Ibid., 12.

32. Hanks, *Struggle for Black Political Empowerment in Three Georgia Counties.*

33. Jeremiah Cotton, "Towards a Theory and Strategy for Black Economic Development," *Race, Politics, and Economic Development* (New York: Verso Press, 1992), 11–31; Mack H. Jones, "The Black Underclass as a Systemic Phenomenon," in ibid., 53–65; William Fletcher and Eugene Newport, "Race and Economic Development: The Need for a Black Agenda," in ibid., b117–130.

34. Friesema developed the term "hollow prize" to describe the fact that African Americans who have become the political elite in cities and counties usually lacked economic power. See Friesema, "Black Control of Central Cities," 75–79. The research of Jones echoed earlier work on the hollow prize thesis. Jones found that blacks in Atlanta had a sizable population and numerous black elected officials by the late 1970s, but most black residents of the city had such a low socioeconomic status that poverty and unemployment levels remained high while median family incomes and minority business enterprises remained low. See Jones, "Black Political Empowerment in Atlanta: Myth and Reality," *Annals of the American Academy of Political and Social Sciences* 439 (September 1978): 90–117.

35. James W. Button, *Blacks and Social Change: The Impact of the Civil Rights Movement in Southern Communities* (Princeton: Princeton University Press, 1989), 11.

36. John P. Pelissero, David B. Holian, and Laura A. Tomaka, "Does Political Incorporation Matter?: The Impact of Minority Mayors over Time," *Urban Affairs Review* 36, 1 (September 2000): 84–92.

37. Robert D. Putnam, *Making Democracy Work: Civic Traditions in Modern Italy* (Princeton: Princeton University Press, 1993), 167.

38. Marion Orr, *Black Social Capital: The Politics of School Reform in Baltimore, 1986–1998* (Lawrence: University Press of Kansas, 1999), 8.

39. Ibid., 14.

40. Ibid., 190.

41. Joyce E. Allen-Smith, "Blacks in Rural America: Socioeconomic Status and Policies to Enhance Economic Well-Being," *Review of Black Political Economy* 22, 4 (Spring 1994): 9.

42. Albert O. Hirschman argues that individuals either "exit" from places when they sense a deteriorating quality of life or remain to engage in "voice" activities such as protests with the intention of improving conditions. See Hirschman. *Exit, Voice and Loyalty: Responses to Declines in Firms, Organizations, and States* (Cambridge: Harvard University Press, 1972).

43. Joint Center for Political and Economic Studies, *Black Elected Officials: A National Roster, 1991; 20th ed.* (Washington, DC: Joint Center for Political and Economic Studies, 1992).

44. John Gaventa, *Power and the Powerlessness: Quiescence and Rebellion in an Appalachian Valley* (Urbana: University of Illinois Press, 1980), vii; Michael Parenti, "Power and Pluralism: A View from the Bottom," *Journal of Politics* 32 (1970): 501–530.

45. Gaventa, *Power and the Powerlessness*, 9; Schattschneider, *Semi-Sovereign People*, 105.

46. Gaventa, *Power and the Powerlessness*, vii. 14.

47. Ibid., 14.

48. Ibid., 23.

49. Delta Council, "1998 Delta Council Annual Report," Unpublished report. www.deltacouncil.org; Delta Council, "2000 Delta Council Annual Report," Unpublished report. www.deltacouncil.org; Delta Council, "2001 Delta Council Annual Report," Unpublished report. www.deltacouncil.org; Delta Council, "2002 Delta Council Annual Report," Unpublished report. www.deltacouncil.org; BF Smith Foundation, "Farmers Advocating Resource Management: Delta FARM Final Report," Unpublished report. (Stoneville, MS: BF Smith Foundation, 2004).

50. The World Bank Group, "How Is Social Capital Measured?" Unpublished Paper www.worldbank.org/poverty/social capital/SChowmeas1.htm.

51. Putnam, "Tuning In, Tuning Out: The Strange Disappearance of Social Capital in America" *PS: Political Science and Politics Internet Edition* 28, 4 (December 1995): 2.

52. Ernesto Cortes Jr., "Reweaving the Fabric: The Iron Rule and the I.A.F. Strategy for Power and Politics," ed. Henry G. Cisneros, *Interwoven Destinies* (New York: Norton, 1993), 299.

53. Putnam, "Bowling Alone: America's Declining Social Capital," *Journal of Democracy* 6 (1995a): 73.

54. Kent E. Portney and Jeffrey M. Berry, "Mobilizing Minority Communities: Social Capital and Participation in Urban Neighborhoods" *American Behavioral Scientist* 40, 5 (March/April 1997): 634.

55. Ibid., 639.

56. Hunter, *Community Power Structure*.

Chapter 2

1. James C. Cobb, *The Most Southern Place on Earth: The Mississippi Delta and the Roots of Regional Identity* (New York: Oxford University Press, 1992); Charles M. Payne, "Men Led, Women Organized," in *Women in the Civil Rights Movement: Trailblazers and Torchbearers, 1941–1965*, eds. Vicki Crawford (Brooklyn: Carlson Publishing, 1990); Rupert Vance, *Human Geography of the South: A Study in Regional Resources and Human Adequacy* (Chapel Hill: University of North Carolina Press, 1935).

2. The core counties are Bolivar, Coahoma, Humphreys, Issaquena, Leflore, Quitman, Sharkey, Sunflower, Tallahatchie, Tunica, and Washington. The fringe counties are Carroll, Holmes, Panola, Tate, Warren, and Yazoo. See John C. Crecink and Roosevelt Steptoe, *Human Resources in the Rural Mississippi Delta-With Emphasis on the Poor Economic Research Service Agricultural Economics Report no. 170* (Washington, DC: U.S. Department of Agriculture, 1970); and Lynn Reinschmidt and Bernal Green, *Structure and Change in Socioeconomic Conditions: The Mississippi Delta.* Mimeo, 1989.

3. Willie Morris, "My Delta. And Yours?" in *A Social and Economic Portrait of the Mississippi Delta*, eds., Arthur G. Cosby Mitchell W. Brackin, T. David Mason, and Eunice R. McCulloch (Mississippi State: Mississippi State University Social Science Research Center, Mississippi Agricultural and Forestry Experiment Station, 1992), 6.

4. William M. Cash and R. Daryl Lewis, *The Delta Council: Fifty Years of Service to the Mississippi Delta* (Stoneville, MS: Delta Council, 1986), 14.

5. Albert B. Nylander III, *Rural Community Leadership Structures in Two Delta Communities.* PhD diss., Mississippi State University, 1998.

6. Clyde Woods, *Development Arrested: The Cotton and Blues Empire of the Mississippi Delta* (New York: Verso Press, 1998), 94.

7. Annie Ruth Wright, former Delta resident, interview, December 6, 2000.

8. Cash and Daryl Lewis, Delta Council, 44.

9. Ibid.

10. Junior White, former Delta resident, interview, December 24, 2000.

11. Eulean Pugh, former Delta resident, interview, December 23, 2000.

12. Ibid.

13. Ludetha Austin, former Delta resident, interview, December 29, 2000.

14. Cobb, Most *Southern Place on Earth*, 71.

15. Ibid., 47.

16. Cynthia M. Duncan, *Worlds Apart: Why Poverty Persists in Rural America* (New Haven, CT: Yale University Press, 1999), 81.

17. Neil R. McMillen, *Dark Journey: Black Mississippians in the Age of Jim Crow* (Urbana-Champaign: University of Illinois Press, 1989), 119.

18. R. Heberle and Udell Jolley, "Mississippi Backwater Study - Yazoo Segment: Report on Social Factors," Unpublished report, November 10, 1940.

19. McMillen, *Dark Journey*, 119.

20. Woods, *Development Arrested*, 92–93.

21. Ibid.

22. Annie Ruth Wright, former Delta resident, interview, December 6, 2000.

23. The Reverend Joe Canada, former Delta resident, interview, December 24, 2000.

24. Woods, *Development Arrested*, 92–93.

25. Ibid., 8.

26. Mary DeLorse Coleman, *Legislators, Law and Public Policy: Political Change in Mississippi and the South* (Westport, CT: Greenwood Press, 1993), 29.

27. Joyce E. Allen-Smith, "Blacks in Rural America: Socioeconomic Status and Policies to Enhance Economic Well-Being," *Review of Black Political Economy* 22, 4 (Spring 1994): 9.

28. Nan Elizabeth Woodruff, "Mississippi Delta Planters and Debates over Mechanization, Labor, and Civil Rights in the 1940s," *Journal of Southern History* 60, 2 (May 1994): 265.

29. Ibid., 266; Woodruff, "Pick or Fight: The Emergency Farm Labor Program in the Arkansas and Mississippi Deltas during World War II," *Agricultural History* 64 (Spring 1990): 74–85.

30. Delta Council, "Addresses Presented to Delta Council Annual Meeting . . . Cleveland, Mississippi, May 3, 1944, and Resolutions Adopted by Ninth Convention," Unpublished paper (Stoneville, MS: Delta Council,

1944); Delta Council, "Delta Council History, 1938-1943," Unpublished paper (Stoneville, MS: Delta Council, 1944).

31. Delta Council, "Delta Survey for a Blueprint for New Horizons Submitted to Mississippi Power and Light Company," Unpublished paper (Stoneville, MS: Delta Council, April 1, 1944), 9.

32. Ibid., 17–18.

33. Woodruff, "Mississippi Delta Planters and Debates over Mechanization, Labor, and Civil Rights in the 1940s," 272.

34. Ibid., 279.

35. Ibid., 278.

36. Ibid., 268.

37. Cash and Lewis, *Delta Council*, 19.

38. Cobb, *Most Southern Place on Earth*, 196.

39. Ibid.

40. Ibid., 185.

41. Ibid.

42. Ibid., 271.

43. David Eugene Conrad, *The Forgotten Farmers: The Story of Sharecroppers in the New Deal* (Urbana: University of Illinois Press, 1965), 52.

44. Cobb, *Most Southern Place on Earth*, 188; Woodruff, "Mississippi Delta Planters and Debates over Mechanization, Labor, and Civil Rights in the 1940s," 264.

45. Cobb, *Most Southern Place on Earth*, 190.

46. Ibid., 189–190.

47. Nylander, *Rural Community Leadership Structures in Two Delta Communities*, 12.

48. Cobb, *Most Southern Place on Earth*, 256.

49. Woods, *Development Arrested*, 10.

50. Mississippi United to Elect Negro Candidates, "To Get that Power: Mississippi United to Elect Negro Candidates," Unpublished pamphlet, 1967.

51. Ralph W. Alewine Jr., "The Changing Characteristics of the Mississippi Delta," in *Farm Labor Developments* (Washington, DC: U.S. Department of Labor, May 1968), 32–37.

52. John Saunders, "A Demography of the Delta," in *A Social and Economic Portrait of the Mississippi Delta,* eds. Arthur G. Cosby and Mitchell W. Brackin, T. David Mason, and Eunice R. McCulloch (Mississippi State: Mississippi State University Social Science Research Center, Mississippi Agricultural and Forestry Experiment Station, 1992), 47.

53. Phyllis Gray-Ray, "Race Relations in the Delta," in ibid., 37.

54. Cash and Lewis, *Delta Council,* 57-58.

55. Duncan, *Worlds Apart,* 93.

56. Gray-Ray, "Race Relations in the Delta," 38.

57. Ibid., 39.

Chapter 3

1. Stephen D. Shaffer and Dale Krane, "Tradition versus Modernity in Mississippi Politics," in *Mississippi Government and Politics: Modernizers versus Traditionalists,* eds. Dale Krane and Stephen D. Shaffer (Lincoln: University of Nebraska Press, 1992), 278.

2. VO Key, *Southern Politics in State and Nation* (New York: Knopf, 1950), 234.

3. Charles E. Menifield, "Mississippi Votes 2000: A Comprehensive Examination of Politics and Elections," Unpublished research report. John C. Stennis Institute of Government, Mississippi State University, 2002.

4. Shaffer and Krane, "Tradition versus Modernity in Mississippi Politics," 280.

5. Ibid.

6. Ibid.

7. William C. Havard, ed. *The Changing Politics of the South* (Baton Rouge: Louisiana State University Press, 1972), 473.

8. Ibid.

9. James W. Silver's text, *Mississippi: The Closed Society* (New York: Harcourt, 1963); reprinted in 1964 and 1966 remains one of the most comprehensive book detailing the conditions of African Americans in Mississippi.

10. Key, *Southern Politics in State and Nation,* 243.

11. Gerald Gabris, "The Dynamics of Mississippi Local Government," 224.

12. U.S. Commission on Civil Rights, *Voting in Mississippi* (Washington, DC: U.S. Government Printing Office, 1965), 3.

13. Havard, *Changing Politics of the* South, 478; Hiram Rhodes Revels (1870–1871) and Blanche Kelso Bruce (1875–1880) served in the U.S. Senate. Revels completed the unexpired term of Jefferson Davis. John Roy Lynch was speaker of the Mississippi House of Representatives from 1872 to 1873 and served three terms in Congress (1872–1876 and 1880–1882). Both James D. Lynch (1870–1872) and James J. Hill (1874–1878) were secretaries of state, and A.K. Davis was lieutenant governor (1874–1875). Hill had also been elected to serve in the Mississippi House of Representatives in 1871 and in the state senate in 1874. See chapter 2, "The Politics of the Disfranchised" in Neil R. McMillen, *Dark Journey: Black Mississippians in the Age of Jim Crow* (Urbana: University of Illinois Press, 1989) and Robert Fulton Holtzclaw's *Black Magnolias: A Brief History of the Afro-Mississippian, 1865–1980* (Shaker Heights, OH: Keeble Press, 1984) for a discussion of the political activities and disfranchisement of African Americans during the late 1800s.

14. Vernon Lane Wharton, *The Negro in Mississippi, 1865–1980* (New York: Harper, 1947), 172.

15. Another purpose of the new Constitution was to end election fraud. However, scholars have questioned whether open and widespread election fraud existed in Mississippi during the late 1800s. See Jack Bass and Walter DeVries, *The Transformation of Southern Politics: Social Change and Politics Consequence since 1945* (New York: Basic, 1976), 192; William Alexander Mabry, "Disfranchisement of the Negro in Mississippi," *Journal of Southern History* 4 (1938): 325; Wharton, *Negro in Mississippi*, 200.

16. *Jackson Daily Clarion-Ledger*, September 11, 1890.

17. Mary DeLorse Coleman, *Legislators, Law and Public Policy: Political Change in Mississippi and the South* (Westport, CT: Greenwood Press, 1993), 29; Clyde M. Woods, *Development Arrested: The Blues and Plantation Power in the Mississippi Delta* (New York: Verso Press, 1998), 89.

18. *Jackson Clarion-Ledger*, September 11, 1890, 6.

19. Woods, *Development Arrested*, 89.

20. In 1954, a constitutional amendment required that prospective voters have the ability to both read and write. Mississippi Constitution, section 244. See Coleman, *Legislators, Law and Public Policy*, 27; Mabry, "Disfranchisement of the Negro in Mississippi," 327; Frank R. Parker, *Black Votes Count: Political Empowerment in Mississippi after 1965* (Chapel Hill: University of North Carolina Press, 1990), 27.

21. In 1960, a "good moral character" requirement for voting was added to the Mississippi Constitution. Mississippi Constitution, section 241A. This clause provided an even greater safeguard to ensure that illiterate whites could vote. In later years, the Mississippi legislature drafted laws that made it easier for whites to intimidate African Americans through threats and/or violence. For example, the state legislature passed a law that required the

names of those taking the voter registration literacy test to be published in local newspapers in 1962. As a result of this law, African Americans who attempted to register to vote faced even greater risks of losing their jobs, safety, and lives. See the U.S. Commission on Civil Rights, *Voting in Mississippi*, 8–9.

22. Parker, *Black Votes* Count, 28.

23. Quoted in U.S. Commission on Civil Rights, *Voting in Mississippi*, 5; Verified by Senator Bilbo, Hearings before the Senate Special Committee to Investigate Senatorial Campaign Expenditures, 79th Cong., 2nd sess. 1946; 350.

24. Mabry, "Disfranchisement of the Negro in Mississippi," 333.

25. Stephen D. Shaffer and Dale Krane, "The Origins and Evolution of a Traditionalistic Society," in *Mississippi Government and Politics: Modernizers versus Traditionalists*, eds. Krane and Shaffer (Lincoln: University of Nebraska Press, 1992), 31.

26. Albert D. Kirwan, *Revolt of the Rednecks: Mississippi Politics, 1876–1925* (Lexington: University of Kentucky Press, 1951), 131.

27. Ibid., 128–129.

28. *Smith v. Allwright* 321 U.S. 646 (1944).

29. U.S. Commission on Civil Rights, *Voting in Mississippi*, 7.

30. Ibid., 7–8.

31. Ibid., 9.

32. Shaffer and Krane, "Origins and Evolution of a Traditionalistic Society," 30.

33. John Dittmer, *Local People: The Struggle for Civil Rights in Mississippi* (Urbana, IL: University of Illinois Press, 1995).

34. Frederick M. Wirt, *We Ain't What We Was: Civil Rights in the New South* (Durham, NC: Duke University Press, 1997), 39.

35. Minion KC Morrison, "Preconditions for Afro-American Leadership: Three Mississippi Towns," *Polity* 17: 3 (Spring 1985): 517.

36. Student Nonviolent Coordinating Committee, "Mississippi Summer Project" Unpublished pamphlet. (Atlanta: Student Nonviolent Coordinating Committee, 1964).

37. *I've Got the Light of Freedom: The Organizing Tradition and the Mississippi Freedom Struggle* (Berkeley: University of California at Berkeley Press, 1995), 255.

38. The Reverend Joe Canada, former Delta resident, interview, December 24, 2000.

39. University of Mississippi Oral History Program, "An Oral History with the Honorable Unita Blackwell," interview with Mike Garvey of the Uni-

versity of Southern Mississippi Center for Oral History and Cultural Heritage (Mayersville, April 21, 1922), 21.

40. Annie Ruth Wright, former Delta resident, interview, December 6, 2000.

41. Payne, *I've Got The Light of Freedom*, 255.

42. U.S. Commission on Civil Rights, *Voting in Mississippi*, 21.

43. See chapter 8, "White Christmas: Boycotts and the Meanings of Shopping, 1960–1990," Ted Ownby, *American Dreams in Mississippi: Consumers, Poverty, and Culture, 1830–1998* (Chapel Hill: University of North Carolina Press, 1999) for a comprehensive discussion of direct action boycotts in Mississippi.

44. Parker, *Black Votes Count*, 2.

45. Marion E. Orr, *Black Social Capital: The Politics of School Reform in Baltimore, 1986–1998* (Lawrence: University Press of Kansas, 1999), 194.

46. Norma Westbrook, Delta resident, interview, December 7, 2000.

47. Alexis de Tocqueville, *Democracy in America*, ed. JP Mayer, trans. George Lawrence (New York: Anchor Books, 1969), 522.

48. Harry Holloway, *The Politics of the Southern Negro: From Exclusion to Big City Organization* (New York: Random House, 1969), 41.

49. Student Nonviolent Coordinating Committee, "Mississippi Summer Project," Unpublished pamphlet. (Atlanta: Student Nonviolent Coordinating Committee, 1964).

50. Mark R. Warren, *Dry Bones Rattling: Community Building to Revitalize American Democracy* (Princeton: Princeton University Press, 2001), 31.

51. Cathy J. Cohen, "Social Capital, Intervening Institutions, and Political Power," Paper presented at the Ford Foundation Conference: "Social Capital in Poor Communities: Building and Utilizing Social Assets to Combat Poverty," Yale University, February 1999.

52. Student Nonviolent Coordinating Committee, *Mississippi Summer Project*.

53. Ibid.

54. Ibid., 14–17.

55. Ibid.

56. Ibid.

57. Robert D. Putnam, "Bowling Alone: America's Declining Social Capital," *Journal of Democracy* 6 (1995a): 73.

58. Holloway, *Politics of the Southern Negro*, 42.

59. Parker, *Black Votes Count*, 15.

60. Ibid., 24.

61. Holloway, *Politics of the Southern Negro*, 43.

62. Ibid., 44.

63. Ibid.

64. Parker, *Black Votes Count*, 25.

65. Ibid.

66. Ibid.

67. Holloway, *Politics of the Southern Negro*, 43.

68. Payne, *I've Got The Light of* Freedom, 237-239.

69. Ibid., 243.

70. Mary Varela, *Holmes County, Mississippi: We Are Not the Minority Race, We Are the Majority Race* (Jackson, MS: K.I.P.C.O., 1967), 3–4.

71. Ibid., 5.

72. Ludetha Austin, former Delta resident, interview, December 6, 2000.

73. Annie Ruth Wright, former Delta resident, interview, December 6,

74. Eulean Pugh, former Delta resident, interview, December 23, 2000.

75. University of Mississippi Oral History Program, "An Oral History with the Honorable Unita Blackwell," interview with Mike Garvey of the University of Southern Mississippi Center for Oral History and Cultural Heritage (Mayersville, April 21, 1922), 22.

76. Eulean Pugh, former Delta resident, interview, December 23, 2000.

77. Ludetha Austin, former Delta resident, interview, December 6, 2000.

78. Ibid.

Chapter 4

1. William Fletcher and Eugene Newport, "Race and Economic Development: The Need for a Black Agenda," in *Race, Politics, and Economic Development*, ed. James B. Jennings (New York: Verso Press, 1992), 117.

2. Bernice Powell-Jackson, "Gambling on Poverty in America," *Michigan Chronicle*, February 7, 1996, 6A.

3. Ibid.

4. Willie Morris, "My Delta. And Yours?" in *A Social and Economic Portrait of the Mississippi Delta*, eds. Arthur G. Cosby, Mitchell W. Brackin, T. David Mason, and Eunice R. McCulloch (Mississippi State: Mississippi State University Social Science Research Center, Mississippi Agricultural and Forestry Experiment Station, 1992), 3–10.

5. James Popkin, "A Mixed Blessing for 'America's Ethiopia,'" *U.S. News and World Report*, March 14, 1994, 52.

6. Kevin Kittredge, "Tunica: 'Nothing Like It: A National Tragedy Congressman States," *Memphis Commercial Appeal*, July 20, 1985, A1.

7. Kaye Dickie, "Hallelujah! Sour Alley Turns Sweet: Sugar Ditch Looking Up," *Memphis Commercial Appeal*, January 11, 1986, A4.

8. Clyde Woods, *Development Arrested: The Blues and Plantation Power in the Mississippi Delta* (New York: Verso Press, 1998), 236.

9. Leo V. Mayer, "Agricultural Change and Rural America," *Annals of the American Academy of Political and Social Science* 529 (September 1993): 80–90.

10. Ibid.

11. Audie Blevins and Katherine Jensen, "Gambling as a Community Development Quick Fix," *ANNALS: American Academy of Political and Social Science* 556 (March 1998): 112–113.

12. Peter K. Eisinger, *The Rise of the Entrepreneurial State* (Madison: University of Wisconsin Press, 1988); John Lyman Mason and Michael Nelson, "The Politics of Gambling in the South," Paper presented at the 1999 annual meeting of the American Political Science Association, Atlanta, September 2–5, 1999, 7.

13. Ranjana G. Madhusudan, "Betting on Casino Revenues: Lessons from State Experiences," *National Tax Journal* 49 (September 1996): 401.

14. Robert Goodman, *The Luck Business: The Devastating Consequences and Broken Promises of America's Gambling Explosion* (New York: Free Press, 1995), 97.

15. Jeffrey L. Pressman, "Preconditions of Mayoral Leadership," *American Political Science Review* 66 (June 1972): 512.

16. Ellen Perlman, "Gambling, Mississippi Style," *Governing Magazine* 8, 7 (April 1995): 40.

17. Mason and Nelson, "Politics of Gambling in the South," 7.

18. Denise von Herrmann, "Casino Gaming in Mississippi: From Backwater to the Big Time," in *Politics in Mississippi*, 2d ed., Joseph B. Parker (Salem, WI: Sheffield Publishing Company, 2001), 303; Perlman, "Gambling, Mississippi Style," 40.

19. Ibid., 303.

20. Mason and Nelson, " Politics of Gambling in the South," 7.

21. John Gnuschke, "The Future of Casino Gambling in Tunica County," *Business Perspectives* 11, 4 (Summer 1999): 4.

22. Mason and Nelson, " Politics of Gambling in the South," 8.

23. Ali A. Abusalih, *Casinos, Tourism Rejuvenation, and Coastal Landscape impacts Biloxi, Mississippi* (Master's thesis, Mississippi State University, 1994).

24. Sharon D. Wright and Richard T. Middleton IV, "Mayor A.J. Holloway and Casino Gambling in Biloxi, Mississippi," in *Governing Middle-Sized Cities: Studies in Mayoral Leadership,* eds. James R. Bowers and Wilbur C. Rich (Boulder: Lynne Rienner Publishers, 2000), 151–166.

25. Ibid.

26. After the legislature voted in 1990 to authorize casinos along the Gulf Coast and along the Mississippi River, riverboat gaming became dockside gaming because the currents in the river and the tides in the Gulf made it too difficult for boats to leave the shore. Moreover, despite the requirement that casinos be located in river or Gulf counties, two casinos operate in Philadelphia (Neshoba County), Mississippi, in the eastern central part of the state. Their owners, the Mississippi Band of Choctaw Indians, were able to open their casinos in Neshoba County because of the Indian Gaming Regulatory Act. This federal law allows tribes to establish casinos on tribal lands if any Class III gaming (which includes casinos and related activities) is legal within the boundaries of a state.

27. Powell-Jackson, "Gambling on Poverty in America," 6A.

28. Perlman, "Gambling, Mississippi Style," 40.

29. The Honorable Bobby E. Williams, Mayor of Tunica, Mississippi, interview, November 1, 1999.

30. Dr. Jeff Wallace, Bureau of Business and Economic Research at the Fogelman Executive Center, University of Memphis, interview, January 4, 2000.

31. Webster Franklin, Director of the Tunica County Chamber of Commerce, interview, March 2, 1999.

32. Dr. Jeff Wallace, Bureau of Business and Economic Research at the Fogelman Executive Center, University of Memphis, interview, January 4, 2000.

33. Butch Reid, Future of Farming on Shaky Ground. *Clarion-Ledger,* December 20, 1999, 1.

34. Ibid.

35. Ibid.

36. Reid, Future of Farming on Shaky Ground; Reid and Butch, "Cotton, Catfish, Cells, Casinos: Delta Struggling to Find Profitable Economic Identity," *Clarion-Ledger*, 1.

37. Anonymous, "Looking Ahead: Tunica Residents Remember the Past, Enjoy the Present, and Look Forward to a Bright Future" *Tunica County: 1996* (Tunica, MS: Tunica Chamber of Commerce), 9.

38. Ibid.

39. Bartholomew Sullivan, "Tunica Landowners Raking in Big Rewards as Values Soar," *Memphis Commercial Appeal*, November 29, 1993, A15.

40. Ibid.

41. James Dunn, Member of the Tunica County Board of Supervisors, interview, April 30, 2004.

42. John Branston, "A Tale of Two Cities," *Memphis Magazine* 21, 4 (July/August 1996), 24.

43. Sullivan, "Tunica Landowners Raking in Big Rewards as Values Soar," A15.

44. Branston, "Tale of Two Cities," 24.

45. Anonymous, "The Mississippi Delta: The Government's Plantations," *The Economist* 324 (July 11, 1992): 26; Butch John, "Lack of Direction Stymies Delta: Shift in Racial Power Has Yet to Produce Unity in Leadership," *Clarion-Ledger*, December 23, 1999 A1.

46. Webster Franklin, Director of the Tunica County Chamber of Commerce, interview, March 2, 1999.

47. Kenneth Murphree, Tunica County Administrator, interview, November 22, 1999.

48. Mississippi Gaming Commission. http//: www.mgc.state.ms.us.

49. Von Herrmann, "Casino Gaming in Mississippi," 308.

50. Ibid., 310.

51. Ibid., 309.

52. Dr. Jeff Wallace, Bureau of Business and Economic Research at the Fogelman Executive Center, University of Memphis, interview, January 4, 2000.

53. Bolivar County African American elected official requesting anonymity, interview, April 30, 2004.

54. Robert Ingram, Director of the Greenwood-Leflore County Industrial Board, interview, April 29, 2004.

55. Von Herrmann, "Casino Gaming in Mississippi," 309–310.

56. James V. Walker, "Tunica County: 10 Years of Gaming Still Paying Off," *Jackson Clarion-Ledger* February 19, 2002.

57. Ibid.

58. Katherine S. Newman, *No Shame in My Game: The Working Poor in the Inner City* (New York: Russell Sage Foundation, 1999).

59. Norma Westbrook, Delta resident, interview, December 7, 2000.

60. Benjamin Schwarz and Christina Schwarz, "Mississippi Monte Carlo," *Atlantic Monthly* 277, 1 (January 1996): 74.

61. James E. Dunn, Member of the Tunica County Board of Supervisors, interview, April 30, 2004.

62. James M. Carlson and Mark S. Hyde, *Doing Empirical Political Research* (Boston: Houghton Mifflin Company, 2003), 347.

63. Ibid., 390.

64. Ibid., 390.

65. Ibid.

66. Yvette Alex-Assensoh, "Race, Concentrated Poverty, Social Isolation, and Political Behavior," *Urban Affairs Review* 33, 2 (November 1997): 209.

67. Devine and Wright, *The Greatest Evils: Urban Poverty and the American Underclass* (New York: Aldine De Gruyter, 1993); Goldsmith and Blakely, *Separate Societies: Poverty and Inequality in U.S. Cities* (Philadelphia: Temple University Press, 1992); Neil J. Kraus. *Race, Neighborhoods, and Community Power, Buffalo Politics, 1934–1997* (Albany: State University of New York Press, 2000), 7; Massey and Denton, *American Apartheid: Segregation and the Making of the Underclass* (Cambridge: Harvard University Press, 1993); William Julius Wilson, *The Truly Disadvantaged: The Inner City, the Underclass, and Public Policy* (Chicago: University of Chicago Press, 1987); Wilson, *When Work Disappears: The World of the New Urban Poor* (New York: Knopf, 1996).

68. Anonymous, "Economic Flatliners- Places Left Behind in Rural America," Unpublished document. http://www.hud.gov/library/bookshelf18/pressrel/leftbehind/nowflat.html.

69. Wilson, *When Work Disappears.*

70. Wilson, *The New Urban Poverty and the Problem, of Race* (Ann Arbor: University of Michigan Press), 1993; Wilson, *The Truly Disadvantaged.*

71. Mary Corcoran, "Rags to Rags: Poverty and Mobility in the United States." *Annual Review of Sociology* 21 (1995): 246.

72. Cynthia M. Duncan, *Worlds Apart: Why Poverty Persists in Rural America* (New Haven: Yale University Press, 1999), 188.

73. John Gaventa, *Power and the Powerlessness: Quiescence and Rebellion in an Appalachian Valley* (Urbana: University of Illinois Press, 1980), 23.

74. Schwarz and Schwarz, "Mississippi Monte Carlo," 74.

75. Bartholomew Sullivan, "On a Roll: Casino Boom Sprays Mississippi with Prosperity," *Memphis Commercial Appeal,* July 24, 1996, A1, A11.

76. Smith Foundation, "Farmers Advocating Resource Management: Delta F.A.R.M." Final Report Unpublished paper. (Stoneville, MS: BF Smith Foundation, 2004); Delta Council, "1998 Delta Council Annual Report," Unpublished report. www.deltacouncil.org; Delta Council, "2000 Delta Council Annual Report," Unpublished report. www.deltacouncil.org; Delta Council, "2001 Delta Council Annual Report," Unpublished report. www.deltacouncil.org; Delta Council, "2002 Delta Council Annual Report," Unpublished report. www.deltacouncil.org.

77. Ken Murphree, Tunica County Administrator, interview, May 18, 2001.

78. Duncan, *Worlds Apart,* 113.

79. Robert A. Dahl, "A Critique of the Ruling Elite Model," *American Political Science Review* 52 (June 1958): 463; G. William Domhoff, *Who Rules America?* (Englewood Cliffs, NJ: Prentice-Hall, 1992); James H. Meisel, *The Myth of the Ruling Class: Gaetano Mosca and the 'Elite': With the First English Translation of the Final Version of the Theory of the Ruling Class* (Ann Arbor: University of Michigan Press, 1962; Roberto Michels, *Political Parties: A Sociological Study of the Oligarchical Tradition of Modern Democracy* (New York: Dover, 1959); C. Wright Mills, *The Power Elite* (London: Oxford University Press, 1956), 3–4; Gaetano Mosca, *The Ruling Class* (New York: McGraw-Hill, 1939); V. Pareto, *The Mind and Society* (London: Cape, 1935).

Chapter 5

1. John Butch, "Lack of Direction Stymies Delta: Shift in Racial Power Has Yet to Produce Unity in Leadership," *Clarion-Ledger,* December 23, 1999, A1.

2. Rufus Browning, Dale Rogers Marshall, and David Tabb, *Protest Is Not Enough: The Struggle of Blacks and Hispanics for Equality in Urban Politics* (Berkeley: University of California Press, 1984).

3. Ibid., "Can People of Color Achieve Power in City Government?," in *Racial Politics in American Cities. The Setting and the Issues, 1ˢᵗ ed.* (New York: Longman, 1990), 12.

4. Ibid., 8–9.

5. Ibid., Can People of Color Achieve Power in City Government?," in *Racial Politics in American Cities, 2d* (New York: Longman, 1997), 8.

6. Ibid., 9.

7. Ibid., 9.

8. Ibid., 9; Sidney Verba, *Elites and the Idea of Equality: A Comparison of Japan, Sweden, and the United States* (Cambridge: Harvard University Press, 1987), 3–4.

9. Albert B. Nylander III, *Rural Community Leadership Structures in Two Delta Communities*, PhD diss., Mississippi State University, 1998, 162, 164.

10. Ibid., 158, 167.

11. Ibid. 166, 167.

12. *Civil Rights Acts of 1957*, 71 Stat. 637; *Civil Rights Acts of 1960*, 74 Stat. 90; U.S. Commission on Civil Rights, *Voting in Mississippi* (Washington, DC: U.S. Government Printing Office, 1965), 8.

13. U.S. Commission on Civil Rights, *Voting in Mississippi*, 8–9.

14. Ibid., 13.

15. Ibid., 16–17; *United States v. Duke* 332 F.2d 759 (5th Cir. 1964).

16. *Voting Rights Act of 1965*, 79 Stat. 437, 42 U.S.C. Section 1973.

17. The U.S. Supreme Court ruled that poll taxes were unconstitutional in the case of *Harper v. State Board of Elections* (1959).

18. Frank R. Parker, *Black Votes Count: Political Empowerment in Mississippi after 1965* (Chapel Hill: University of North Carolina Press, 1990), 30.

19. U.S. Commission on Civil Rights, *Political Participation: A Study of the Participation by Negroes in the Electoral and Political Processes in 10 Southern States since Passage of the Voting Rights Act of 1965* (Washington, DC: U.S. Government Printing Office, 1968), 15.

20. Theodore J. Davis Jr., "Black Political Representation in Rural Mississippi," in *Blacks in Southern Politics*, eds. Laurence W. Moreland, Robert P. Steed, and Tod A. Baker (New York: Praeger Publishers, 1987), 149.

21. Browning, Marshall, and Tabb, "Can People of Color Achieve Power in City Government?," in *Racial Politics in American Cities*, 2d ed., 10.

22. Minion K. C. Morrison found that African Americans who won elective offices had similar backgrounds. They were not a part of an earlier generation of black activists, had a higher socioeconomic status than other community residents, were young and charismatic, had participated in civil rights protests, and wanted to serve the needs of the black community. See Morrison, "Preconditions for Afro-American Leadership: Three Mississippi Towns," *Polity* 17:3 (Spring 1985): 509.

23. Ibid., 510.

24. Ibid., 519.

25. Sylvia Reedy Gist, *Educating a Southern Rural Community: The Case of Blacks in Holmes County, Mississippi, 1870 to Present, Vols. 1 and 2.* PhD diss., University of Chicago, 1994, 215–216.

26. Ibid., 235–236.

27. Gist, *Educating a Southern Rural Community*, 223–224.

28. Ibid.

29. Anonymous, "The Mississippi Delta: The Government's Plantations," *Economist* 324, 7767 (July 11, 1992): 26.

30. Davis, "Black Political Representation in Rural Mississippi," 154–156.

31. Parker, *Black Votes Count*, 30–31.

32. Lawrence J. Hanks, *The Struggle for Black Political Empowerment in Three Georgia Counties* (Knoxville: University of Tennessee Press, 1987), xi–xii.

33. Verba, *Elites and the Idea of Equality*, 3–4.

34. Parker, *Black Votes Count*, 1, 3; U.S. Commission on Civil Rights, *Political Participation*, 25.

35. U.S. Commission on Civil Rights, *Political Participation*, 22.

36. *Jackson Daily News,* January 14, 1966.

37. *Connor v. Johnson* 11 Race Rel. L. Rep. 1859 (S.D. Miss. 1966).

38. House Bill No. 911, Miss. Laws, 1966, ch. 616, approved April 7, 1966, codified as Miss. Code section 3305 (Supp. 1966).

39. Id at 498–99.

40. Clyde Woods, *Development Arrested: The Blues and Plantation Power in the Mississippi Delta* (New York: Verso Press, 1998), 223.

41. Ibid., 215.

42. Parker, *Black Votes Count*, 51.

43. Ibid., 53.

44. Gerald Gabris, "The Dynamics of Mississippi Local Government," in *Mississippi Government and Politics: Modernizers versus Traditionalists*, eds. Dale Krane and Stephen D. Shaffer (Lincoln: University of Nebraska Press, 1992), 232.

45. Ibid., 235; Bill Hicks and Joseph B. Parker, "Local Government in Mississippi," in *Politics in Mississippi, 2d ed.*, ed. Joseph B. Parker (Salem: Sheffield Publishing Company, 2001), 209.

46. Parker, *Black Votes Count*, 54.

47. Ibid., 73–74.

48. *Fairley v. Patterson* 282 F. Supp. 164 (S.D. Miss. 1967) (three-judge court), rev'd sub nom. *Allen v. State Board of Elections* 393 U.S. 544 (1969).

49. *Bunton v. Patterson* 281 F. Supp. 918 (S.D. Miss 1967) (three-judge court), rev'd sub nom. *Allen v. State Board of Elections* 393 U.S. 544 (1969).

50. *Whitley v. Johnson* 260 F. Supp. 630 (S.D. Miss. 1966) (three-judge court), 296 F. supp. 630 (S.D. Miss. 1967) (three-judge court) rev'd sub nom. *Allen v. State Board of Elections* 393 U.S. 544 (1969).

51. *Allen v. State Board of Elections* 393 U.S. 544 (1969).

52. Ibid.

53. Ibid.

54. Gokhan R. Karahan, Laura Razzolini, and William F. Shughart II, "No Pretense to Honesty: County Governmental Corruption in Mississippi," Unpublished paper, May 2003.

55. Stephen D. Shaffer and Dale Krane, "Tradition versus Modernity in Mississippi Politics," in *Mississippi Government and Politics: Modernizers Versus Traditionalists*, eds. Krane and Shaffer (Lincoln: University of Nebraska Press, 1992), 284.

56. Hanks, *Struggle for Black Political Empowerment in Three Georgia Counties*, xi–xii.

57. Davis, "Black Political Representation in Rural Mississippi," 149.

58. Woods, *Development Arrested*, 215–216.

59. James C. Cobb, *The Most Southern Place on Earth: The Mississippi Delta and the Roots of Regional Identity* (New York: Oxford University Press, 1992), 247–248; Gabris, "Dynamics of Mississippi Local Government," 239; Parker, *Black Votes Count*, 199–203; Woods, *Development Arrested*, 216.

60. Woods, *Development Arrested*, 221.

61. Ibid., 326.

62. Ibid., 325.

63. Penda Hair, *Louder than Words: Lawyers, Communities and the Struggle for Justice*, Unpublished report (Mahwah, NJ: Rockefeller Foundation, 2004), 69.

64. Gabris, "Dynamics of Mississippi Local Government," 239.

65. Shaffer and Krane, "Tradition versus Modernity in Mississippi Politics," 280.

66. Riva Brown, "Racial Divisions Deep; Is There Hope?" *Clarion Ledger Internet Edition*, December 23, 1999, 1–7.

67. Former Tunica County elected official requesting anonymity, interview, October 29, 1999.

68. Sharon Grandberry, Tunica County Circuit Cout Clerk, interview, January 5, 2000.

69. James Dunn, Member of the Tunica County Board of Supervisors, interview, April 30, 2004.

70. Hair, *Louder than Words*, 64.

71. Former Tunica County elected official requesting anonymity, interview, October 29, 1999.

72. Sharon Grandberry, Tunica County Circuit Court Clerk, interview, January 5, 2000.

73. Browning, Marshall, and Tabb, "Can People of Color Achieve Power in City Government?" in *Racial Politics in Ameican Cities*, 2d ed., 9.

74. John Gaventa, *Power and the Powerlessness: Quiescence and Rebellion in an Appalachian Valley* (Urbana: University of Illinois Press, 1980), vii.

75. Ibid., 23.

76. Hair, *Louder than Words*, 70.

77. Ibid.

78. Ibid.

79. Ibid., 71.

80. Ibid., 75.

81. *Richard Gardner et al. v. Tallahatchie County, Mississippi et al.* No. 2:91CV146-EMB (United States District Court for the Northern District of Mississippi Delta Division 1997).

82. Hair, *Louder than Words*, 64, 76.

83. Ibid., 76.

84. Jeremiah Cotton, "Towards a Theory and Strategy for Black Economic Development," *Race, Politics, and Economic Development* (New York: Verso Press, 1992), 11–31; Mack H. Jones, "The Black Underclass as a Systemic Phenomenon," in *Race, Politics, and Economic Development* (New York: Verso Press, 1992), 53–65; William Fletcher and Eugene Newport, "Race and Economic Development: The Need for a Black Agenda," in *Race, Politics, and Economic Development*, ed. James B. Jennings (New York: Verso Press, 1992), 117–130.

85. Jennings, *Race, Politics, and Economic Development*, 5.

86. Verba, *Elites and the Idea of Equality*, 48.

87. H. Paul Friesema, "Black Control of Central Cities: The Hollow Prize," *American Institute of Planners Journal* 35 (March 1969): 75–79; Minion K. C. Morrison, *Black Political Mobilization* (New York: State University of New York Press, 1986).

88. Davis, "Black Political Representation in Rural Mississippi," 158.

89. William Julius Wilson, *The Truly Disadvantaged: The Inner City, the Underclass, and Public Policy* (Chicago: University of Chicago Press, 1987).

Chapter 6

1. Alexis de Tocqueville, *Democracy in America*, ed. JP Mayer. Trans. George Lawrence (New York: Anchor Books, 1969), 522.

2. James S. Coleman, *Foundations of Social Theory* (Cambridge: Harvard University Press, 1990); Glenn C. Loury, "Why Should We Care about Group Inequality?" *Social Philosophy and Policy* 5 (Autumn 1987): 249–271.

3. De Tocqueville, *Democracy in America*, 522; Ross Gittell and Avis Vidal, *Community Organizing: Building Social Capital as a Development Strategy* (Thousand Oaks, CA: Sage Publications, 1998), 14; Putnam, "Bowling Alone: America's Declining Social Capital," *Journal of Democracy* 6 (1995a): 65–78; Robert D. Putnam, *Making Democracy Work: Civic Traditions in Modern Italy* (Princeton: Princeton University Press, 1993), 167; Putnam, "Tuning In, Tuning Out: The Strange Disappearance of Civic America," *PS: Political Science and Politics* 28, 4 (December 1995): 664.

4. Mark S. Granovetter, "The Strength of Weak Ties," *American Journal of Sociology* 78, 6 (May 1973): 1360–1380.

5. Putnam, "Bowling Alone: America's Declining Social Capital," 73.

6. Kent E. Portney and Jeffrey M. Berry, "Mobilizing Minority Communities: Social Capital and Participation in Urban Neighborhoods," *American Behavioral Scientist* 40, 5 (March/April 1997).

7. Putnam, "Tuning In, Tuning Out," 667.

8. Ibid., 675.

9. Ibid., 669

10. Ibid., 680.

11. Ibid., 670.

12. Portney and Berry, "Mobilizing Minority Communities."

13. Ernesto Cortes Jr., "Reweaving the Fabric: The Iron Rule and the IAF Strategy for Power and Politics," in Henry G. Cisneros, ed., *Interwoven Destinies* (New York: Norton, 1993), 294–319; Portney and Berry, "Mobilizing Minority Communities."

14. Portney and Berry, "Mobilizing Minority Communities," 632.

15. Cathy J. Cohen, "Social Capital, Intervening Institutions, and Political Power," Paper presented at the Ford Foundation Conference: "Social Capital in Poor Communities: Building and Utilizing Social Assets to Combat Poverty," Yale University, February 1999.

16. Marion E. Orr, *Black Social Capital: The Politics of School Reform in Baltimore, 1986–1998* (Lawrence: University Press of Kansas, 1999), 9, 41.

17. Ibid., 9.

18. Ibid., 194.

19. Gittell and Thompson, "Making Social Capital Work: Social Capital and Community Economic Development," in *Social Capital and Poor Communities*, eds. Susan Saegert, Thompson, and Mark R. Warren (New York: Russell Sage Foundation, 2001), 120–122.

20. Warren, Thompson, and Saegert, "The Role of Social Capital in Combating Poverty," in *Social Capital and Poor Communities*, eds. Saegert, Thompson, and Warren (New York: Russell Sage Foundation, 2001), 4; Gittell and Thompson, "Making Social Capital Work: Social Capital and Community Economic Development," ibid., 122.

21. Cathy J. Cohen, "Social Capital, Intervening Institutions, and Political Power," in ibid., 279.

22. Ibid.

23. Ibid., 280.

24. Ibid., 278.

25. Warren, *Dry Bones Rattling: Community Building to Revitalize American Democracy* (Princeton: Princeton University Press, 2001), 9.

26. Ibid., 33.

27. Orr, *Black Social Capital*, 194.

28. Ibid., 186.

29. Cynthia M. Duncan, "Social Capital in America's Poor Rural Communities," in *Social Capital and Poor Communities*, 65.

30. Tunica County, Mississippi resident requesting anonymity, interview, June 1, 2000.

31. Ibid.

32. Shelia Hardwell Byrd, "After 7 Years, Few in Delta Zone Feel Empowered," *Memphis Commercial Appeal Internet Edition,* June 24, 2001, 2.

33. Lee Powell, ed., *The Mississippi Delta: Beyond 2000 Interim Report* (Washington, DC: U.S. Department of Transportation, 1998), III.

34. Clyde Woods, *Development Arrested: The Blues and Plantation Power in the Mississippi Delta* (New York: Verso Press, 1998), 23.

35. Governor Bill Clinton of Arkansas, Chairman of the Lower Mississippi Delta Development Commission to President George Bush, October 15, 1989; reprinted in *Lower Mississippi Delta Development Commission, Body of the Nation* (Memphis: Lower Mississippi Delta Development Commission, 1989), n.p.

36. Powell, *Mississippi Delta,* 2.

37. Anonymous, "The Mississippi Delta: The Government's Plantations," *Economist* 324, 7767 (July 11, 1992): 26.

38. Woods, *Development Arrested,* 237.

39. Ibid., 23.

40. Powell, ed., *Mississippi Delta,* 4.

41. Ibid., 13.

42. Shelia Hardwell Byrd, "After 7 Years, Few in Delta Zone Feel Empowered," *Memphis Commercial Appeal Internet Edition,* June 24, 2001, 2.

43. Powell, ed., *Mississippi Delta,* 41.

44. Ibid., 15.

45. Ibid.

46. Riva Brown, "Racial Divisions Deep; Is There Hope?" *Clarion Ledger Internet Edition,* December 23, 1999, 5.

47. Byrd, "After 7 Years, Few in Delta Zone Feel Empowered," 1.

48. Bolivar County resident requesting anonymity, interview, June 1, 2003.

49. Byrd, "After 7 Years, Few in Delta Zone Feel Empowered," 1.

50. Mario Rossilli, "A Laboratory of Program after Program, Promise after Promise," *Clarion Ledger Internet Edition,* December 19, 1999, 4.

51. Ibid.

52. Byrd, "After 7 Years, Few in Delta Zone Feel Empowered," 1.

53. Ibid., 2.

54. Black elected official in the Mississippi Delta requesting anonymity, interview, May 6, 2004.

55. Warren, *Dry Bones Rattling*, 25.

56. John Gaventa, *Power and the Powerlessness: Quiescence and Rebellion in an Appalachian Valley* (Urbana: University of Illinois Press, 1980), 9; EE Schattschneider, *The Semi-Sovereign People: A Realist's View of Democracy in America* (New York: Holt, 1960), 105.

57. The author did an extensive reading of the 1992–2004 minutes of meetings of the Tunica County Board of Supervisors.

58. James Dunn, Member of the Tunica County Board of Supervisors, interview, April 30, 2004.

59. Reid Jones, John Thornell, and Gene Hamon, "Educational Attainment in the Delta," in *A Social and Economic Portrait of the Mississippi Delta*, eds. Arthur G. Cosby, Mitchell W. Brackin, T. David Mason, and Eunice R. McCulloch (Mississippi State: Mississippi State University Social Science Research Center, Mississippi Agricultural and Forestry Experiment Station, 1992), 91; Benjamin Schwarz and Christina Schwarz, "Mississippi Monte Carlo," *Atlantic Monthly* 277, 1 (January 1996): 74.

60. Schwarz and Schwarz, "Mississippi Monte Carlo," 74.

61. Thomas Nolan Touchstone, "The Report of a Study of the Tunica County Schools" (Jackson: State Department of Education, 1949), 26.

62. Eulean Pugh, former Delta resident, interview, December 23, 2000.

63. Nsombi Lambright, *Community Organizing for School Reform in the Mississippi Delta*, Unpublished report for the Southern ECHO Organization, August 2001, 20.

64. *Brown v. Board of Education of Topeka Kansas (Brown II)* 347 U.S. 483 (1954); Laura Parker, "Abandoned Education: Tunica's Schools Struggle with Leftovers and Neglect," *APF Reporter* 18, 2 (1997): 20.

65. Parker, "Abandoned Education: Tunica's Schools Struggle with Leftovers and Neglect," 20.

66. *Brown v. Board of Education of Topeka Kansas (Brown II)* 349 U.S. 294 (1955).

67. Parker, "Abandoned Education: Tunica's Schools Struggle with Leftovers and Neglect," 20.

68. Ibid., 19.

69. *Alexander v. Holmes* 396 US 19; 90 S.Ct. 29 (1969).

70. Brooks, Taylor, Owner of the *Tunica Times* newspaper, interview, December 28, 2000.

71. Parker, "Abandoned Education: Tunica's Schools Struggle with Leftovers and Neglect," 22.

72. *Green v. County School Board* 391 U.S. 430 (1968) struck down freedom of choice plans. The case, *United States of America v. Tunica County School District* 421 F.2d 1236 (1970), upheld *Green* and ordered the county's school board to submit a public school desegregation plan by February 1, 1970.

73. Penda Hair, *Louder than Words: Lawyers, Communities, and the Struggle for Justice,* Unpublished report (Mahwah, NJ: Rockefeller Foundation, 2004), 68.

74. Laura Parker, "Abandoned Education: Tunica's Schools Struggle with Leftovers and Neglect," 21.

75. The PEER Committee, "The PEER Committee Report to the Mississippi Legislature: A Review of Tunica County School District's Administrative and Instructional Spending," Unpublished document, July 8, 1997, 3.

76. Schwarz and Schwarz, "Mississippi Monte Carlo," 81.

77. Lambright, *Community Organizing for School Reform in the Mississippi Delta,* 20.

78. Ibid.

79. Bolivar County resident requesting anonymity, interview, June 1, 2003.

80. Mary Williams Walsh, "Casino Booms Throws Poor County into Debate over Region's Future," *St. Louis Post-Dispatch,* December 3, 1999, A19.

81. Anonymous, "Housing Development and Resegregation: A Report from Activists Working in Tunica County, Mississippi," *Rural Policy Matters: A Newsletter of Rural School and Community Action* 1:6 (July 1999): 1–2.

82. Lambright, *Community Organizing for School Reform in the Mississippi Delta,* 21.

83. Edward Jackson, "Disparity in a Town's Schools Seen by Some as Revived Segregation," *Memphis Commercial Appeal,* September 3, 1999.

84. Rufus Browning, Dale Rogers Marshall, and David Tabb, "Can People of Color Achieve Power in City Government?," in *Racial Politics in American Cities, 1st ed.,* eds. Browning, Marshall, and Tabb (New York: Longman, 1990), 12.

85. Tallahatchie County resident requesting anonymity, interview, May 14, 2004.

86. Lambright, *Community Organizing for School Reform in the Mississippi Delta,* 10.

87. An apartment complex has replaced the substandard houses in Sugar Ditch Alley. Future plans include airport expansion, golf courses, hotels, resorts, retirement homes, RV parks, subdivisions, theaters, and theme parks. In other cities, development strategies have resulted in "black removal" from prime locations. Because of high property values and rents as well as a lack of low-income housing in redeveloped communities, black citizens have had to find housing in other areas.

88. Warren, *Dry Bones Rattling*, 9.

89. Lambright, *Community Organizing for School Reform in the Mississippi Delta*, 14.

90. Tallahatchie County resident seeking anonymity, interview, May 18, 2004.

91. Lambright, *Community Organizing for School Reform in the Mississippi Delta*, 14.

92. Tallahatchie County resident seeking anonymity, interview, May 14, 2004.

93. Ibid., May 18, 2004.

94. Lambright, *Community Organizing for School Reform in the Mississippi Delta*, 15.

95. Ibid.

96. Tallahatchie Education and Redistricting Committee Member requesting anonymity, interview, May 17, 2004.

97. Ibid.

98. Ibid.

99. Lambright, *Community Organizing for School Reform in the Mississippi Delta*, 15.

100. Ibid.

101. Ibid., 5.

102. Tallahatchie Education and Redistricting Committee Member requesting anonymity, interview, May 17, 2004.

103. Lambright, *Community Organizing for School Reform in the Mississippi Delta*, 16.

104. Ibid.

105. Ibid.

106. Ibid.

107. Tallahatchie Education and Redistricting Committee Member requesting anonymity, interview, May 17, 2004.

108. Lambright, *Community Organizing for School Reform in the Mississippi Delta*, 23.

109. Tallahatchie Education and Redistricting Committee Member requesting anonymity, interview, May 17, 2004.

110. Lambright, *Community Organizing for School Reform in the Mississippi Delta*, 24.

111. Ross Gittell and J. Phillip Thompson, "Making Social Capital Work: Social Capital and Community Economic Development," in *Social Capital and Poor Communities*, eds. Susan Saegert and Mark R. Warren (New York: Russell Sage Foundation, 2001), 120–122.

112. De Tocqueville, *Democracy in America*, 522.

113. Putnam, "Tuning In, Tuning Out: The Strange Disappearance of Civic America," *PS: Political Science and Politics* 28, 4 (December 1995).

114. Laura Parker, author of several articles on school disparities in the Mississippi Delta requesting anonymity, interview, December 3, 1999.

115. Ibid.

116. Bryan Gruley, "Mississippi's Prison-Building Spree Creates Glut of Lockups and Struggle for Convicts," *Wall Street Journal Internet Edition*, September 6, 2001, 2.

117. James Dunn, Member of the Tunica County Board of Supervisors, interview, April 30, 2004.

118. Clay Harden, "Road to Casino Work Long, Taxing for Many Deltans," *Clarion-Ledger Internet Edition*, January 13, 2003, 1.

119. Mississippi Delta elected official requesting anonymity, interview, April 29, 2004.

120. Guillame Debre, "Town Needs Revitalizing? Build a Prison. The 'Not in My Backyard' Attitude Is Largely Gone: Prisons Mean Jobs, Infrastructure, and Investment," *Christian Science Monitor Internet Edition*, April 5, 2000, 2.

121. John Butch, "Poor Counties See Inmates as Ticket to Freedom," *Clarion Ledger Internet Edition*, December 20, 1999, 1.

122. Ibid., 3.

123. Ted Evanoff, "Delta's Manufacturing Base Needs New Technology, Employee Skills," *Commercial Appeal Internet Edition*, October 14, 1990, 2.

124. Mississippi Legislature 2001 Regular Session. House Bill 1652.

125. Anonymous, *Education v. Incarceration: A Mississippi Case Study*, Research Report (Charlotte, NC: Grassroots Leadership, 2001), 3.

126. Otey Sherman, Tallahatchie County, Mississippi Industrial Development Authority, interview, May 4, 2004.

127. Peter T. Kilborn, "Delta Town's Hopes Are as Scarce as Inmates," *New York Times Internet Edition*, November 24, 2001, 2.

128. Mr. Otey Sherman, Tallahatchie County, Mississippi Industrial Development Authority, interview, May 4, 2004.

129. Peter T. Kilborn, "Delta Town's Hopes Are as Scarce as Inmates," *New York Times Internet Edition*, November 24, 2001, 2.

130. Otey Sherman, Tallahatchie County, Mississippi Industrial Development Authority, interview, May 4, 2004.

131. Andy Kanengiser, "Tutwiler Prison Survives, to Take Hawaiian Inmates," *Clarion-Ledger Internet Edition*, January 28, 2004, 2.

132. Tonyia Rawls, "$45 Million to Mississippi Private Prisons at Expense of Educational Spending," Unpublished paper, http://grassrootsleadership.org, 1.

133. Ibid., 2.

Chapter 7

1. Albert B. Nylander III, *Rural Community Leadership Structures in Two Delta Communities*, PhD diss., Mississippi State University, 1998.

2. Richard I. Zweigenhaft and G. William Domhoff, *Diversity in the Power Elite: House Women and Minorities Reached the Top* (New Haven: Yale University Press, 1998).

3. H. Paul Friesema, "Black Control of Central Cities: The Hollow Prize," *American Institute of Planners Journal* 35 (March 1969): 75–79.

4. C. Wright Mills, *The Power Elite* (London: Oxford University Press, 1956), 3–4.

5. Rufus Browning, Dale Rogers Marshall, and David Tabb, "Can People of Color Achieve Power in City Government?" in *Racial Politics in American Cities*, 2d ed., eds. Browning, Marshall, and Tabb (New York: Longman, 1997), 8.

6. Lawrence J. Hanks, *The Struggle for Black Political Empowerment in Three Georgia Counties* (Knoxville: University of Tennessee Press, 1987).

7. G. William Domhoff, *Who Rules America?* (Englewood Cliffs, NJ: Prentice-Hall, 1992); James H. Meisel, *The Myth of the Ruling Class: Gaetano*

Mosca and the "Elite": With the First English Translation of the Final Version of the Theory of the Ruling Class (Ann Arbor: University of Michigan Press, 1962); Roberto Michels, *Political Parties: A Sociological Study of the Oligarchical Tradition of Modern Democracy* (New York: Dover, 1959); Mills, *Power Elite*; Gaetano Mosca, *The Ruling Class* (New York: McGraw-Hill, 1939); V. Pareto

8. John Gaventa, *Power and the Powerlessness: Quiescence and Rebellion in an Appalachian Valley* (Urbana: University of Illinois Press, 1980), 9; EE Schattschneider, *The Semi-Sovereign People: A Realist's View of Democracy in America* (New York: Holt, 1960), 105.

9. Shelia Hardwell Byrd, "After 7 Years, Few in Delta Zone Feel Empowered," *Memphis Commercial Appeal Internet Edition*, June 24, 2001, 1; Mario Rossilli, "A Laboratory of Program after Program, Promise after Promise," *Clarion Ledger Internet Edition*, December 19, 1999, 4.

APPENDIX A

QUESTIONS FOR POLITICAL FIGURES
AND COMMUNITY ACTIVISTS

Has an African American mayor ever been elected in your town?

Has an African American mayoral candidate ever made a credible bid
for the mayor's office (almost won)?

Do African Americans serve on the town's aldermanic board?
If so, when was the first black alderman elected?

Do African Americans serve on the county board of supervisors?
If so, when were they elected?

Are there any other powerful African American politicians?

Does Tunica County's lack of political power contribute to the remaining high poverty rates?

Why is there so much poverty in the Delta?

Should current race relations be classified as good or strained? Why?

Have African Americans and white community residents worked together on any community development projects? Why or why not?

Who are the most influential business-people?

Who are the most influential families?

Who are the most influential politicians?

Do the members of the wealthiest families determine the winners of local offices?

Have the members of the wealthiest families exhibited any opposition to black political officeholding?

Have the members of the wealthiest families exhibited any opposition to initiatives favored by black politicians to uplift black low-income residents?

What have been the greatest obstacles for black candidates in local and countywide elections?

Do African American voters have a high turnout in local elections? Why or why not?

Are there any influential black political or community development organizations in the town and county?
How long have they existed and what activities have they been involved in?
How successful have they been in "getting what they want"?

What role have churches played in mobilizing African Americans for political or community activism?

What was the role of the mayor and other political figures in bringing casinos to Delta counties?

What benefits has your county received from legalized gaming?

In what ways have the poorest residents benefited from gaming?

Have landowning elites opposed any measures to use gaming revenues to benefit the poor?

Why did such a high poverty rate remain after gaming delivered millions of revenues into the state and into the Delta region?

What other industries have been pursued (other than the gaming industry) in your county?

If your town or county is pursuing prisons as a strategy for economic development, why is this the case?

APPENDIX B

QUESTIONS FOR COMMUNITY ACTIVISTS
AND SCHOOL BOARD MEMBERS

What percentage of revenues is devoted to public schools?

What are most of the revenues being used for?

How many public schools are there?

What is their racial makeup and overall condition?

How many school board members are there?

What is the racial makeup of the school board?

Which issues are the most divisive for school board members and community residents?

In Tunica County, what are the goals of the Concerned Citizens for a Better Tunica County?

Who are its leaders?

Why was it formed and when?

Why do they oppose the new elementary school's location?

How have they mobilized Tunica County residents to fight the location?

Have they solicited assistance from national or regional organizations, or from national political figures?

What other industries have been pursued (other than the gaming industry) in your county?

If your town or county is pursuing prisons as a strategy for economic development, why is this the case?

Why is there so much poverty in the Delta?

Should current race relations be classified as good or strained? Why?

Have African Americans and white community residents worked together on any community development projects? Why or why not?

APPENDIX C

QUESTIONS FOR FORMER AND CURRENT MISSISSIPPI DELTA RESIDENTS

What were conditions like in Mississippi during the era of segregation?

What was a typical workday for a sharecropper?

How were sharecroppers kept indebted?

Who were the most influential business-people?

Who were the most influential families?

Who were the most influential politicians?

How did business-people and politicians maintain the status quo?

Did the members of wealthy landowning families exhibit any opposition to black political officeholding?

Did the members of wealthy landowning families exhibit any opposition to initiatives to uplift black low-income residents?

What were the greatest obstacles for black candidates in local and countywide elections?

What community empowerment organizations exist in your county? Are you a member of one? Why or why not?

What political organizations exist in your county?

Are you a member of one?

Which are most effective-community or political organizations?

What benefits have you received from black elected officials?

What disappointments have you had in their leadership?

Would you say that most of the members of the black community trust each other? Work together to accomplish goals? Care about their community?

Why is there so much poverty in the Delta?

Should current race relations be classified as good or strained? Why?

Have African Americans and white community residents worked together on any community development projects? Why or why not?

APPENDIX D

QUESTIONS FOR PLANTATION ELITES AND JOURNALISTS

Are there any other powerful African American politicians?

Who are the most influential business-people?

Who are the most influential families?

Did local elites resist new nonagricultural industries before the legalization of gaming?

How did casino owners convince the members of the wealthiest families, politicians, and citizens that gaming would be advantageous?

What benefits have each of these groups received from gaming?

Have the elites done anything to oppose casino gaming?

Have they made any efforts to keep African Americans from benefiting from gaming revenues?

Does Tunica County's lack of political power contribute to the remaining high poverty rates?

What changes have casino owners and other "outsiders" made in the Delta-that is, threatened the status quo?

What efforts have poor African Americans made to reap more of gaming's benefits?

What substantive benefits have the poor in the Delta gained from gaming?

Why is there so much poverty in the Delta?

Should current race relations be classified as good or strained? Why?

Have African Americans and white community residents worked together on any community development projects? Why or why not?

BIBLIOGRAPHY

Books and Articles

Alex-Assensoh, Yvette. Race, Concentrated Poverty, Social Isolation, and Political Behavior. *Urban Affairs Review* 33, 2 (November 1997): 209–227.

Allen-Smith, Joyce E. "Blacks in Rural America: Socioeconomic Status and Policies to Enhance Economic Well-Being." *Review of Black Political Economy* 22, 4, (Spring 1994): 7–29.

Anonymous, *Education v. Incarceration: A Mississippi Case Study Research Report* (Charlotte, NC: Grassroots Leadership, 2001), 1–5.

Anonymous. *Jackson Daily Clarion-Ledger*, September 11, 1890.

Anonymous. "Looking Ahead: Tunica Residents Remember the Past, Enjoy the Present, and Look Forward to a Bright Future." *Tunica County: 1996* (Tunica, MS: Tunica Chamber of Commerce), 9–14.

Anonymous. "Modern Tunica Has Historic Background: Busy Little Delta City in Romantic Area." *Memphis Commercial Appeal* January 1, 1940.

Anonymous. "The Mississippi Delta: The Government's Plantations." *The Economist* 324, 7767 (July 11, 1992): 26.

The Associated Press. "Delta Still Sings the Blues after Speech." *Memphis Commercial Appeal Internet Edition*, January 29, 2000, 1–2.

Bass, Jack and Walter DeVries. *The Transformation of Southern Politics: Social Change and Politics Consequence since 1945* (New York: Basic, 1976).

Blair, John P. *Local Economic Development: Analysis and Practice* (Thousand Oaks, CA: Sage Publications, 1995).

Blevins, Audie and Katherine Jensen. "Gambling as a Community Development Quick Fix." *ANNALS: American Academy of Political and Social Science* 556 (March 1998): 109–123.

Branston, John. "A Tale of Two Cities." *Memphis Magazine* 21, 4 (July/August 1996): 24–29, 50.

Brown, Riva. "Racial Divisions Deep; Is There Hope?" *Clarion Ledger Internet Edition,* December 23, 1999, 1–7.

Browning, Rufus, Dale Rogers Marshall, and David Tabb. "Can People of Color Achieve Power in City Government? The Setting and the Issues." In *Racial Politics in American Cities, 2d ed.,* eds. Browning, Marshall, and Tabb (New York: Longman, 1997), 3–14.

Ibid., "Mobilization, Incorporation, and Policy in Ten California Cities." In *Racial Politics in American Cities, 2d ed.,* eds. Browning, Marshall, and Tabb (New York: Longman, 1997), 15–37.

Ibid., *Protest Is Not Enough: The Struggle of Blacks and Hispanics for Equality in Urban Politics* (Berkeley: University of California Press, 1984).

Butch, John. "Lack of Direction Stymies Delta: Shift in Racial Power Has Yet to Produce Unity in Leadership." *Clarion-Ledger,* December 23, 1999, A1.

Ibid., "Pockets of Success Overshadowed by Staggering Poverty." *Clarion-Ledger,* December 19, 1999, 1-11.

Button, James W. *Blacks and Social Change: The Impact of the Civil Rights Movement in Southern Communities* (Princeton: Princeton University Press, 1989).

Carlson, James M. and Mark S. Hyde. *Doing Empirical Political Research* (Boston: Houghton Mifflin Company, 2003).

Cobb, James C. *The Most Southern Place on Earth: The Mississippi Delta and the Roots of Regional Identity* (New York: Oxford University Press, 1992).

Cohen, Cathy J. "Social Capital, Intervening Institutions, and Political Power." In *Social Capital and Poor Communities,* eds. Susan Saegert, J. Phillip Thompson, and Mark R. Warren (New York: Russell Sage Foundation, 2001), 267–289.

Coleman, James S. *Foundations of Social Theory* (Cambridge: Harvard University Press, 1990).

Coleman, Mary DeLorse. *Legislators, Law and Public Policy: Political Change in Mississippi and the South* (Westport, CT: Greenwood Press, 1993).

Conrad, David Eugene. *The Forgotten Farmers: The Story of Sharecroppers in the New Deal* (Urbana: University of Illinois Press, 1965).

Corcoran, Mary. "Rags to Rags: Poverty and Mobility in the United States." *Annual Review of Sociology* 21 (1995): 237–267.

Cortes Jr., Ernesto. "Reweaving the Fabric: The Iron Rule and the I.A.F. Strategy for Power and Politics." In *Interwoven Destinies,* ed. Henry G. Cisneros (New York: Norton, 1993), 294–319.

Cotton, C. Richard. "Casinos Paying Off for Tunica's Schools." *Memphis Commercial Appeal,* April 4, 1996, A1.

Cotton, Jeremiah. "Towards a Theory and Strategy for Black Economic Development." In *Race, Politics, and Economic Development* (New York: Verso Press, 1992), 11–31.

Dahl, Robert A. "A Critique of the Ruling Elite Model" *American Political Science Review* 52 (June 1958): 463–469.

Ibid., *Who Governs: Democracy and Power in an American City* (New Haven: Yale University Press, 1961).

Danzinger, Sheldon and Ann Chih Lin. *Coping with Poverty: The Social Context of Neighborhood, Work, and Family in the African American Community* (Ann Arbor: University of Michigan Press, 2000).

Davis, Theodore J. Jr. "Black Political Representation in Rural Mississippi." In *Blacks in Southern Politics,* eds. Laurence W. Moreland, Robert P. Steed, and Tod A. Baker (New York: Praeger Publishers, 1987), 149–159.

De Tocqueville, Alexis. *Democracy in America* Edited by JP Mayer. Translated by George Lawrence (New York: Anchor Books, 1839; 1969).

Debre', Guillaume. "Town Needs Revitalizing? Build a Prison. The 'Not in My Backyard' Attitude Is Largely Gone: Prisons Mean Jobs, Infrastructure, and Investment." *Christian Science Monitor Internet Edition,* April 5, 2000, 1–3.

Devine, JA and JD Wright. *The Greatest Evils: Urban Poverty and the American Underclass* (New York: Aldine De Gruyter, 1993).

Dickie, Kaye. "Hallelujah! Sour Alley Turns Sweet: Sugar Ditch Looking Up." *Memphis Commercial Appeal,* January 11, 1986, A1, A4.

Dittmer, John. *Local People: The Struggle for Civil Rights in Mississippi* (Urbana: University of Illinois Press, 1995).

Dolbeare, Kenneth and Murray Edelman. *American Politics, 3rd ed.* (Lexington, MA: Heath, 1971).

Domhoff, G. William. *The Higher Circles.* (New York: Vintage Books, 1971).

Ibid., *Who Rules America?* (Englewood Cliffs, NJ: Prentice-Hall, 1992).

Duncan, Cynthia M. "Social Capital in America's Poor Rural Communities." In *Social Capital and Poor Communities,* eds. Susan Saegert, J. Philip Thompson, and Mark R. Warren (New York: Russell Sage Foundation, 2001), 60–86.

Duncan, Cynthia M. *Worlds Apart: Why Poverty Persists in Rural America* (New Haven, CT: Yale University Press, 1999).

Eisinger, Peter K. *The Politics of Displacement: Racial and Ethnic Transition in Three American Cities* (New York: Academic Press, 1980).

Erie, Steven P. "Big-City Rainbow Politics: Machines Revividus?" In *The Politics of Urban America: A Reader*, eds. Dennis R. Judd and Paul P. Kantor (Needham Heights, MA: Allyn and Bacon, 1998), 106–121.

Evanoff, Ted. "Delta's Manufacturing Base Needs New Technology, Employee Skills." *Commercial Appeal Internet Edition*, October 14, 1990, 1–4.

Faust, Fred. "Hard-Luck Southern Casino Bets Its Future on Casinos." *St. Louis Post-Dispatch*, May 15, 1995, 12BP–15BP.

Fletcher, William and Eugene Newport. "Race and Economic Development: The Need for a Black Agenda." In *Race, Politics, and Economic Development*, ed. James B. Jennings (New York: Verso Press, 1992), 117–130.

Friesema, H. Paul. "Black Control of Central Cities: The Hollow Prize." *American Institute of Planners Journal* 35 (March 1969): 75–79.

Furuseth, Owen. "Uneven Social and Economic Development." In *Contemporary Rural Systems in Transition. Vol 2, Economy and Society*, eds. IR Bowler, CR Bryant, and MD Nellis (London: CAB International, 1992), 17–28.

Gabris, Gerald. "The Dynamics of Mississippi Local Government." In *Mississippi Government and Politics: Modernizers Versus Traditionalists*, eds. Dale Krane and Stephen D. Shaffer (Lincoln: University of Nebraska Press, 1992), 223–248.

Galston, William A. and Karen J. Baehler. *Rural Development in the United States: Connecting Theory, Practice and Possibilities* (Washington, DC: Island Press, 1995).

Gaventa, John. *Power and the Powerlessness: Quiescence and Rebellion in an Appalachian Valley* (Urbana: University of Illinois Press, 1980).

Gittell Marilyn, Isolda Ortega-Bustamente, and Tracy Steffy. "Social Capital and Social Change: Women's Community Activism" *Urban Affairs Review* 36, 2 (November 2000): 123–147.

Gittell, Marilyn, Kathe Newman, Janice Brockmeyer, and Robert Lindsay. "Expanding Civic Opportunity Urban Empowerment Zones" *Urban Affairs Review* 33, 4 (March 1998): 530–558.

Gittell, Ross and Avis Vidal. *Community Organizing: Building Social Capital as a Development Strategy* (New York: Sage Publications), 1998.

Gittell, Ross and J. Phillip Thompson. "Making Social Capital Work: Social Capital and Community Economic Development." In *Social Capital and Poor Communities*, eds. Susan Saegert, Thompson, and Mark R. Warren (New York: Russell Sage Foundation, 2001), 115135.

Glover, Glenda and J. Paul Brownridge. *Enterprise Zones.* In *Economic Development in Local Government: A Handbook for Public Officials and Citizens,* ed. Roger L. Kemp (Jefferson, NC: McFarland and Company, 1995), 181–186.

Gnuschke, John. "The Future of Casino Gambling in Tunica County." *Business Perspectives* 11, 4 (Summer 1999): 2–5.

Goldsmith,WW and EJ Blakely. *Separate Societies: Poverty and Inequality in U.S. Cities* (Philadelphia: Temple University Press, 1992).

Goodman, Robert. *The Luck Business: The Devastating Consequences and Broken Promises of America's Gambling Explosion* (New York: Free Press, 1995).

Granovetter, Mark S. "The Strength of Weak Ties." *American Journal of Sociology* 78, 6 (May 1973): 1360–1380.

Greenberg, Pam. "Not Quite the Pot of Gold." *State Legislatures* 18 (December 1992): 24–27.

Gruley, Bryan. "Mississippi's Prison-Building Spree Creates Glut of Lockups and Struggle for Convicts." *Wall Street Journal Internet Edition,* September 6, 2001, 1–8.

Hacker, Andrew. *Two Nations, Black and White, Separate, Hostile, Unequal* (New York: Andrew, Scribners, 1992).

Hanks, Lawrence J. *The Struggle for Black Politics Empowerment in Three Georgia Counties* (Knoxville: University of Tennessee Press, 1987).

Harden, Clay. "Road to Casino Work Long, Taxing for Many Deltans." *Clarion-Ledger Internet Edition,* January 13, 2003, 1–4.

Harding, Alan. "Elite Theory and Growth Machines." In *Theories of Urban Politics,* eds. David Judge, Gerry Stoker, and Harold Wolman (Thousand Oaks, CA: Sage Publications, 1995), 35-53.

Harris, William C. *The Day of the Carpetbagger: Republican Reconstruction in Mississippi* (Baton Rouge: Louisiana State University Press, 1979).

Hathom, Clay. "Tunica Begins Year's Celebration." *Memphis Commercial Appeal* March 3, 1988.

Havard, William C. ed. *The Changing Politics of the South* (Baton Rouge: Louisiana State University Press, 1972).

Hicks, Bill and Joseph B. Parker. "Local Government in Mississippi." In *Politics in Mississippi.* 2d ed., ed. Joseph B. Parker (Salem, WI: Sheffield Publishing Company, 2001), 181–202.

Hirschman, Albert O. *Exit, Voice and Loyalty: Responses to Declines in Firms, Organizations, and States* (Cambridge: Harvard University Press, 1972).

Holloway, Harry. *The Politics of the Southern Negro: From Exclusion to Big City Organization* (New York: Random, 1969).

Holtzclaw, Robert Fulton. *Black Magnolias: A Brief History of the Afro-Mississippian, 1865–1980* (Shaker Heights: Keeble Press, 1984).

Howland, Marie. "Applying Theory to Practice in Rural Economies." In *Theories of Local Economic Development: Perspectives from across the Disciplines*, eds. Richard D. Bingham and Robert Meier (Newbury Park, NY: Sage Publications, 1993).

Hunter, Floyd. *Community Power Structure* (Chapel Hill: University of North Carolina Press, 1953).

Jenkins, Joseph Craig and Charles Perrow. "Insurgency of the Powerless: Farm Worker Movements (1946–1972)." *American Sociological Review* 42, 2 (1977): 248–268.

Jennings, James B. and Mel King. *From Access to Power: Black Politics in Boston* (Cambridge: Schenkman Books, 1983).

Jennings, James B. *Race, Politics, and Economic Development* (New York: Verso Press, 1992).

John, Butch. "Lack of Direction Stymies Delta: Shift in Racial Power Has Yet to Produce Unity in Leadership," *Clarion Ledger*, December 23, 1999, A1–3.

John, Butch. "Poor Counties See Inmates as Ticket to Freedom," *Clarion Ledger Internet Edition*, December 20, 1999, 1–3.

Joint Center for Political and Economic Studies. *Black Elected Officials: A National Roster, 1991; 20th ed.* (Washington, DC: Joint Center for Political and Economic Studies, 1992).

Ibid., *1993; 21st ed.* (Washington, DC: Joint Center for Political and Economic Studies, 1994).

Jones, Mack H. "Black Political Empowerment in Atlanta: Myth and Reality" *Annals of the American Academy of Political and Social Sciences* 439 (September 1978): 90–117.

Ibid., "The Black Underclass as a Systemic Phenomenon." In *Race, Politics, and Economic Development* (New York: Verso Press, 1992), 53–65.

Judd, Dennis R. and Todd Swanstrom. *City Politics: Private Power and Public Policy* (New York: HarperCollins College Publishers, 1994).

Judge, David. "Pluralism." In *Theories of Urban Politics*, eds. David Judge, Gerry Stoker, and Harold Wolman (Thousand Oaks, CA: Sage Publications, 1995), 13–34.

Kanengiser, Andy. "Tutwiler Prison Survives, to Take Hawaiian Inmates." *Clarion-Ledger Internet Edition*, January 28, 2004, 1–3.

Kelley, Brian. "Rebuilding Rural America: The Southern Development Bancorporation." *Annals of the American Academy of Political and Social Science* 529 (September, 1993): 113–127.

Kelley, Richard. "Casinos Helping Upgrade Tunica Infrastructure." *Memphis Commercial Appeal*, November 30, 1993, A8.

Ibid., "Gambling Puts Tunica on Path for Change." *Memphis Commercial Appeal*, October 18, 1992, A1, A22.

Kemp, Roger L., ed. *Economic Development in Local Government: A Handbook for Public Officials and Citizens* (Jefferson, NC: McFarland and Company, 1995).

Key, VO *Southern Politics in State and Nation* (New York: Knopf, 1950).

Kilborn, Peter T. "Delta Town's Hopes Are as Scarce as Inmates." *New York Times Internet Edition*, (November 24, 2001) 1–4.

Kirwan, Albert D. *Revolt of the Rednecks: Mississippi Politics, 1876–1925* (Lexington: University of Kentucky Press, 1951).

Kittredge, Kevin. "Tunica: 'Nothing Like It': 'A National Tragedy Congressman States." *Memphis Commercial Appeal*, July 20, 1985, A1, A4.

Kraus, Neil J. *Race, Neighborhoods, and Community Power, Buffalo Politics, 1934–1997* (Albany: State University of New York Press, 2000).

Larsen, Michael D. "Gaming Industry Development: A Comparison of Three States." *Economic Development Review* 13, 4 (Fall 1995): 4–8.

Levine, Marc V. "Downtown Redevelopment as an Urban Growth Strategy: A Critical Appraisal of the Baltimore Renaissance." *Journal of Urban Affairs* 9, 2 (1987): 103–123.

Loury, Glenn C. "Why Should We Care about Group Inequality?" *Social Philosophy and Policy* 5 (Autumn 1987): 249–271.

Lyson, Thomas A. "Economic Development in the Rural South: An Uneven Past-An Uncertain Future." In *The Rural South in Crisis: Challenges for the Future*, ed. Lionel J. Beaulieu (Boulder, CO: Westview Press, 1988).

McCarthy, John D. and Mayer N. Zald. *The Trend of Social Movements in America: Professionalization and Resource Mobilization* (Morristown, NJ: General Learning Press), 1973.

McMillen, Neil R. *Dark Journey: Black Mississippians in the Age of Jim Crow* (Urbana-Champaign: University of Illinois Press, 1989).

Mabry, William Alexander. "Disfranchisement of the Negro in Mississippi." *Journal of Southern History* 4 (1938): 318–333.

Madhusudan, Ranjana G. "Betting on Casino Revenues: Lessons from State Experiences" *National Tax Journal* 49 (September 1996): 401–412.

Massey, DS and NA Denton. *American Apartheid: Segregation and the Making of the Underclass* (Cambridge: Harvard University Press, 1993).

Matthews, Donald R. and James W. Protho. *Negroes and the New Southern Politics* (New York: Harcourt, Brace, and World, 1966).

Mayer, Leo V. "Agricultural Change and Rural America" *Annals of the American Academy of Political and Social Science* 529 (September, 1993): 79–91.

Meisel, James H. *The Myth of the Ruling Class: Gaetano Mosca and the 'Elite': With the First English Translation of the Final Version of the Theory of the Ruling Class* (Ann Arbor: University of Michigan Press, 1962).

Meyer-Arendt, Klaus. "Casino Gaming in Mississippi: Location, Location, Location." *Economic Development Review* 13, 4 (Fall 1995): 27–33.

Michels, Roberto. *Political Parties: A Sociological Study of the Oligarchical Tradition of Modern Democracy* (New York: Dover, 1959).

Mollenkopf, John. *The Contested City* (Princeton: Princeton University Press, 1983).

Morrison, Minion K. C. *Black Political Mobilization* (Albany: State University of New York Press, 1985).

Ibid., "Preconditions for Afro-American Leadership: Three Mississippi Towns." *Polity* 17: 3 (Spring 1985): 504–529.

Mosca, Gaetano. *The Ruling Class* (New York: McGraw-Hill, 1939).

Moyser, George and Margaret Wagstaffe. "Studying Elites: Theoretical and Methodological Issues." In *Research Methods for Elite Studies*, eds. George Moyser and Margaret Wagstaffe (London: Allen and Unwin, 1987), 1-24.

Nadel, Siegfried Frederick. "The Concept of Social Elites." *International Social Science Bulletin* 8, 3 (1956): 413–424.

Nelson Jr., William E. *Black Atlantic Politics: Dilemmas of Power Empowerment in Boston and Liverpool* (Albany: State University of New York Press, 2000).

Newman, Katherine S. *No Shame in My Game: The Working Poor in the Inner-City* (New York: Knopf and Russell Sage Foundation, 1999).

Oberschall, Anthony. "The Los Angeles Riot of August 1965." In *The Black Revolt*, ed. James A. Geschwender (Englewood Cliffs, NJ: Prentice-Hall, 1971), 264–284.

Ochrym, Ronald G. "Gambling in Atlantic City: The 'Grand Vision' Blurs." *National Civic Review* (December 1983): 591–596.

Orr, Marion E. *Black Social Capital: The Politics of School Reform in Baltimore,* 1986-1998 (Lawrence: University Press of Kansas, 1999).

Ownby, Ted. *American Dreams in Mississippi: Consumers, Poverty, and Culture, 1830–1998* (Chapel Hill: University of North Carolina Press, 1999).

Parenti, Michael. *Democracy for the Few: 2d ed.* New York: St. Martin's, 1977).

Ibid., "Power and Pluralism: A View from the Bottom" *Journal of Politics* 32 (1970): 501–530.

Pareto, V. *The Mind and Society* (London: Cape, 1935).

Parker, Frank R. *Black Votes Count: Political Empowerment in Mississippi after 1965* (Chapel Hill: University of North Carolina Press, 1990).

Parker, Laura. "Abandoned Education: Tunica's Schools Struggle with Leftovers and Neglect." *APF Reporter* 18, 2 (1997): 17–22.

Payne, Charles M. *I've Got the Light of Freedom: The Organizing Tradition and the Mississippi Freedom Struggle* (Berkeley: University of California at Berkeley Press, 1995).

Pelissero, John P. David B. Holian, and Laura A. Tomaka. "Does Political Incorporation Matter?: The Impact of Minority Mayors over Time." *Urban Affairs Review* 36, 1 (September 2000): 84–92.

Perlman, Ellen. "Gambling, Mississippi Style." *Governing Magazine* 8, 7 (April 1995): 40.

Pinderhughes, Dianne M. *Race and Ethnicity in Chicago Politics: A Re-Examination of Pluralist Theory* (Urbana: University of Illinois Press, 1987).

Polsby, Nelson. *Community Power and Political Theory* (New Haven: Yale University Press, 1963).

Popkin, James. "A Mixed Blessing for 'America's Ethiopia.'" *U.S. News and World Report,* March 14, 1994, 52–54.

Portney, Kent E., and Jeffrey M. Berry. "Mobilizing Minority Communities: Social Capital and Participation in Urban Neighborhoods." *American Behavioral Scientist* 40, 5 (March/April 1997): 632–644.

Powell-Jackson, Bernice. "Gambling on Poverty in America." *Michigan Chronicle,* February 7, 1996, 6A.

Pressman, Jeffrey L. "Preconditions of Mayoral Leadership." *American Political Science Review* 66 (June 1972): 511–524.

Putnam, Robert D. "Bowling Alone: America's Declining Social Capital." *Journal of Democracy* 6 (1995a): 65–78.

Ibid., *Making Democracy Work: Civic Traditions in Modern Italy* (Princeton: Princeton University Press, 1993).

Ibid., "Tuning In, Tuning Out: The Strange Disappearance of Social Capital in America." *PS: Political Science and Politics Internet Edition* 28, 4 (December 1995): 1–23.

Reid, Bruce. "Future of Farming on Shaky Ground." *Clarion-Ledger,* December 20, 1999, 1.

Reid, Bruce and John Butch. "Cotton, Catfish, Cells, Casinos: Delta Struggling to Find Profitable Economic Identity." *Clarion-Ledger Internet Edition,* December 20, 1999, 1–3.

Rich, Wilbur C. "The Politics of Casino Gambling: Detroit Style." *Urban Affairs Quarterly* 26, 2 (December 1990): 274–298.

Rosenfeld, Stuart A. "The Tale of Two Souths." In *The Rural South in Crisis: Challenges for the Future,* ed. Lionel J. Beaulieu (Boulder, CO: Westview Press, 1988), 279–296.

Rossilli, Mario. "A Laboratory of Program after Program, Promise After Promise." *Clarion Ledger Internet Edition,* December 19, 1999, 1–5.

Rubenstein, Joseph. "Casino Gambling in Atlantic City: Issues of Development and Redevelopment." *Annals of the American Academy of Political and Social Science* 474 (July 1984): 61–71.

Salter, Sid. "Democratic Republican Strategists Are All Plotting How to Win Mississippi's Rural Vote: Study Shows Rural Women Voters Are Deciding Election Winners" *Clarion Ledger Internet Edition,* January 19, 2003, 1–4.

Saunders, John. "A Demography of the Delta." In *A Social and Economic Portrait of the Mississippi Delta,* eds. Arthur G. Cosby, Mitchell W. Brackin, T. David Mason, and Eunice R. McCulloch (Mississippi State, MS: Mississippi State University Social Science Research Center, Mississippi Agricultural and Forestry Experiment Station, 1992).

Schattschneider, EE *The Semi-Sovereign People: A Realist's View of Democracy in America* (New York: Holt, Rinehart, and Winston, 1960).

Schwarz, Benjamin and Christina Schwarz. "Mississippi Monte Carlo." *Atlantic Monthly* 277, 1 (January 1996): 67–82.

Shaffer, Stephen D. and Dale Krane. "The Origins and Evolution of a Traditionalistic Society." In *Mississippi Government and Politics: Modernizers versus Traditionalists,* eds. Dale Krane and Stephen D. Shaffer (Lincoln: University of Nebraska Press, 1992), 24–42.

Ibid., "Tradition versus Modernity in Mississippi Politics." In *Mississippi Government and Politics: Modernizers Versus Traditionalists*, edited by Dale Krane and Stephen D. Shaffer (Lincoln: University of Nebraska Press, 1992), 270–288.

Silver, James W. *Mississippi: The Closed Society* (New York: Harcourt, Brace, and World, 1963, 1964, and 1966).

Slater, Courtenay M. and George E. Hall, eds. "States and Counties: Poverty, Housing, and Disability." In *1993 County and City Extra. Annual Metro, City and County Data Book* (Lanham, MD: Bernan Press, 1993).

Stone, Clarence N. "Race and Regime in Atlanta." In *Racial Politics in American Cities, 2d ed.*, edited by Rufus Browning, Dale Rogers Marshall, and David Tabb (New York: Longman, 1997).

Ibid., *Regime Politics: Governing Atlanta, 1946–1988* (Lawrence: University of Kansas Press, 1989).

Sullivan, Bartholomew. "Clinton Talks about Better Days Ahead in Clarksdale." *Memphis Commercial Appeal Internet Edition*, July 7, 1999, 1–3.

Ibid., "On a Roll: Casino Boom Sprays Mississippi with Prosperity." *Memphis Commercial Appeal*, July 24, 1996, A1, A11.

Ibid., "Tunica Landowners Raking in Big Rewards as Values Soar." *Memphis Commercial Appeal*, November 29, 1993, A15.

Tantillo, Charles. *A Unique Tool of Urban Redevelopment: Casino Gambling in Atlantic City* (Rutgers: Center for Urban Policy Research, Rutgers University, 1981).

Verba, Sidney. *Elites and the Idea of Equality: A Comparison of Japan, Sweden, and the United States* (Cambridge: Harvard University Press, 1987).

Von Herrmann, Denise. "Casino Gaming in Mississippi: From Backwater to the Big Time." In *Politics in Mississippi. 2d ed.*, Joseph B. Parker (Salem, WI: Sheffield Publishing Company, 2001), 301–321.

Walker, James V. "Tunica County: 10 Years of Gaming Still Paying Off." *Jackson Clarion-Ledger*, February 19, 2002.

Warren, Mark R. *Dry Bones Rattling: Community Building to Revitalize American Democracy* (Princeton: Princeton University Press, 2001).

Warren, Mark R., J. Phillip Thompson, and Susan Saegert. "The Role of Social Capital in Combating Poverty." In *Social Capital and Poor Communities*, eds. Susan Saegert, J. Phillip Thompson, and Mark R. Warren (New York: Russell Sage Foundation, 2001), 1–28.

Wharton, Vernon Lane. *The Negro in Mississippi, 1865–1980* (New York: Harper, 1947).

Wilson, William Julius. *The New Urban Poverty and the Problem, of Race* (Ann Arbor, MI: University of Michigan Press, 1993).

Ibid., *The Truly Disadvantaged: The Inner City, the Underclass, and Public Policy* (Chicago: University of Chicago Press, 1987).

Ibid., *When Work Disappears: The World of the New Urban Poor* (New York: Knopf, 1996).

Wirt, Frederick M. *The Politics of Southern Equality* (Chicago: Aldine, 1970).

Ibid., *We Ain't What We Was: Civil Rights in the New South* (Durham, NC: Duke University Press, 1997).

Woodruff, Nan Elizabeth. "Mississippi Delta Planters and Debates over Mechanization, Labor, and Civil Rights in the 1940s." *Journal of Southern History* 60, 2 (May 1994): 263–284.

Ibid., "Pick or Fight: The Emergency Farm Labor Program in the Arkansas and Mississippi Deltas during World War II." *Agricultural History* 64 (Spring 1990): 74–85.

Woods, Clyde. *Development Arrested: The Blues and Plantation Power in the Mississippi Delta* (New York: Verso Press, 1998).

Wright, Sharon D. *Race, Power, and Political Emergence in Memphis* (New York: Garland Publishing, 2000).

Wright, Sharon D. and Richard T. Middleton IV. "Mayor A.J. Holloway and Casino Gambling in Biloxi, Mississippi." In *Governing Middle-Sized Cities: Studies in Mayoral Leadership*, eds. James R. Bowers and Wilbur C. Rich (Boulder, CO: Lynne Rienner Publishers, 2000), 151–166.

Zweigenhaft, Richard I. and G. William Domhoff. *Diversity in the Power Elite: House Women and Minorities Reached the Top* (New Haven: Yale University Press, 1998).

Court Cases

Allen v. State Board of Elections, 393 U.S. 544 (1969).

Alexander v. Holmes, 396 U.S. 19; 90 S.Ct. 29 (1969).

Brown v. Board of Education of Topeka Kansas, 347 U.S. 483 (1954).

Brown v. Board of Education of Topeka Kansas (Brown II), 349 U.S. 294 (1955).

Bunton v. Patterson, 281 F.Supp. 918 (S.D. Miss. 1967) (three-judge court), rev'd sub nom. *Allen v. State Board of Elections*, 393 U.S. 544 (1969).

Connor v. Johnson, 11 Race Rel. L. Rep. 1859 (S.D. Miss.1966).

Fairley v. Patterson, 282 F.Supp. 164 (S.D. Miss. 1967) (three-judge court), rev'd sub nom. *Allen v. State Board of Elections*, 393 U.S. 544 (1969).

Green v. County School Board, 391 U.S. 430 (1968).

Richard Gardner, et al v. Tallahatchie County, Mississippi et al., No. 2:91CV146-EMB (United States District Court for the Northern District of Mississippi Delta Division 1997).

United States v. Duke, 332 F.2d 759 (5th Cir. 1964).

United States of America v. Tunica County School District, 421 F.2d 1236 (1970).

Whitley v. Johnson, 260 F. Supp. 630 (S.D. Miss. 1966) (three-judge court), 296 F. Supp. 630 (S.D. Miss. 1967) (three-judge court) rev'd sub nom. *Allen v. State Board of Elections*, 393 U.S. 544 (1969).

Dissertations, Oral Histories, Theses, and Unpublished Papers

Abusalih, Ali A. *Casinos, Tourism Rejuvenation, and Coastal Landscape Impact Biloxi, Mississippi* (Master's Thesis, Mississippi State University, 1994).

Alewine Jr., Ralph W. "The Changing Characteristics of the Mississippi Delta." *Farm Labor Developments* (Washington, DC: U.S. Department of Labor, May 1968), 32–37.

Anonymous. "Effects of Tourism as a Tool for Rural Economic Development. Hearing before the Subcommittee on Procurement, Taxation and Tourism of the Committee on Small Business." (House of Representatives, 103rd, 1st Sess., October 4, 1993 (Washington, DC: U.S. Government Printing Office: 1994).

Anonymous. "Housing Development and Resegregation: A Report from Activists Working in Tunica County, Mississippi." *Rural Policy Matters: A Newsletter of Rural School and Community Action* 1:6 (July 1999): 1–2.

Anonymous. "Looking Ahead: Tunica Residents Remember the Past, Enjoy the Present, and Look Forward to a Bright Future." (Tunica: Tunica County Chamber of Commerce, 1996), 9–14.

Anonymous. "Testimony of Webster Franklin, Executive Director, Chamber of Commerce, Tunica County, Mississippi before the Small Business Committee" (House of Representatives. 103rd Cong., 2d., September 21, 1994 (Washington, DC: U.S. Government Printing Office, 1994).

BF Smith Foundation. "Farmers Advocating Resource Management: Delta F.A.R.M. Final Report." Unpublished paper (Stoneville, MS: BF Smith Foundation, 2004).

Campbell, Charles, Kathie S. Gilbert, and Paul W. Grimes. "Human Capital: Characteristics of the Labor Force." In *A Social and Economic Portrait of the Mississippi Delta,* eds. Arthur G. Cosby, Mitchell W. Brackin, T. David Mason, and Eunice R. McCulloch (Mississippi State: Mississippi State University Social Science Research Center, Mississippi Agricultural and Forestry Experiment Station, 1992).

Cash, William M. and R. Daryl Lewis. *The Delta Council: Fifty Years of Service to the Mississippi Delta* (Stoneville, MS: Delta Council, 1986).

Delta Council. "Addresses Presented to Delta Council Annual Meeting . . . Cleveland, Mississippi, May 3, 1944, and Resolutions Adopted by Ninth Convention." (Stoneville, MS: Delta Council, 1944).

Ibid., "1998 Delta Council Annual Report." Unpublished report. www.delta council.org.

Ibid., "2000 Delta Council Annual Report." Unpublished report. www.delta council.org.

Ibid., "2001 Delta Council Annual Report." Unpublished report. www.delta council.org.

Ibid., "2002 Delta Council Annual Report." Unpublished report. www.delta council.org.

Ibid., "Delta Council History, 1938–1943" (Stoneville, MS: Delta Council, 1944).

Ibid., "Delta Survey for a Blueprint for New Horizons Submitted to Mississippi Power and Light Company" (Stoneville, MS: Delta Council, April 1, 1944).

Edgell, David L. "Testimony before the Subcommittee on Procurement, Taxation, and Tourism of the U.S. House of Representatives Committee on Small Business" (Washington, DC: U.S. Department of Commerce, October 4, 1993), 1–16.

Forgotson, CB. "In the Big Easy." In *Forum for Applied Research and Public Policy: A Publication of the University of Tennessee Energy, Environment and Resources Center and Oak Ridge National Laboratory* 11 (Summer 1996): 105–106.

Franklin, Webster. "Along the Mississippi." In *Forum for Applied Research and Public Policy: A Publication of the University of Tennessee Energy, Environment and Resources Center and Oak Ridge National Laboratory* 11 (Summer 1996): 106–108.

Gist, Sylvia Reedy. *Educating a Southern Rural Community: The Case of Blacks in Holmes County, Mississippi, 1870 to Present, Vols. 1 and 2.* PhD dissertation, University of Chicago, 1994.

Gray-Ray, Phyllis. "Race Relations in the Delta." In *A Social and Economic Portrait of the Mississippi Delta*, eds. Arthur G. Cosby, Mitchell W. Brackin, T. David Mason, and Eunice R. McCulloch (Mississippi State: Mississippi State University Social Science Research Center, Mississippi Agricultural and Forestry Experiment Station, 1992), 29–94.

Grisham, Vaughn L. Jr. "Leadership in the Mississippi Delta." In *A Social and Economic Portrait of the Mississippi Delta*, eds., Arthur G. Cosby, Mitchell W. Brackin, T. David Mason, and Eunice R. McCulloch (Mississippi State: Mississippi State University Social Science Research Center, Mississippi Agricultural and Forestry Experiment Station, 1992), 179–191.

Gustke, Larry D. *Improving Rural Tourism Extension and Research in the South, Final Report Submitted to H. Doss Brodnax Jr., Director, Southern Rural Development Center, March 29, 1993*, 1–15.

Hair, Penda. *Louder than Words: Lawyers, Communities and the Struggle for Justice* Unpublished report (Mahwah, NJ: Rockefeller Foundation, 2004).

Hearings before the Senate Special Committee to Investigate Senatorial Campaign Expenditures, 79th Con., 2d sess. 350 (1946).

Heberle, R. and Udell Jolley. "Mississippi Backwater Study–Yazoo Segment: Report on Social Factors." Unpublished report, November 10, 1940.

Hoppe, RA "Economic Structure and Change in Persistently Low-Income Nonmetro Counties." In *Rural Development Research Report 50* (Washington, DC: Economic Research Service, U.S. Department of Agriculture, 1985).

Joint Center for Political and Economic Studies. "Black Elected Officials Roster of Mississippi Black Elected Officials-Latest Data-May 2004-Joint Center.xls." Unpublished report (Washington, DC, 2004).

Jones, Reid, John Thornell, and Gene Hamon. "Educational Attainment in the Delta." In *A Social and Economic Portrait of the Mississippi Delta*, eds. Arthur G. Cosby, Mitchell W. Brackin, T. David Mason, and Eunice R. McCulloch (Mississippi State: Mississippi State University Social Science Research Center, Mississippi Agricultural and Forestry Experiment Station, 1992), 90–103.

Karahan, Gokhan R., Laura Razzolini, and William F. Shughart II. "No Pretense to Honesty: County Governmental Corruption in Mississippi." Unpublished paper, May 2003.

Lambright, Nsombi. "Community Organizing for School Reform in the Mississippi Delta." Unpublished report for the Southern E.C.H.O. Organization, August, 2001, 1–27.

Lower Mississippi Delta Development Commission. *The Delta Initiatives: Realizing the Dream. Fulfilling the Potential: A Report by the Lower Mississippi Delta Development Commission* (Memphis: Lower Mississippi Delta Development Commission, 1990).

Mason, John Lyman and Michael Nelson. "The Politics of Gambling in the South." Paper presented at the 1999 annual meeting of the American Political Science Association, Atlanta, September 2–5, 1999.

Menifield, Charles E. "Mississippi Votes 2000: A Comprehensive Examination of Politics and Election" Unpublished research report. John C. Stennis Institute of Government, Mississippi State University, 2002.

Mississippi United to Elect Negro Candidates. "To Get that Power: Mississippi United to Elect Negro Candidates." Unpublished pamphlet, 1967.

Morris, Willie. "My Delta. And Yours?" In *A Social and Economic Portrait of the Mississippi Delta,* eds. Arthur G. Cosby, Mitchell W. Brackin, T. David Mason, and Eunice R. McCulloch. (Mississippi State: Mississippi State University Social Science Research Center, Mississippi Agricultural and Forestry Experiment Station, 1992).

Nylander III, Albert B. *Rural Community Leadership Structures in Two Delta Communities.* PhD dissertation, Mississippi State University, 1998.

Powell, Lee, ed. "The Mississippi Delta: Beyond 2000 Interim Report" (Washington, DC: US Department of Transportation, 1998).

Rawls, Tonyia. "$45 Million to Mississippi Private Prisons at Expense of Educational Spending." Unpublished paper, http://grassrootsleadership.org, 1–3.

Student Nonviolent Coordinating Committee. "Mississippi Summer Project." Unpublished pamphlet (Atlanta: Student Nonviolent Coordinating Committee, 1964).

The World Bank Group. "How Is Social Capital Measured?" Unpublished paper. www.worldbank.org/poverty/social capital/SChowmeas1.htm.

Touchstone, Thomas Nolan. "The Report of a Study of the Tunica County Schools" (Jackson: State Department of Education, 1949), 26.

University of Mississippi Center for Population Studies. *Population Changes for Mississippi Places 1980, 1990, and 2000.* www.olemiss.edu/depts/sdc/citychg.pdf.

University of Mississippi Oral History Program. "An Oral History with the Honorable Unita Blackwell." Interview with Mike Garvey of the University of Southern Mississippi Center for Oral History and Cultural Heritage (Mayersville; April 21, 1922), 1–59.

U.S. Commission on Civil Rights. *Political Participation: A Study of the Participation by Negroes in the Electoral and Political Processes in 10 Southern States since Passage of the Voting Rights Act of 1965* (Washington, DC: U.S. Government Printing Office, 1968).

Ibid., *Voting in Mississippi* (Washington, DC: US Government Printing Office, 1965).

Special Collections Libraries

Delta State University, Cleveland, Mississippi

Mississippi Valley Collection, University of Memphis

University of Florida, Gainesville

University of Michigan, Ann Arbor

University of Mississippi, Oxford

INDEX